B L U E P R I N T S
Junior Geography
Resource Bank

Stephen Scoffham

Sue Thomas

Stanley Thornes (Publishers) Ltd

Do you receive *BLUEPRINTS NEWS*?

Blueprints is an expanding series of practical teacher's ideas books and photocopiable resources for use in primary schools. Books are available for separate infant and junior age ranges for every core and foundation subject, as well as for an ever widening range of other primary teaching needs. These include **Blueprints Primary English** books and **Blueprints Resource Banks**. **Blueprints** are carefully structured around the demands of the National Curriculum in England and Wales, but are used successfully by schools and teachers in Scotland, Northern Ireland and elsewhere.

Blueprints provide:
- *Total curriculum coverage*
- *Hundreds of practical ideas*
- *Books specifically for the age range you teach*
- *Flexible resources for the whole school or for individual teachers*
- *Excellent photocopiable sheets – ideal for assessment and children's work profiles*
- *Supreme value.*

Books may be bought by credit card over the telephone and information obtained on **(01242) 577944**. Alternatively, photocopy and return this **FREEPOST** form to receive **Blueprints News**, our regular update on all new and existing titles. You may also like to add the name of a friend who would be interested in being on the mailing list.

Please add my name to the **BLUEPRINTS NEWS** mailing list.

Mr/Mrs/Miss/Ms _____

Home address _____

_____ Postcode _____

School address _____

_____ Postcode _____

Please also send **BLUEPRINTS NEWS** to:

Mr/Mrs/Miss/Ms _____

Address _____

_____ Postcode _____

To: Marketing Services Dept., Stanley Thornes Ltd, FREEPOST (GR 782), Cheltenham, GL50 1BR

First published in 1994 by:
Stanley Thornes (Publishers) Ltd
Ellenborough House
Wellington Street
CHELTENHAM GL50 1YD
England

A catalogue record for this book is avilable from the British Library.

ISBN 0–7487–1758–7

Typeset by Tech-Set, Gateshead, Tyne and Wear.
Printed in Great Britain at The Bath Press, Avon.

96 97 98 99 00 / 10 9 8 7 6 5 4 3 2

CONTENTS

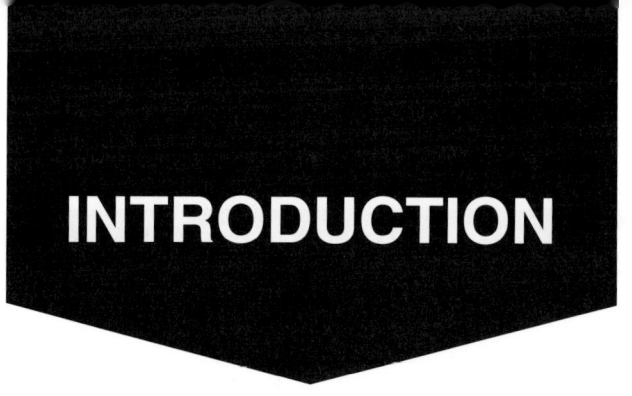

INTRODUCTION

The **Blueprints** *Geography Resource Banks* have been devised to provide an encyclopaedic resource of photocopiable material for teachers of geography in primary schools. The *Junior Resource Bank* provides material for 7–11 year olds, the *Infant Resource Bank* for 5–7 year olds. The books can be used alongside all UK geography curricula and are designed, unlike conventional worksheets, to provide materials which can be used with great flexibility to meet individual classroom needs.

The Junior Geography Resource Bank

The book provides 106 photocopiable copymasters together with teacher's notes, a topic index and a curriculum matrix linking the material to the National Curriculum for England, Wales and Northern Ireland, and the 5–14 Guidelines for Scotland.

The book is divided into fifteen sections, each of which covers a major geographical theme and which provide direct links to familiar junior school topics. The sections are:

- Land and sea
- Rivers and water
- Weather
- Volcanoes and earthquakes
- Rocks and soils
- Houses and streets
- Towns and cities
- Moving around
- Food and crops
- Natural resources
- Making things
- Habitats
- Pollution
- Conservation
- Maps and plans

There are blank maps of the UK and other parts of the world at the back of the book. You can use these to make up your own worksheets and in conjunction with projects on places beyond the local area.

The material covers all appropriate aspects of geography for the junior age range. There is a careful balance of physical, human and environmental geography. Mapwork and fieldwork skills are treated in context whenever possible. Special attention has also been given to the study of named places, which satisfies the requirement for case studies and knowledge of the wider world in all the UK curricula. The localities chosen are: Canterbury in Kent, Keswick in Cumbria, London (UK), and Nairobi (Kenya).

In addition, some individual sheets also consider specific events and places. For example, the section on the weather includes a description of Hurricane Joan striking the coast of Nicaragua in 1988. Similarly, the section on volcanoes gives an account of the birth of Paricutin, a volcano in Mexico.

Using the copymasters

The sheets provide a huge bank of picture information, process diagrams, maps, templates and source material which you can call upon as you wish. The sheets can be used to:

- introduce geographical vocabulary
- practise map and atlas skills
- prompt discussion and research
- provide information and ideas
- make classroom wall displays
- develop studies of places and themes
- assess geographical skills and knowledge.

You may find it helpful to discuss the content of each sheet with the children before starting any activity. As well as using them for reference, the children will want to colour many of the sheets. They can also cut them up for sequencing activities, individual booklets, class scrapbooks and games. Depending on the needs of your class, you may want to adapt the sheets or turn them into workcards. This approach can help to provide for differentiation.

In order to make them as flexible as possible, you will find that the sheets do not carry specific instructions for use. Instead you will find a range of concise suggestions on how to use each sheet in the teacher's notes, along with a sentence summarising the main geographical idea. One suggestion is to make wall displays using an OHP. This is particularly useful for creating large wall maps using Copymasters 97–108. Make a transparency from the Copymaster and, using the OHP, project it onto a wall (the further from the wall you are, the larger the projected image). You can then draw around the image and use it as you wish.

The notes also identify cross curricular links. History, art, maths, data handling, IT, science, technology, English and environmental education are all considered. This emphasises that geography is a synthesis subject providing a unique bridge between the humanities and science.

Using the copymasters in lesson planning

The topic index allows you to find all the sheets that could be useful for a cross curricular topic. For example, if you were doing a project on 'The environment', the topic index directs you to 'Land and sea', 'Rivers and water', 'Rocks and soils' and 'Natural resources'. This makes the material quick and easy to access.

There is also a matrix showing how the main themes in the book relate to the National Curriculum Orders for England, Wales, Scotland and Northern Ireland. This highlights the breadth and balance of the material and will help in whole school planning.

TOPIC INDEX

PRIMARY CURRICULUM COVERAGE FOR ENGLAND AND WALES, SCOTLAND AND NORTHERN IRELAND

● Major focus
○ Minor focus

	Land and sea	Rivers and water	Weather	Volcanoes and earthquakes	Rocks and soils	Houses and streets	Towns and cities	Moving around	Food and crops	Natural resources	Making things	Habitats	Pollution	Conservation	Maps and plans	Blank maps
ENGLAND AND WALES																
Geographical skills		○	○			○		○	○					○	●	○
Places	○	○	○	○			●		○		○			●	○	○
Physical geography themes	●	●	●	●	●					○						
Human geography themes						●	●	●	●	●	●					
Environmental geography themes					○			○			●	●	●	●		
SCOTLAND																
Aspects of the physical and built environment	○		●		○	●	●									
Ways in which places have affected people and people have used and affected places		○	○			○			○	●	○	●	○	●		
Locations, linkages and networks							○	●							○	
Making and using maps						○		○	○					○	●	●
NORTHERN IRELAND																
AT1 Methods of geographical enquiry						○		○	○					○	●	●
AT2 Physical environments	●	●	●	●	●						○					
AT3 Human environments						●	●	●	●	●	●					
AT4 Place and space								○						○	○	●
AT5 Issues in a changing world								○					●	●		

TEACHER'S NOTES

LAND AND SEA

Copymaster 1 (Rainforest)
In the rainforest the trees create a dense layer of foliage called a canopy. Very little light reaches the forest floor.

● Discuss the way the rainforest forms different layers of vegetation as shown on the sheet.
● Blank out the creatures and get the children to draw their own versions of the pictures in the empty boxes.
● Use the sheet to help make a 'Save the Rainforest' poster. **(Technology link)**
● Put the sheets together in a row to make a class frieze.

Copymaster 2 (Deserts)
Most deserts are rocky and bare. People, plants and creatures have to survive in the heat with very little water.

● Get the children to make their own annotated diagram of the camel, house or date palm. They could then write a sentence or two of explanation underneath. **(Assessment)**
● Design a 'desert' symbol for use on a world map. See **Copymaster 26** (World climate).
● Read to the children accounts and stories of desert life. They might make comparisons with their own environment following the approach used by Nigel Gray in *A Country Far Away* (Andersen, 1988).
● Make a painting, or 3-D model in a box, of a desert scene.

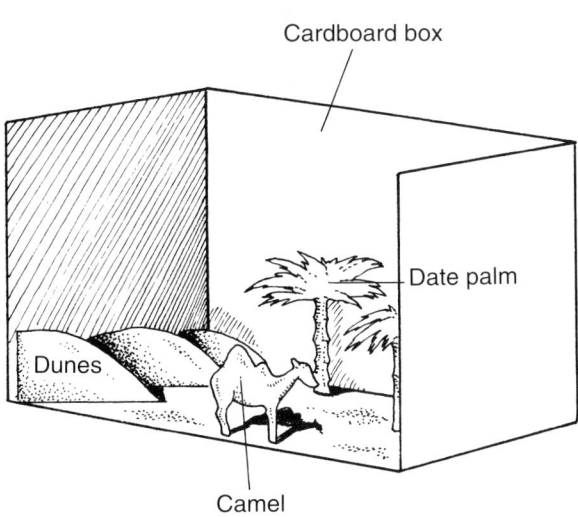

Cardboard box

Date palm

Dunes

Camel

Copymaster 3 (Grasslands)
Grasslands are often on flat plains far from the sea. Rainfall is low but there is a wet season and a dry season.

● List the different names for grasslands around the world and the continent where each name is used.
● Using an OHP, enlarge one of the cross sections to create a class wall display.
● Find out more about the different animals in the African savanna. You might also make a study of a game reserve, perhaps as part of a project on Kenya.

Copymaster 4 (Mountains)
The vegetation changes as you climb higher up a mountain and the air gets thinner.

● Get the children to annotate the picture using the information panel. They could also add some extra drawings of their own.
● Ask the children to imagine they are mountaineers. What changes would they notice as they climb a high mountain?
● Draw a map of the scene shown on the sheet and invent names for the different places.

Copymaster 5 (Antarctica)
The seas around Antarctica are rich in marine life. However, the food chain is very short and life is delicately balanced.

● Cut out the pictures of the creatures to make a wildlife collage. Books such as *Antarctica* by Helen Coucher (Deutsch, 1990) are useful for extending the work.
● Write a description of Antarctica using the pictures and information on the sheet, and the information on climate on **Copymaster 25**.
● Find out more about Antarctica as a research project. Greenpeace (Canonbury Villas, London N1 2PN) are a valuable contact.
● Set up a role-play exercise to discuss the arguments for and against keeping Antarctica as a wilderness or world park. **(Environmental education link)**

Copymaster 6 (Caves)
Caves are most often found in limestone areas where rainwater dissolves the rocks. In Britain, the most

1

famous caves are in the Pennines and Mendip Hills (Somerset).

- Ask the children to list and describe in a few words each of the features shown on the sheet.
- Colour the diagrams.
- Make up adventure stories about exploring a cave.
- Blank out the explanatory sentences. Get the children to explain how caves are formed. **(Assessment)**

Copymaster 7 (Cliffs)
Resistant rocks jut out as cliffs and headlands around the coast. They are shaped and worn away by the pounding of strong waves.

- Discuss the four different pictures and what they show. **(History link)**
- Remove one of the pictures from the sequence and get the children to make their own drawing of the missing picture.
- Ask the children to describe what they think will happen to the cliff in the next 200 years.
- Find out about famous cliffs around the British Isles.

Copymaster 8 (The sea bed)
Water covers two-thirds of the earth's surface. There are mountains, plains and deep trenches beneath the sea. In some places raised areas of land appear as islands.

- Colour and list the plants and creatures on the sheet.
- Using the sheet, make a sea bed or ocean poem. **(English link)**
- Working from an atlas, make labelled maps of different islands around the world. See if the children can sort them into groups: coral islands, volcanic islands, other islands.
- Find out more about an individual island, such as St Lucia, for which there is a special study pack. Contact the Geographical Association, 343 Fulwood Road, Sheffield S10 3BP for further details.

Copymaster 9 (Natural wonders)
The earth is a remarkable planet. There is a huge variety of natural forms. In some places there are spectacular weather conditions.

- Colour the pictures.
- The drawings could be cut out and arranged around a world map. See **Copymaster 106** (The world).
- Make a collection of photographs of natural wonders for a class book or wall display.
- Divide the children into groups and ask them to find out more about one of the things shown on the sheet as a research project.

RIVERS AND WATER

Copymaster 10 (A river system)
Rivers shape the land, cutting valleys and gorges, and building up plains and mudflats.

- Remove the labels from the picture and get the children to write the words in the correct places. **(Assessment)**
- Write a short account of the journey of the river shown on the sheet. The children might like to imagine they are fish swimming downstream.
- Find a river on an Ordnance Survey map of your area. Follow its course and note down the different features that are shown.
- Using the symbols from the bottom of the sheet, make up a map of an imaginary river.

Copymaster 11 (Great rivers)
Rivers are important for agriculture and industry in all parts of the world.

- Colour the map.
- Draw a bar graph to show the length of each river. **(Maths link)**

The World's Longest Rivers	
Nile	6695 km
Amazon	6570 km
Mississippi	6020 km
Yangtze	5471 km
Murray - Darling	3717 km
Volga	3688 km

- Compile a computer database about different rivers around the world. List: the name of the river, its length, the sea or ocean it flows into, the countries through which it passes and any dams, waterfalls or other important features.
- Using the reference books, get the children to find out more about one of the rivers shown on the sheet.
- Blank out the numbers on the map so that the children have to identify the rivers themselves. **(Assessment)**

Copymaster 12 (The Nile)

The world's first great civilisations grew up on the banks of the Nile, Euphrates and Indus between 4,000 and 5,000 years ago. They all depended on irrigation for their survival.

- Ask the children to cut out the pictures and arrange them to make a picture strip, starting with the picture of Lake Victoria.
- Using **Copymaster 10** (A river system) identify the features of a river system on the map of the Nile.
- Enlarge the map of the Nile using an OHP for use in a class wall display.

Copymaster 13 (Floods on the Mississippi)

The floods on the Mississippi in summer 1993 were the worst in living memory.

- Write a report about the floods using the names of places from the map.
- Make a set of drawings to go with the descriptions.
- Compile a newspaper about the flood using a computer program such as Front Page Extra. **(IT link)**

Copymaster 14 (Controlling floods)

Floods occur when there is more water in a river than it can carry away. Although floods have always occurred, they have been made much worse in recent years as trees have been cleared and soils left exposed to the rain.

- Look carefully at the pictures on the sheet. Why are different flood control measures needed?

- Using **Copymaster 13** (Floods on the Mississippi) what might be done to control floods on the Mississippi?
- Using a map of your area, discuss which local places suffer from flooding. Mark them on a map. Why do these places flood and what can be done about it?

Copymaster 15 (The water cycle)

The sun provides the energy to drive the water cycle.

- Discuss the sheet and get the children to colour the pictures.
- Cut out the drawings to make a picture strip.
- Blank out two of the drawings on the sheet and ask the children to complete the empty boxes. **(Assessment)**
- Discuss what would happen if the trees were cut down in the mountains. **(Environmental education link)**

Copymaster 16 (Water supply system)

Drinking water comes either from rivers or is pumped from rocks underground. This sheet shows how water is cleaned, treated, stored and piped to our homes.

- Colour the route the water takes on the diagram.
- Blank out the descriptions and get the children to write their own captions for the pictures.
- Using a map of your area, identify water towers, water works and reservoirs.
- Use this sheet to help with a study of local services.

Copymaster 17 (Water in the home)

In Britain we use an average of 150 to 170 litres of water per person per day.

- Colour the route of the water pipes on the diagram.
- Make a list of all the machines and equipment in the home which use water.
- Working from the figures on the sheet, make a bar chart to show the amount of water used for different daily activities.
- Write a report suggesting how people could reduce their water consumption.

WEATHER

Copymaster 18 (Clouds)

There are three basic types of clouds: cirrus, cumulus and stratus. When 'nimbus' is added as a prefix or suffix, it indicates rain clouds.

- Use the sheet to help the children to identify the different clouds they can see. **(Science link)**
- Make a daily weather chart recording the type of cloud and amount of cloud cover in your area using the symbols from the bottom of the sheet.
- Collect photographs of different clouds, make a wall display and label the photographs.
- Blank out some of the captions or drawings on the sheet and get the children to complete the gaps. **(Assessment)**

Copymaster 19 (Wind speed)

The Beaufort scale was devised by Admiral Beaufort in 1805 and is measured in knots.

- Get the children to write a description to go with each picture.
- Devise pictures for intermediate points on the scale as follows: force 1 light air, force 3 gentle breeze, force 5 fresh breeze, force 7 near gale, force 9 strong gale, force 11 violent storm.
- Record the wind speed in your area over a period of a week or a fortnight using the Beaufort scale.

Copymaster 20 (Wind direction)

The direction of the wind can be recorded on a rose

diagram. This is rather like a bar graph, but with a separate column for each compass point.

- Discuss the three wind roses. Which place has the most west winds? Which place has the most south winds?
- Get the children to design a simple wind direction indicator of their own such as a wind sock or weather vane. **(Technology link)**
- Record the direction of the wind in your own area over a 21-day period and discuss how it compares with the places on the sheet.

Copymaster 21 (Types of air)
The air masses that affect the weather in the British Isles come from Greenland, Asia, North Africa and the Caribbean.

- Colour land and sea on the map.
- Discuss the wind direction that would bring each air mass to the British Isles.
- Cut out the pictures at the bottom on the sheet and arrange them round the map.
- Using an atlas, name the place where each air mass originates.

Copymaster 22 (Hurricanes)
Hurricanes develop over warm, tropical seas in the late summer and early autumn. They quickly lose their energy when they reach the land.

- Use this sheet in conjunction with **Copymaster 23** (Hurricane Joan).
- Find Nicaragua on the map. Which other countries are affected by hurricanes?
- What are tropical storms called in other parts of the world?
- Using the diagram discuss the structure of a hurricane.

Copymaster 23 (Hurricane Joan)
There have been a number of very serious hurricanes in recent years. Hurricane Gilbert which struck Jamaica in 1988 was the most powerful ever recorded.

- Make up a diary describing how Hurricane Joan affected Bluefields.
- Devise a warning poster telling people how to prepare themselves for a hurricane. **(Assessment)**
- Make a list of all the jobs that would need to be done after a hurricane disaster.

Copymasters 24 and 25 (Different climates 1 and 2)
There are distinctive differences between the hot desert, rainforest, polar and temperate climates as the temperature and rainfall graphs on these sheets show.

- Discuss the graphs with the children. See that they understand that the lines show temperature and the blocks show rainfall. Which place is wettest? Which place is driest? Which place is coldest?
- Complete the climate graph and description for London working from the figures in the table below.

Month	Rainfall	Temperature
Jan.	55 mm	6° C
Feb.	40 mm	7° C
Mar.	35 mm	10° C
Apr.	40 mm	13° C
May	45 mm	17° C
June	45 mm	20° C
Jul.	55 mm	22° C
Aug.	60 mm	21° C
Sept.	50 mm	19° C
Oct.	55 mm	14° C
Nov.	65 mm	10° C
Dec.	50 mm	7° C

- Colour and cut out the climate graph for each place and arrange it round a world map as a wall display. See **Copymaster 26** (World climate).
- Design a piece of clothing suitable for each climate. **(Technology link)**
- Ask the children to write a description of each climate using just the temperature and rainfall graphs.

Copymaster 26 (World climate)
Climate regions are usually defined in terms of average temperatures and rainfall.

- Use this sheet in conjunction with **Copymasters 24 and 25**.
- Colour the symbols in the key and on the map.
- Name the continents on the map.

VOLCANOES AND EARTHQUAKES

Copymaster 27 (The story of a volcano)
Paricutin is famous because it gave scientists a rare chance to study the birth of a volcano.

- Cut out the pictures and arrange them along a timeline. **(History link)**

- Get the children to write their own accounts of the story of Paricutin using the pictures and captions.
- Colour the pictures and make a 'triangle model' by cutting round the outside of the picture panels and fixing the bottom flap underneath the top edge.

Copymaster 28 (Mount Etna)
Mount Etna is continually active, but people live on the slopes because volcanic soil is particularly fertile.

● Make a list of the crops grown on Mount Etna. What grows in each 1,000 metre band?
● Make up a map of Mount Etna and the surrounding crops and villages using the information on the sheet.
● Make a stand-up model of Etna by cutting out the shape of the mountain and folding along the base line (0 metres).

Copymaster 29 (Famous volcanoes)
There are about 650 active volcanoes in the world. The majority are found in a 'Ring of Fire' around the shores of the Pacific Ocean.

● Make up a volcano quiz using the information on the sheet.
● Build up a volcano datafile using a computer database. Name the volcano, the country it is in and why it is famous. **(IT link)**
● Mark the location of the different volcanoes on a world map using **Copymaster 108** (World map).
● If any volcanoes happen to be in the news at the time, make a display of newspaper cuttings about them.

Copymaster 30 (Earthquake model)
Earthquakes are caused by sudden movements of the earth's crust along the junctions between the plates.

● Colour the two pictures and cut them out. Cut and fold the top picture along the lines indicated. To complete the model, glue the two side panels of the top picture onto the bottom picture so that the As and Bs match up.

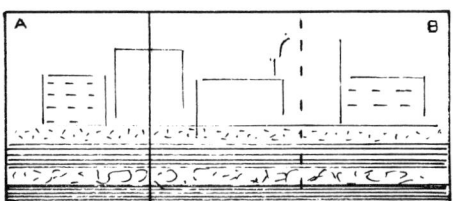

Copymaster 31 (Measuring earthquakes)
There are two scales for measuring earthquakes. The Richter scale measures the power of the seismic waves. The Mercalli scale measures the effect on people and buildings.

● Get the children to make a second picture to show the different stages in the scale.
● Blank out the descriptions on the sheet and get the children to write down in their own words what each point on the scale means.
● Read to the children an account of what happens during an earthquake. *Earthquake* by Ruskin Bond (Julia MacRae, 1989) is a good starting point.
● Devise a drama or role play about what would happen if a powerful earthquake hit your school. **(English link)**

Copymaster 32 (Earthquake disasters)
Earthquakes can often happen without warning, killing large numbers of people.

● Use the information on the sheet to write an account of the problems that earthquakes can cause.
● Devise a radio message to warn people that an earthquake is expected.
● A simple earthquake game could be devised using a dice and squares or spaces on a track.

ROCKS AND SOILS

Copymaster 33 (How rocks are formed)
Although there are hundreds of different kinds of rock, they can all be classified into one of three groups: igneous, sedimentary or metamorphic.

● Use the sheet as the basis for an introductory lesson on rock types. **(Science link)**
● Get the children to find out more about each rock type, working in groups.

- Set up a class rock display.
- Use **Copymasters 27** (The story of a volcano) and **28** (Mount Etna) as part of a further study on igneous rocks.

Copymaster 34 (Useful rocks)
Rocks are important to people in many different ways.

- Blank out the name of each item and ask the children to complete the sheet using the drawings to help them.
- Provide the children with a collection of rocks and get them to arrange them in order of hardness.
- Sort the rocks into a number of different groups according to colour, texture and shape. **(Science link)**

Copymaster 35 (Old and new rocks)
Rocks can be divided into categories according to their age. The oldest rocks on Earth are about 4,000 million years old.

- Cut out the drawings of different life forms and arrange them along a timeline.
- Discuss the way life has evolved and organisms have become more complex.
- Make a class fossil collection with labels describing the rocks.

Copymaster 36 (Soil formation)
It takes about 50 years for 1 cm of soil to form.

- Make the pictures into a zig zag book. First cut them out. Then tape them together and add a cover.
- Blank out the descriptions and ask the children to say what each picture shows.
- Get the children to add arrows linking the drawings together in the correct sequence to show soil formation. **(Assessment)**

Copymaster 37 (Creatures in the soil)
Worms and other creatures help to keep a soil healthy.

- Collect a bucket of garden soil and identify the creatures living in it, using the sheet for reference.
- Make a minibeast mobile as an artwork display.
- Study one of the creatures in detail as part of a science project. **(Science link)**

Copymaster 38 (Soil profile)
Cross sections are used to show the structure of the soil.

- Colour and cut out the drawings. Then fold along the dotted lines and glue down the flap to make a free-standing model.
- Collect some soil samples from different places in your locality, shake each one with some water in a jam jar and allow it to settle into layers. Compare the different results.
- Set up a wormery using alternate layers of sand and soil and record how the layers become mixed together over a period of time.

Copymaster 39 (Soil at risk)
Apart from the produce of the sea, all the food we eat depends on the soil.

- Colour the land and sea on the map.
- Cut out the drawings at the bottom of the sheet and attach them to the correct place on a world map as part of a class wall display.
- Write a report about the problems of soil erosion and the ways in which it can be prevented. **(Environmental education link)**

HOUSES AND STREETS

Copymaster 40 (House types)
Houses make an important contribution to the character of an area. There are considerable variations in building materials, design and overall arrangement.

- Use the sheet to help develop the children's vocabulary.
- Cut out the pictures and arrange them in the correct places on a map of your area.
- Take photographs of different house types for a wall display.
- Make a survey of the houses which the children live in and display the results on a bar chart. **(Maths link)**

Copymaster 41 (House plans)
Individual house plans are a distinctive feature on large-scale maps.

- Working from a large-scale map of your area, try to identify some of the different types of houses that are shown.
- Colour a map of your area to show different house types using the sheet as a key.

- Make up a map of an imaginary street working from the house plans. **(Assessment)**

Copymaster 42 (Houses in towns)
The style and design of houses has changed considerably over the years. This sheet contains a range of examples from Canterbury in Kent dating from the Elizabethan period onwards. The topic index identifies the other sheets giving information about Canterbury.

- Get the children to draw lines from the notes to the correct part of each drawing.
- Enlarge the drawings and timeline using an OHP, and get the children to set up a wall display of houses through the ages.
- Visit any historic buildings in your area. Compile a collection of field sketches and photographs of the visits.

Copymaster 43 (Homes around the world)
The design of a house is influenced by the climate in the area and the building materials available.

● Make a fact file for each home listing the climate, materials, country and the main features of the building.

House Fact File

Type of house	Brick
Climate	Temperate
Country	UK
Main features	Large windows for light. Chimneys for heating

● Use **Copymasters 24** and **25** to find out about the different climates.
● Make a survey of the different building materials which are used in houses in your area.
● Ask the children to write a sentence or two about how each house is designed to suit the climate. **(Assessment)**

Copymaster 44 (Traditional homes)
In the past, people had to use whatever materials they could find for their houses. Nowadays concrete, glass and plastic are used all over the world.

● Use **Copymasters 40** and **43** to compare the traditional houses with modern homes.
● List some of the things which are part of a modern home but missing in the traditional house.
● Make a model of a tent using cloth, or a wood house using match sticks. **(Technology link)**

Copymaster 45 (Under the street)
A large number of services are supplied to modern houses.

● Colour the key and diagram.
● Discuss the inputs (telephone, electricity, gas and water) and outputs (foul sewer and rain water sewer) for the house in the diagram.
● Make a collection of rubbings of traps and covers in your area. **(Art link)**

Copymaster 46 (Street furniture)
The things which are added to a street for people to use are known as street furniture.

● Make a survey of street furniture in your area – get the children to tick or colour a box for each item that they find.
● The results can be presented as bar charts or pie charts. Use a computer data handling program if you can.
● Record the location of post boxes and telephone kiosks on a map of your area. Where would be the best place for a new box or kiosk?

TOWNS AND CITIES

Copymaster 47 (Towns in Scotland)
Settlements develop for a variety of different reasons.

● Colour the map and pictures.
● Draw lines from the pictures to the towns on the map and discuss why each one has developed.
● The pictures can be cut out and used as symbols around a map of your own area in the same way.

Copymaster 48 and 49 (Places in London and Places in Nairobi)
All major cities have a similar range of buildings but they also have distinctive features.

● Compare the two sheets. In what ways are London and Nairobi similar? In what ways are they different?
● Discuss each building or place. Why is it important?
● Design tourist postcards of London and Nairobi. **(Assessment)**
● Make a collage of pictures of each of the cities. Add any other images you can find.

Copymaster 50 (Transport in Nairobi)
The streets of Nairobi are often noisy and congested.

● Compare journeys in Nairobi with journeys in a city in the UK.

● Make drawings of the different types of transport used in your area.
● Blank out the pictures of the taxi and hand cart, and get the children to complete the sheet with their own drawings. **(Assessment)**

Copymaster 51 (Moving to Nairobi)
All over the developing world cities are growing rapidly as industrialisation gains momentum.

● Read the sheet carefully. The left-hand column gives a number of reasons why people are being driven into towns, while the right-hand column explains why they are attracted and positively want to go there.
● Use the sheet as the basis for a short role-play. What problems do the children think people face when they arrive in a large city for the first time? **(English link)**
● The sheet illustrates the changes that are happening in most cities in the developing world. You can adapt it to suit a number of different places.

Copymaster 52 (Great cities)
By the year 2000 over half of the world's population will be living in cities.

● Colour land and sea on the map. Which continents appear to have the most large cities?

● Complete the bar chart of city populations.
● Make a list of great cities, putting them in rank order according to size. **(Maths link)**

Copymaster 53 (Famous buildings)
There are famous buildings in cities all over the world.

● Cut out the pictures for a wall display. Add photographs of other buildings.
● Using an atlas, name the country where each famous building is found.
● Find out more about each building as a research exercise. **(English link)**

MOVING AROUND ▶

Copymaster 54 (Road signs)
Road signs are designed to be as clear and as unambiguous as possible.

● Colour the signs. Warnings and orders all have red margins. Information signs are mainly blue and rectangular in shape. Check in *The Highway Code* for colours.
● Devise a route in your own area working from a map. Add any road signs that might be needed.
● Organise a short walk in the local environment and record the signs that you come across.

Copymaster 55 (Travelling by rail)
Most large towns in Britain are connected to the rail network. The diagram on the sheet shows routes and travel times from London.

● Make a list of places which are more than 2 hours by train from London. Write them out in rank order.
● Record the time it takes to reach different places on a computer database.
● Add information about the distance to each place working from a road atlas.
● Draw a map of Britain showing the actual routes the railways take. Why don't they always take the most direct route?

Copymaster 56 (Ferry routes)
There are many different ferry routes between the UK and the mainland of Europe.

● Make a chart listing the different routes shown on the sheet.
● Add an extra column to the chart naming the sea which the ferry crosses.
● Colour the countries on the map.
● Compile a list of ferry services on a country by country basis. **(IT link)**

Copymaster 57 (Crossing the world)
The main world air routes are in Europe and North America. In some places there is now a severe shortage of air space.

● Measure the distance from London to Nairobi and London to Melbourne.
● Work out how long each flight would take at 700 kph.
● Make a collection of photographs of different types of civilian aircraft for a wall display.

Copymaster 58 (Crossing obstacles)
Mountains, hills, rivers and marshes can be major obstacles to land transport.

● Devise a map symbol for each obstacle using the empty circle beside each drawing.
● Working from a map of your area find examples of the different features shown on the sheet.
● Divide the children into groups and ask them to make a model of one of the features. **(Technology link)**

Copymaster 59 (Bridges and tunnels)
There are many famous bridges and tunnels in the UK.

● Draw lines linking each picture to the correct place on the map.
● Say what obstacle each bridge or tunnel is overcoming in the space provided below each picture.
● Use the empty box to add another example of your own.
● Find out about famous bridges and tunnels around the world.

Copymaster 60 (Types of transport)
There are advantages and disadvantages to every form of transport.

● Debate the advantages and disadvantages of each type of transport.

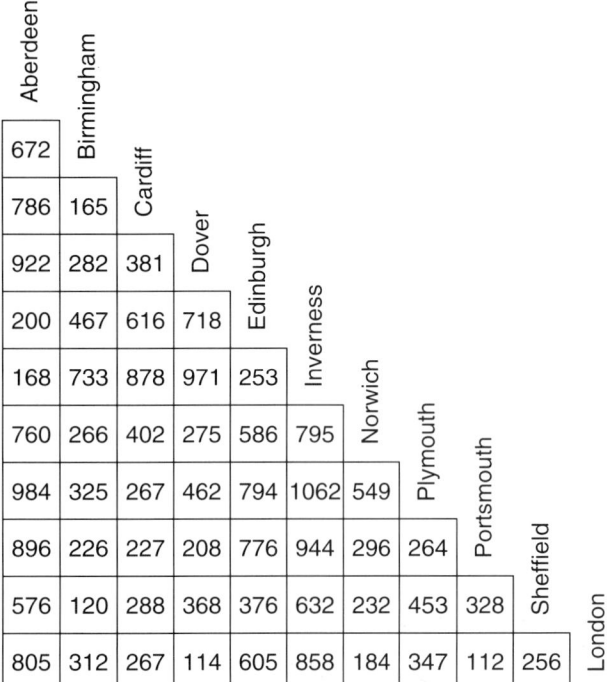

Aberdeen										
672	Birmingham									
786	165	Cardiff								
922	282	381	Dover							
200	467	616	718	Edinburgh						
168	733	878	971	253	Inverness					
760	266	402	275	586	795	Norwich				
984	325	267	462	794	1062	549	Plymouth			
896	226	227	208	776	944	296	264	Portsmouth		
576	120	288	368	376	632	232	453	328	Sheffield	
805	312	267	114	605	858	184	347	112	256	London

Table of distances between towns (kilometres)

- Make up an imaginary journey to an Alpine resort or some other holiday destination. Compare the land and air routes. What are the advantages of each?
- Blank out some of the information on the sheet and get the children to complete it. **(Assessment)**

Copymaster 61 (Transport problems)
More people and goods are being transported now than ever before.

- Make up a similar set of headlines about transport problems in your area.
- Devise a transport problems board game. **(Technology link)**
- Select one of the headlines and write a short article to go with it. **(Creative writing)**

FOOD AND CROPS

Copymaster 62 (Sheep farming in the Lake District)
Sheep farming is the main activity in the hills of western Britain where the rainfall is high and the soil is too poor for crops.

- Use the centre of the dial for adding information about the seasons or weather.
- Get the children to draw up a table of jobs which have to be done each season.

Marked in spring

Fleece sheared in summer

Hooves trimmed in August

Grazed in mountains in summer

Sheep Fact File

- Make a sheep fact file on a folded sheet of card cut out in the shape of a sheep.
- Divide the children into small groups and get them to find out more about one particular months' activity.

Copymaster 63 (A crop farm in Kent)
In southern and eastern England there is more sunshine than in the west and many farmers grow crops.

- Colour the key and the map.
- Work out the numbers of hectares for each crops and draw a graph to show the totals.
- Find out what each crop is used for.
- Collect some stems of wheat, barley and oats and put them out on a display table so the children can see the difference. **(Science link)**

Copymaster 64 (Farm products)
In order to produce food and crops (outputs) a farm requires a range of resources (inputs).

- Divide the children into groups and ask them to find out more about one of the inputs.
- Use the sheet as the basis for a class wall display in which inputs and outputs are clearly labelled.
- Make a diagram of inputs and outputs for (a) a sheep farm and (b) a crop farm.

Copymaster 65 (Growing rice)
Rice is the main food crop in the monsoon lands of south-east Asia.

- Cut out the pictures and make a zig zag book telling the story of rice. Add a cover and title. Use the reverse side of the book for a similar story sequence of a UK garden crop.
- Blank out three of the pictures and get the children to make their own drawings.
- Compile some recipes that use rice, working from a recipe book.

Copymaster 66 (Oranges from Israel)
The UK grows about 60 per cent of its own food. The rest is brought by ship or aeroplane.

- Make a list of jobs which have to be done to bring oranges to a British supermarket.
- Using an atlas, make a map of the route by sea from Tel Aviv to Southampton.
- Make a collection of labels from orange juice products.
- Blank out some of the descriptions and ask the children to complete the story. **(Assessment)**

Copymaster 67 (Food from around the world)
The food that we buy comes from many different parts of the world.

- Make up a symbol for each crop.
- Make a large wall map as a class display and pin the symbols in the correct places.
- Select one crop and find out more about it.
- Visit a local food shop and make a survey of where each product comes from.

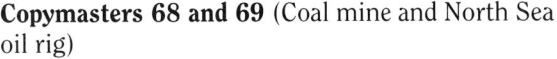

NATURAL RESOURCES

Copymasters 68 and 69 (Coal mine and North Sea oil rig)
Both coal and oil were formed about 300 million years ago. Coal is formed from trees that have been submerged by water and covered by sand and mud. Oil is made from plankton that fell to the sea bed and became buried by sand and mud.

- Get the children to label the diagrams using the lists at the bottom of the sheets.
- Write a few sentences explaining what each diagram shows. **(Assessment)**
- Get the children to imagine what it would be like to work down a mine or on a rig. Write an account.

Copymaster 70 (Stone quarry)
Whereas coal often occurs deep under the ground and has to be mined, stone is usually found near the surface and can be quarried.

- Make a model of a quarry in a cardboard box. **(Art link)**
- Discuss the effects of quarrying on the landscape. **(Environmental education link)**
- Make a survey of materials in and around your school that might have come from a quarry.

Copymaster 71 (Resources worldwide)
Natural resources are distributed very unevenly around the world.

- Make a fact file for each of the different resources. Find out what they are used for.
- Discuss what might happen if supplies of different resources run out.
- Make up a 'Save Energy' poster. **(Environmental education link)**

Copymaster 72 (Forestry)
Forests cover about one third of the world's land surface, but they are disappearing fast due to commercial pressures.

- Colour the pictures.
- Cut out each panel, together with a flap and fold along the lines to make a free standing 'triangle' model. (See notes for **Copymaster 27**.)
- Make a list of things you can find in your classroom that are made of wood.
- Find out more about hardwoods using **Copymaster 1** (Rainforest).

Copymaster 73 (Food from the sea)
Fish are a valuable source of food. However, drift nets and large modern fishing fleets are now depleting the oceans at an alarming rate.

- Add some more fish to the drawings.
- Make up a simple food chain using the drawings on the sheet.
- Discuss the problem of overfishing. Why do some people think drift nets should be banned?

MAKING THINGS

Copymaster 74 (Making paper in the USA)
Paper is essential to modern life.

- Use the sheet to introduce a project on paper.
- Make a survey of all the things in the classroom that are made of paper.
- Blank out some of the captions or drawings and ask the children to fill in the gaps.

Copymaster 75 (Making pencils in Keswick)
The first pencils ever made were produced in Keswick in the Lake District in the sixteenth century using local supplies of graphite. You can use this sheet as part of a place study of Keswick and the Lake District.

- Discuss the equipment and jobs needed in a pencil factory.
- Set up a simple pencil production line by dividing the children into groups each with a separate task. **(History link)**
- Find California, Sri Lanka, China and Korea on a world map. How might wooden slats and graphite be transported to Keswick?

Copymaster 76 (Making wool clothes in Scotland)
Wool has excellent insulation properties as it traps air between the fibres.

- Use this sheet as part of a project on clothes. **(Science link)**
- Make a list of all the different tasks required to make a jumper.
- Discuss the difference between natural and man-made fibres. Make a chart of materials used in the clothes you are wearing today.
- Collect some raw sheep's wool from fences and try carding and spinning it.
- Find out about sheep farming using **Copymaster 62** (Sheep farming in the Lake District).

Copymaster 77 (Making iron and steel in Wales)
Although the iron and steel industry is now in decline, it played a crucial role from the late eighteenth century until well after the Second World War.

- Discuss the different stages in the process and get the children to colour the diagrams.

● Find out where iron ore and coal might come from using **Copymaster 63** (Resources worldwide).
● Using a magnet, make a survey of iron and steel objects in the classroom. Could these objects be made of any other materials?

Copymaster 78 (Making electricity)
The amount of electricity that people use is one way of measuring economic development.

● Working from the sheet, get the children to explain how electricity is made and transmitted to our homes.
● Identify the pylon lines and any power stations and transmission points marked on an Ordnance Survey map of your area.

● Make a list of safety rules and precautions to do with electricity. **(Science link)**

Copymaster 79 (Using oil)
Out of every 100 barrels of oil, 88 are used to produce energy. The rest are made into chemicals and other products.

● Blank out the labels and get the children to complete the sheet, working from a list on the blackboard.
● Making a class collage or wall display showing how we use oil.
● Find out how oil is obtained using **Copymaster 61** (North Sea oil rig).

HABITATS

Copymaster 80 (Oak tree)
An oak tree can support nearly 150 different species. This means it is a particularly valuable habitat, or place for natural life.

● Discuss the idea of habitat. Where would each creature on the sheet live?
● Cut out the pictures and glue them onto the tree where they belong.
● Working in groups, get the children to make an oak tree 'advent calender' showing the different creatures from the sheet in a suitable place.

Copymaster 81 (Threatened creatures)
Half of all the world's plant and animal species could become extinct within the next 60 years.

● Draw lines linking each picture to the correct part of the world map.
● Discuss why creatures are becoming extinct. Does it matter? **(Environmental education link)**
● Make up a 'Save these creatures' poster.
● Find out what is being done to protect endangered animals such as whales and elephants.

Copymaster 82 (Threatened landscape)
Cutting down trees is seriously affecting the soil in many parts of the world.

● Colour the pictures and arrows.
● Blank out the centre picture in each sequence and ask the children to complete it for themselves. **(Assessment)**
● Set up a display of newspaper cuttings about current environmental disasters.
● Use the sheet in conjunction with **Copymaster 51** (Moving to Nairobi) and **Copymaster 72** (Forestry)

POLLUTION

Copymaster 83 (Pollution problems)
Any change in the environment which affects the health of people, plants or creatures is known as pollution.

● List all the things which are labelled in the picture. Say what problems each one causes.

● Take one example and make a detailed study of the problem and possible solutions.
● Collect photographs which show different types of pollution.
● Devise a 'pollution trail' linking together different examples of pollution in the area around your school.

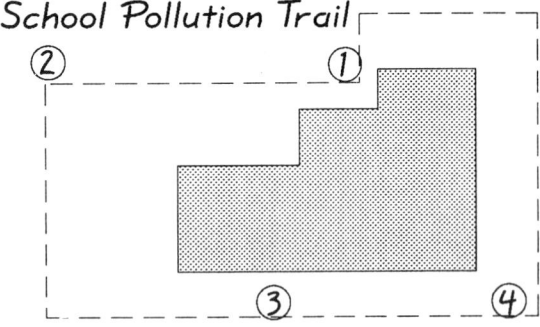

School Pollution Trail

① Corner where litter collects

② Border fence

③ Smell from traffic

④ Noise from cars

Copymaster 84 (Water pollution)
Several million tonnes of oil spill into the sea each year, either from accidents or as ships wash out their tanks.

● Discuss the picture. Why does oil pollution matter?
● Think of three reasons why there have been oil tanker disasters in the English Channel. Answers could include the number of ships in the area, the rocky coastline, carelessness and strong winds and storms.

● Debate the advantages and disadvantages of using oil. See **Copymaster 71** (Resources worldwide).

Copymaster 85 (Air pollution)
Air pollution is becoming an increasingly serious problem, especially in industrialised countries.

● Use the sheet to introduce a project on air pollution.
● Make a list of the causes and consequences of acid rain.
● Write a report about the things which are causing air pollution in your area.
● Carry out an air quality survey using different types of lichen as indicators. **(Science link)** Show the results on a map.

Copymaster 86 (Global warming)
The world is now warmer than at any time since the last Ice Age 10,000 years ago and temperatures seem to be rising steadily.

● Colour the diagram and world map.
● Working from the sheet get the children to write a newspaper report about what causes global warming and how it might affect us.
● Discuss the effects on your own region of rising sea levels. Which areas might be flooded? What would be the consequences? Use a map to help gather information.

CONSERVATION

Copymaster 87 (Improving the school environment)
There are many different ways of improving the school environment.

● Make a survey of ten children. Ask them to select the three changes they would most like to see. Record the answers by ticking the empty boxes under each picture.
● Design a symbol for each change.
● Identify sites around the school where each change could happen. Attach the symbols to the correct place on a plan to show your results.

Copymaster 88 (Recycling)
Most waste products can be recycled. Not only does this reduce the demand on natural resources, it helps to solve the problem of waste disposal.

● Colour the pictures and arrows.
● Make a list of things which can be recycled. Say what they can be turned into.
● Put up a wall display about recycling based on the sheet.

Copymaster 89 (National parks)
National parks were established in England and Wales in 1949. They cover 9 per cent of the country.

● Colour the land, sea and parks shown on the map.

● Mark your town on the map. List the parks within a radius of 100 km, 200 km and so forth.
● Blank out the numbers and letters on the map and ask the children to work them out for themselves from the key.
● Use this sheet to introduce a more detailed study of the Lake District, Keswick and Derwent Water.

Copymaster 90 (Keswick)
Keswick is an old market town and the centre of the northern Lake District.

● Complete the key on the map.
● Make a list of the different places and things visitors could do in and around Keswick.
● Plan a timetable to show how you would spend the day if you were visiting the area on holiday.

Copymaster 91 (Derwent Water)
The Lake District is a heavily glaciated landscape and the lakes have been formed by the action of glaciers.

● List the features shown in the pictures. Try to identify them on the map of the area around Keswick. See **Copymaster 91** (Keswick).
● Study one of the pictures carefully. Write a description for a tourist brochure.
● Design a postcard of Keswick and Derwent Water. **(Assessment)**

MAPS AND PLANS

Copymaster 92 (Classroom plan)
Plans are drawn from an overhead perspective and show a small area in a considerable detail.

• Cut out the tables and other furniture and arrange them so that there is room for 30 children in the class. (Work on the basis that three children can sit along the edge of a table and one at each end.)
• Make drawings on the plan of any other pieces of furniture which might be needed.
• Make a plan of your classroom.

Copymaster 93 (Canterbury street plan)
Many of the visitors to Canterbury find their way round using a street plan.

• Link each drawing to the correct place on the plan.
• Get the children to devise a short illustrated brochure advertising Canterbury to tourists.
• Devise a trail linking together the places shown in the drawings.
• Make up a Canterbury postcard.

Copymaster 94 (Picture map)
Picture maps are often used on postcards and tourist guides.

• Colour the drawings, cut them out and glue them on the map at the correct points.
• Make up a route which links together some or all of the things shown on the map. Approximately how long is the journey?
• Discuss with the children the things they might show on a picture map of their home region. How can they decide what to choose? Get them to make drawings of the places they eventually select and make their own picture maps.

Copymaster 95 (Map symbols)
Ordnance Survey map symbols are designed to be as clear and simple as possible.

• Blank out the descriptions to see if the children can identify the symbols on their own.
• Get the children to cut out the symbols and use them on a map they have made up themselves.
• Study an Ordnance Survey map of your area and list the grid squares where each symbol on the sheet is used.
• Make drawings of some more map symbols, using the key on an Ordnance Survey map.

Copymasters 96–106 (Blank maps)
These maps are drawn to different scales. They are based on projections which show the area and shape of land as accurately as possible.

• Add rivers, mountains and other landscape features with the help of an atlas.
• Mark major cities and places that are in the news.
• Identify, colour and name specific countries.
• Make a collection of stamps from different countries and arrange them round one of the continent maps.
• Enlarge the maps using an OHP for a wall display.
• Select a continent and make a collage showing the main types of vegetation – forest, grassland, desert, mountains and so on.
• Make a transparent grid overlay or add lines of latitude and longitude so that the children can give the coordinates for specific places.
• Use the maps to introduce the study of a locality in an economically developing country.
• Make a display of artefacts from different countries around the world and arrange along with the relevant maps.
• Measure distances from place to place across the maps using the scale.
• Plan journeys from one place to another using the maps as stimulus.

Rainforest

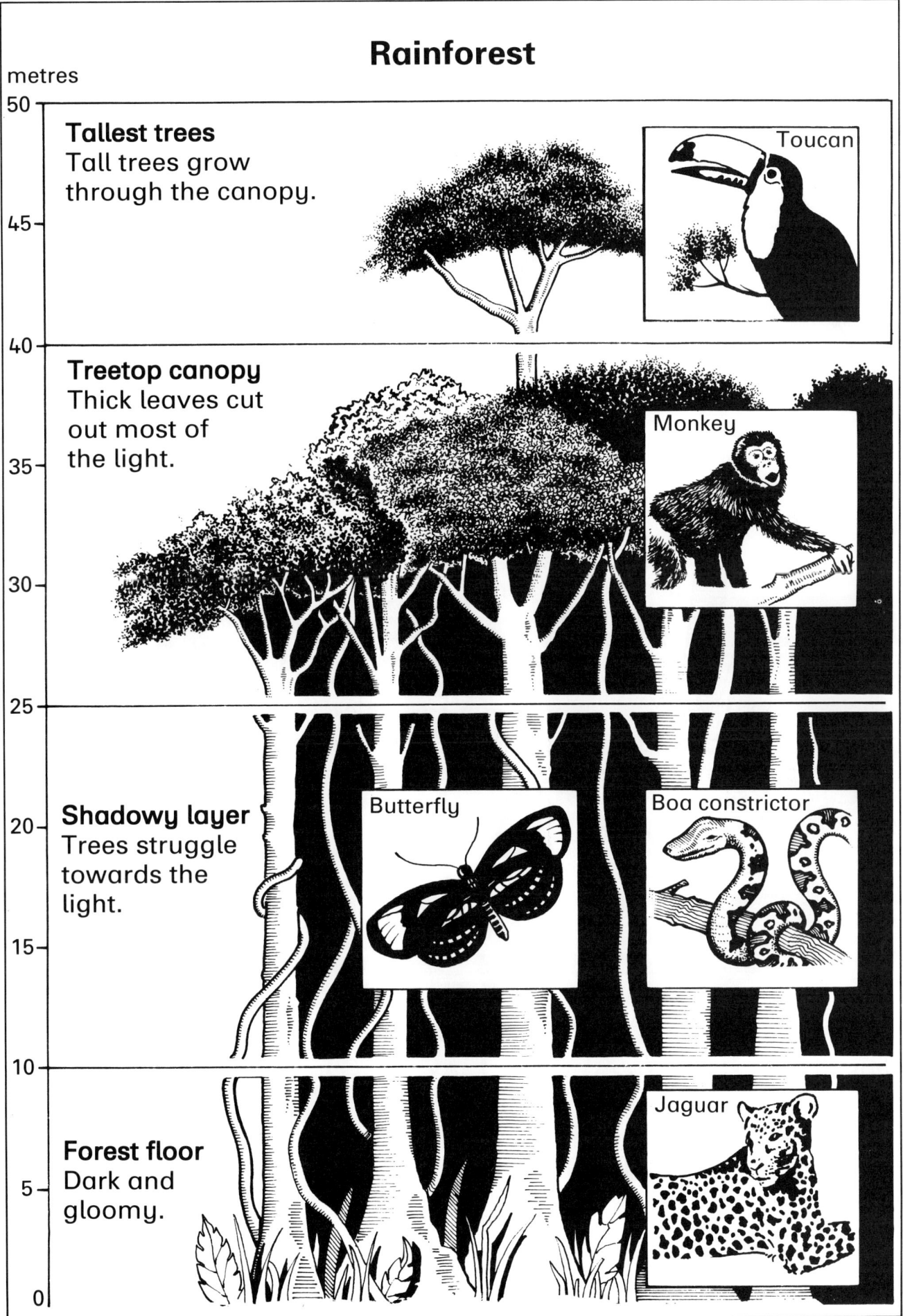

metres

50

Tallest trees
Tall trees grow
through the canopy.

Toucan

45

40

Treetop canopy
Thick leaves cut
out most of
the light.

Monkey

35

30

25

Shadowy layer
Trees struggle
towards the
light.

Butterfly

Boa constrictor

20

15

10

Forest floor
Dark and
gloomy.

Jaguar

5

0

Copymaster 1

Deserts

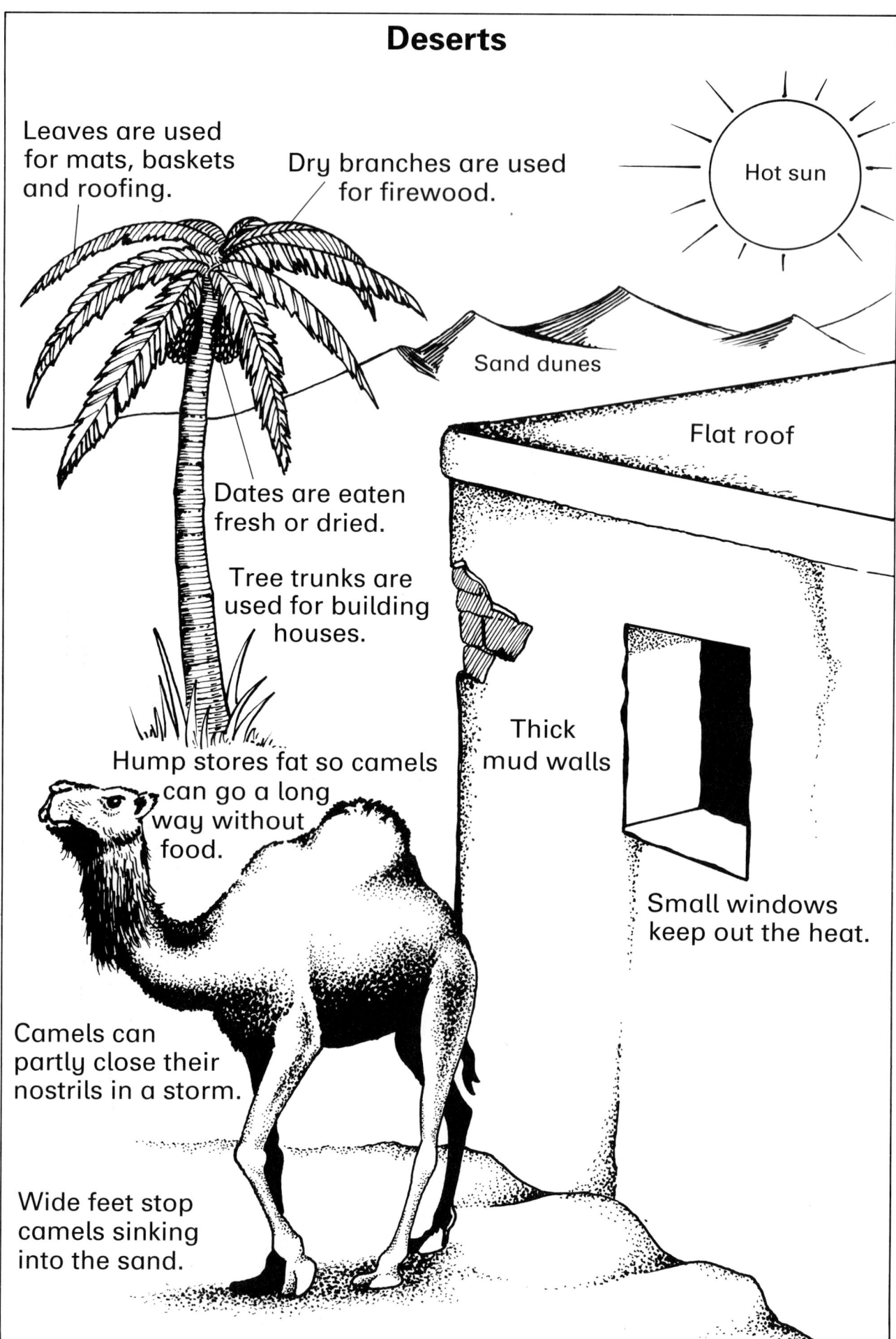

Leaves are used for mats, baskets and roofing.

Dry branches are used for firewood.

Hot sun

Sand dunes

Flat roof

Dates are eaten fresh or dried.

Tree trunks are used for building houses.

Thick mud walls

Hump stores fat so camels can go a long way without food.

Small windows keep out the heat.

Camels can partly close their nostrils in a storm.

Wide feet stop camels sinking into the sand.

Grasslands

American prairie

Bison Antelope Jack rabbit

River

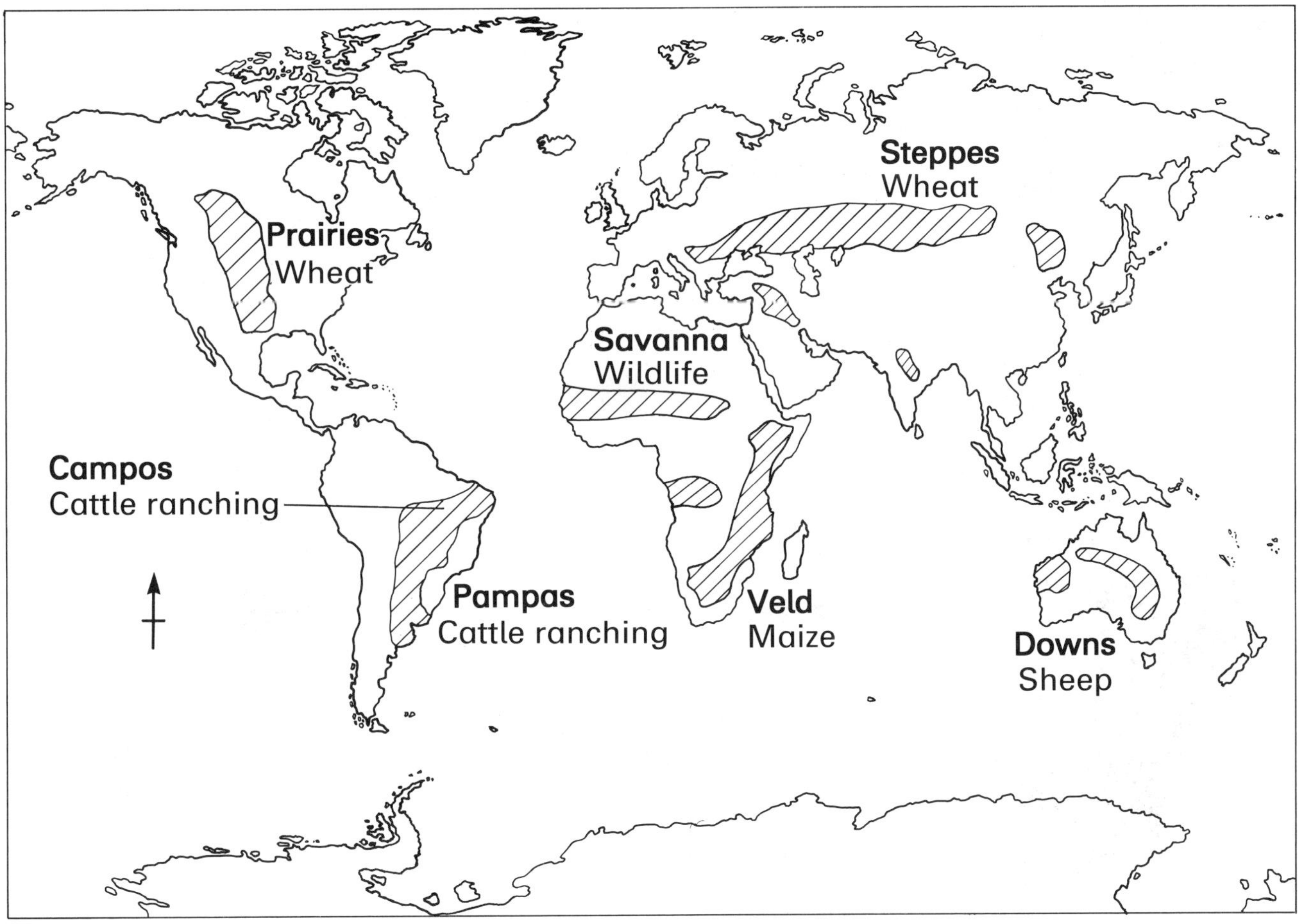

Map

Prairies
Wheat

Steppes
Wheat

Savanna
Wildlife

Campos
Cattle ranching

Pampas
Cattle ranching

Veld
Maize

Downs
Sheep

African savanna

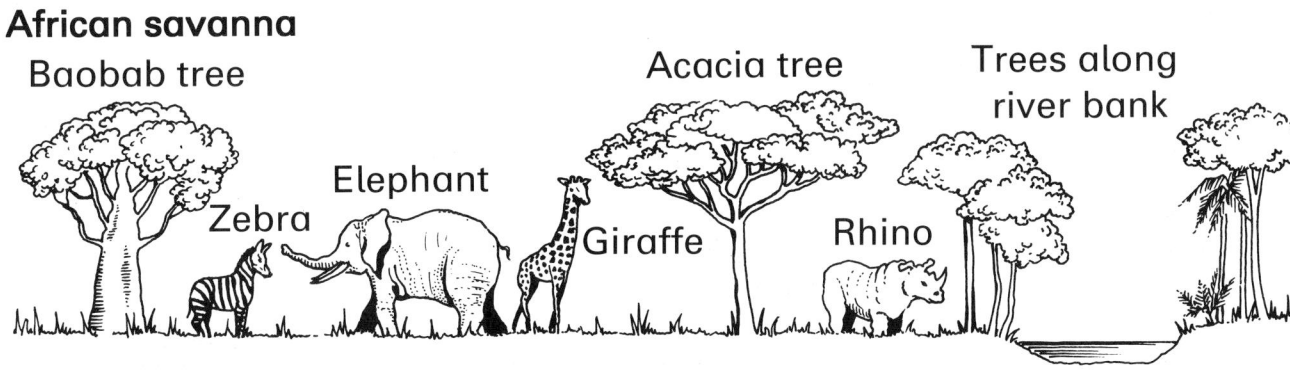

Baobab tree

Acacia tree

Trees along
river bank

Elephant

Zebra

Giraffe

Rhino

Copymaster 3

Mountains

Permanent snow

Butterfly

Lichen

Alpine layer

Eagle

Edelweiss

Evergreen trees

Pine

Bear

Deciduous trees

Beech

Squirrel

Tropical forest

Mahogany

Elephant

Antarctica

Penguin

Gull

Albatross

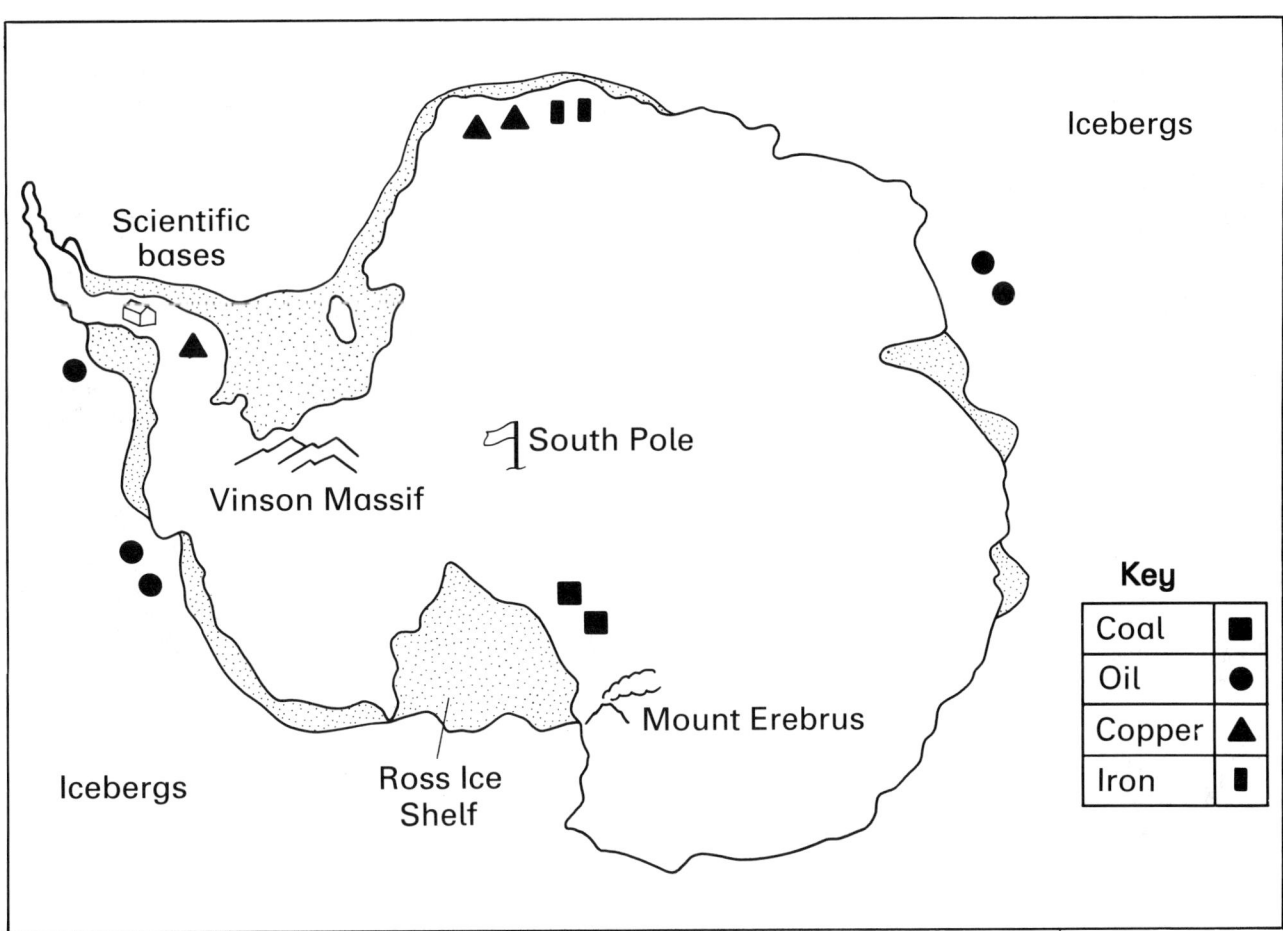

Scientific bases

Icebergs

South Pole

Vinson Massif

Mount Erebrus

Ross Ice Shelf

Icebergs

Key

Coal	■
Oil	●
Copper	▲
Iron	▮

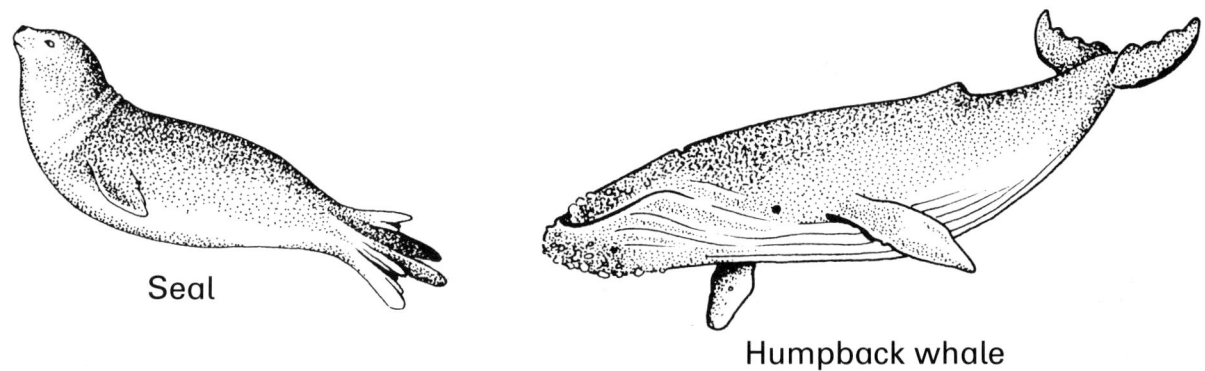

Seal

Humpback whale

Copymaster 5

Caves

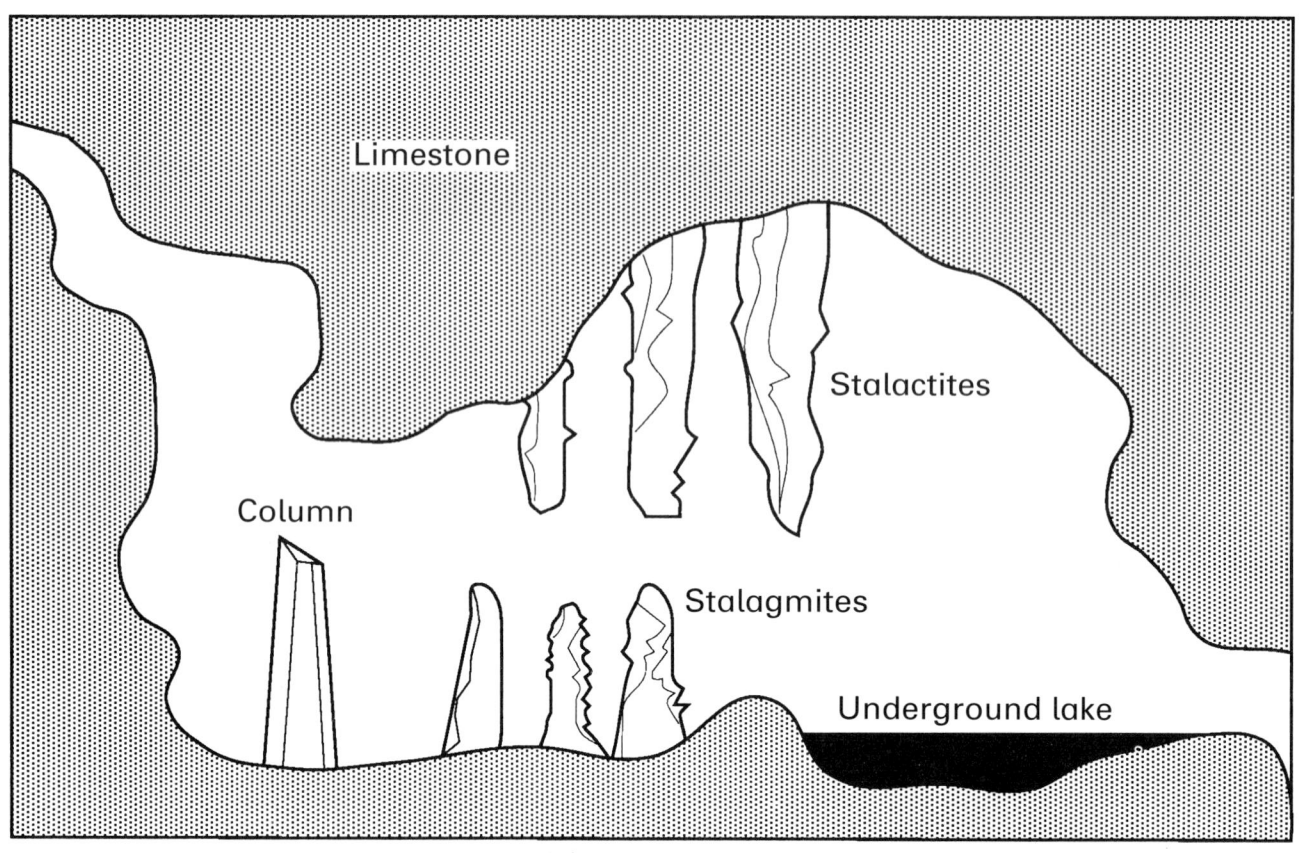

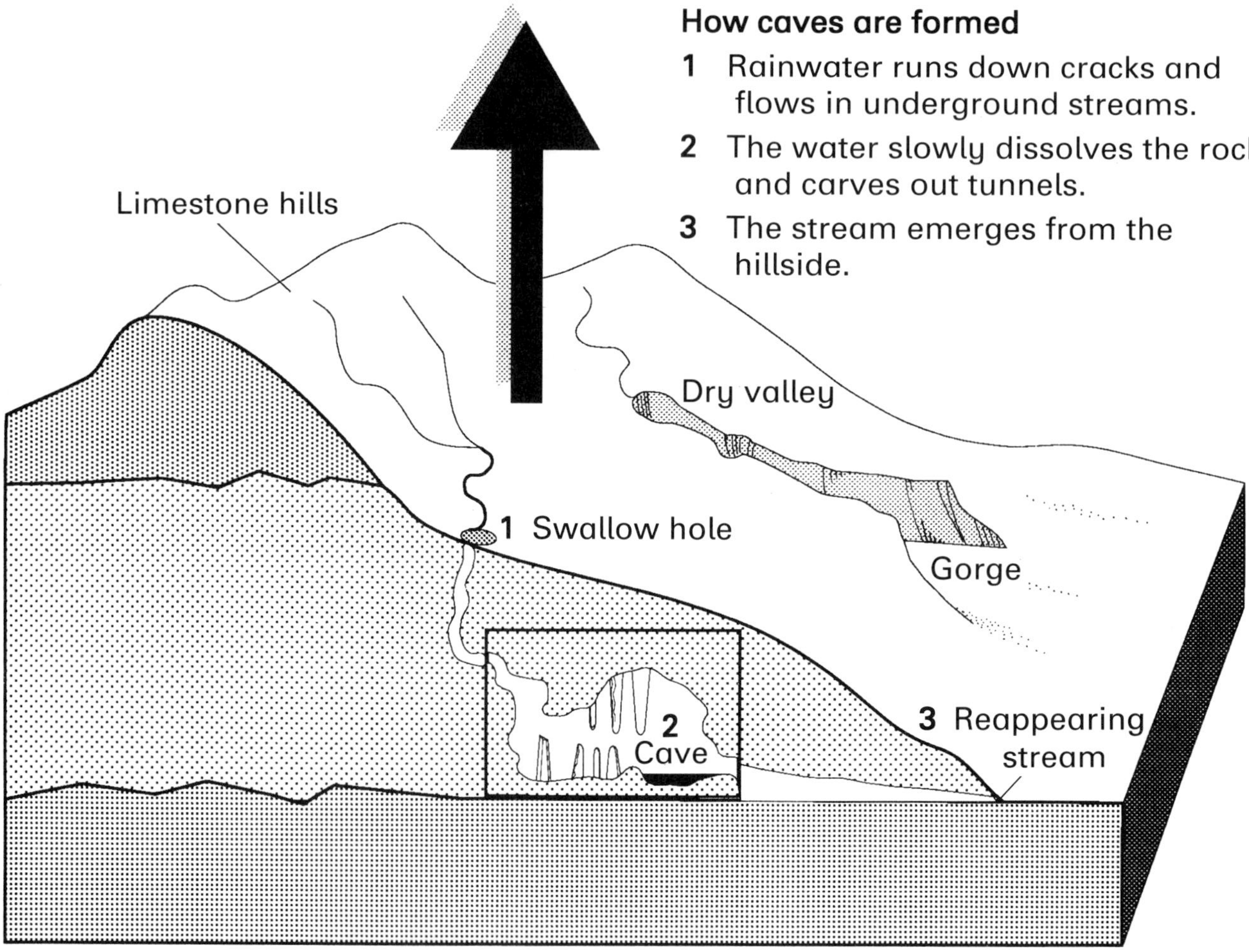

How caves are formed

1 Rainwater runs down cracks and flows in underground streams.

2 The water slowly dissolves the rock and carves out tunnels.

3 The stream emerges from the hillside.

Limestone

Stalactites

Column

Stalagmites

Underground lake

Limestone hills

Dry valley

1 Swallow hole

Gorge

2 Cave

3 Reappearing stream

Cliffs

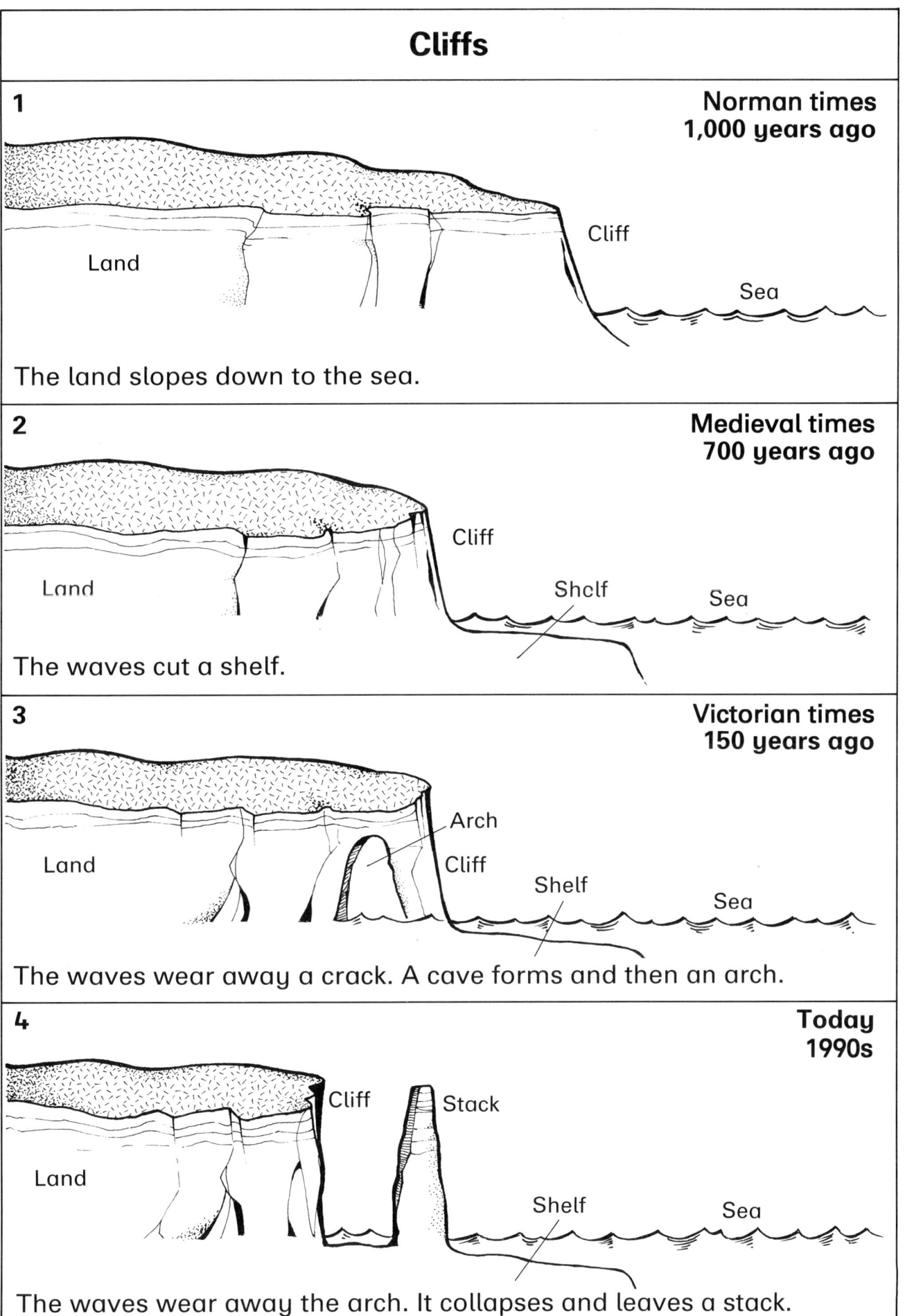

1   **Norman times**
1,000 years ago

Land   Cliff

Sea

The land slopes down to the sea.

2   **Medieval times**
700 years ago

Land   Cliff

Shelf   Sea

The waves cut a shelf.

3   **Victorian times**
150 years ago

                          Arch

Land   Cliff

Shelf   Sea

The waves wear away a crack. A cave forms and then an arch.

4   **Today**
1990s

Cliff   Stack

Land

Shelf   Sea

The waves wear away the arch. It collapses and leaves a stack.

The sea bed

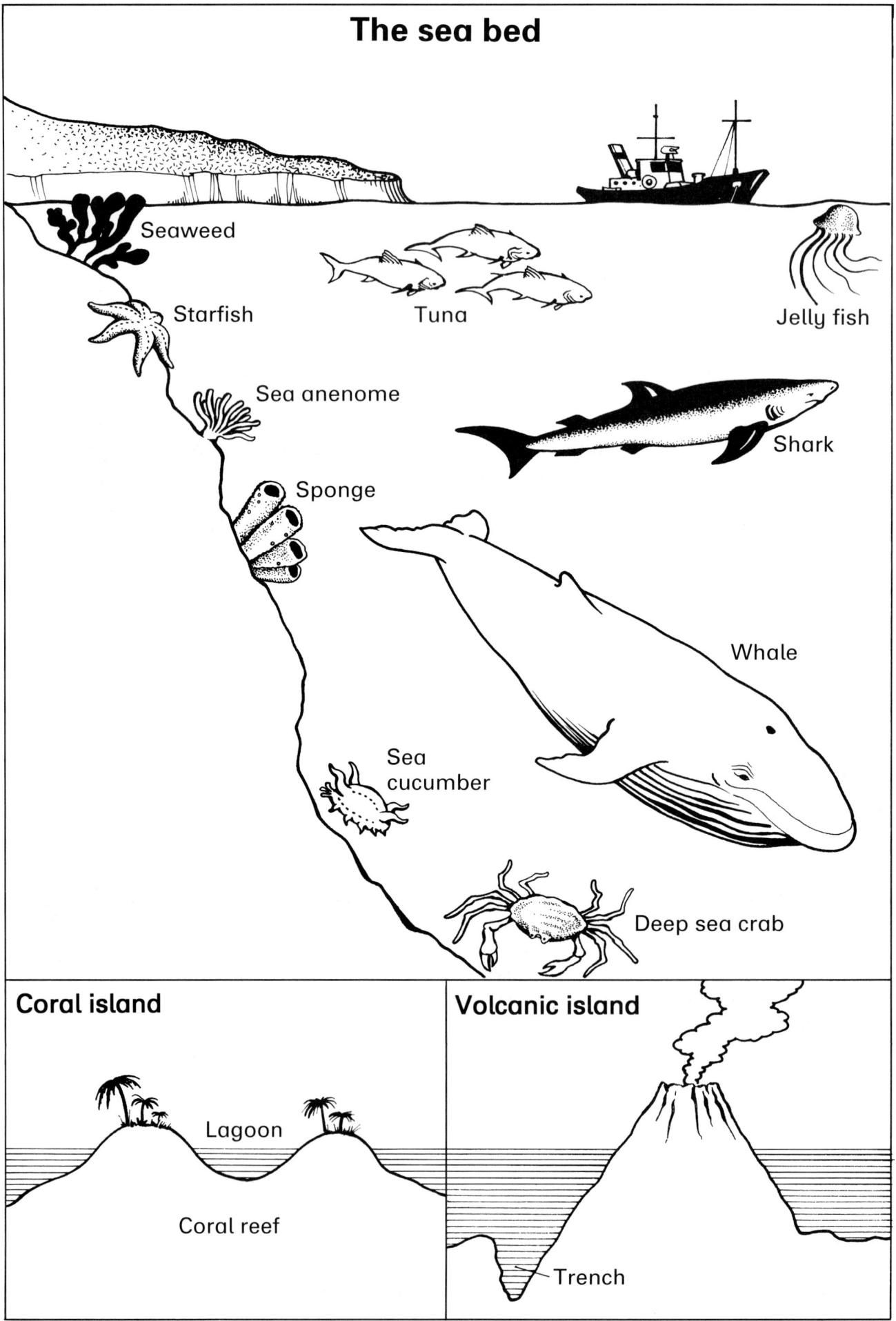

Seaweed

Starfish

Tuna

Jelly fish

Sea anenome

Shark

Sponge

Whale

Sea cucumber

Deep sea crab

Coral island

Lagoon

Coral reef

Volcanic island

Trench

Natural wonders

Mount Fujiyama, Japan

Victoria Falls, Zimbabwe

Giant's Causeway, Northern Ireland

Geysers, New Zealand

Grand Canyon, USA

Coral Island, Pacific Ocean

Northern Lights, Russia

Icebergs, Antarctica

A river system

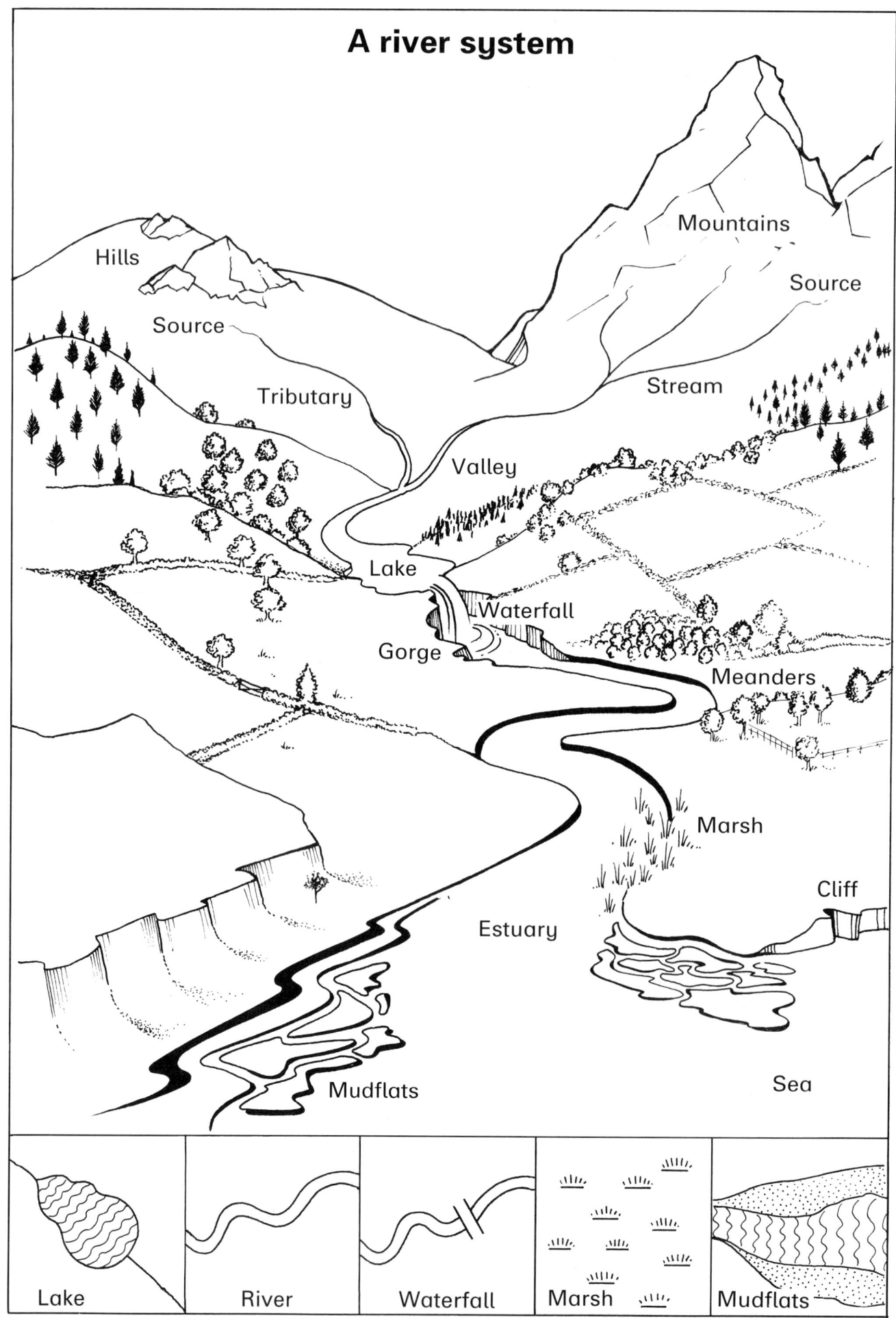

Mountains

Hills

Source

Source

Tributary

Stream

Valley

Lake

Waterfall

Gorge

Meanders

Marsh

Cliff

Estuary

Mudflats

Sea

| Lake | River | Waterfall | Marsh | Mudflats |

Copymaster 10

Great rivers

1 Mississippi
6020 km long
The Mississippi flows across the great plains of the United States of America (USA).

2 Volga
3688 km long
The Volga flows into the Caspian Sea and is used by ships.

3 Yangtze
5471 km long
The Yangtze is China's largest river and may soon be dammed to make electricity

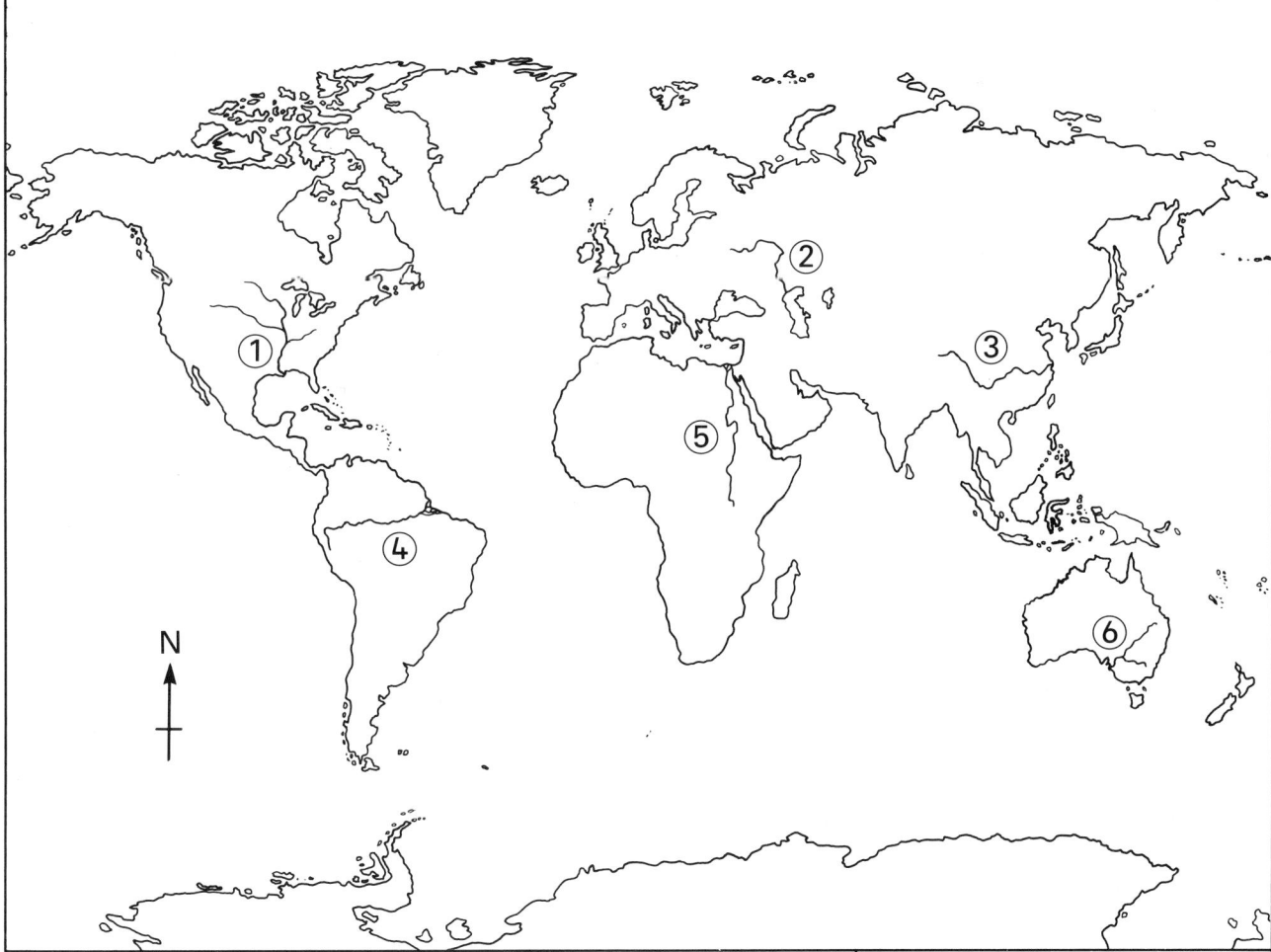

4 Amazon
6570 km long
The Amazon carries more water than any other river in the world.

5 Nile
6695 km long
The Nile is the longest river in the world. It brings water to the fields of Egypt.

6 Murray–Darling
3717 km long
In Australia two large rivers (the Murray and Darling) join together before they reach the sea.

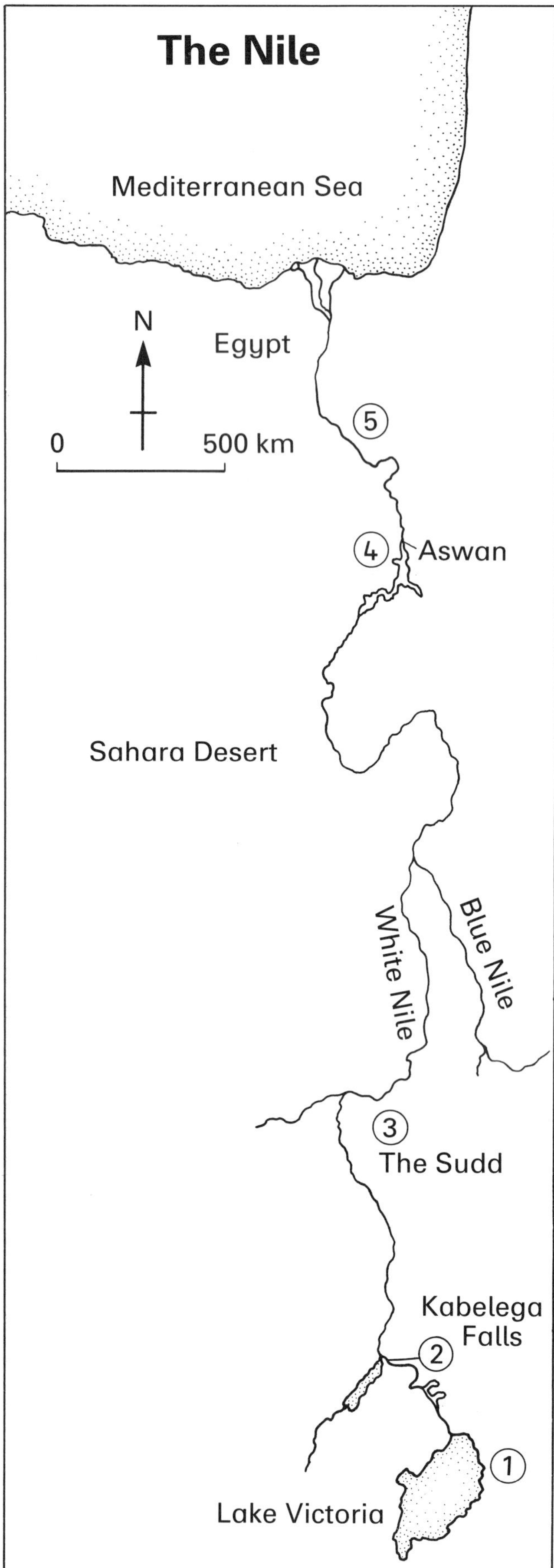

The Nile

Mediterranean Sea

N

Egypt

⑤

0   500 km

④ Aswan

Sahara Desert

White Nile

Blue Nile

③
The Sudd

Kabelega
Falls
②

①

Lake Victoria

5 In Egypt water from the Nile is used for farming.

4 The Aswan Dam was built in 1965 to control floods and make electricity.

3 Half the water is lost in a huge swamp called the Sudd.

2 It tumbles over the Kabalega Falls.

1 The White Nile rises around Lake Victoria.

Floods on the Mississippi

1 June 1993
Many days of very heavy rain in the mid west of the USA.

2 1 July
Maize and soya bean crops ruined by floods.

3 5 July
Rivers break their banks.

4 15 July
50,000 people left homeless. 250,000 without drinking water.

5 18 July
Water in the Mississippi 14 metres higher than normal.

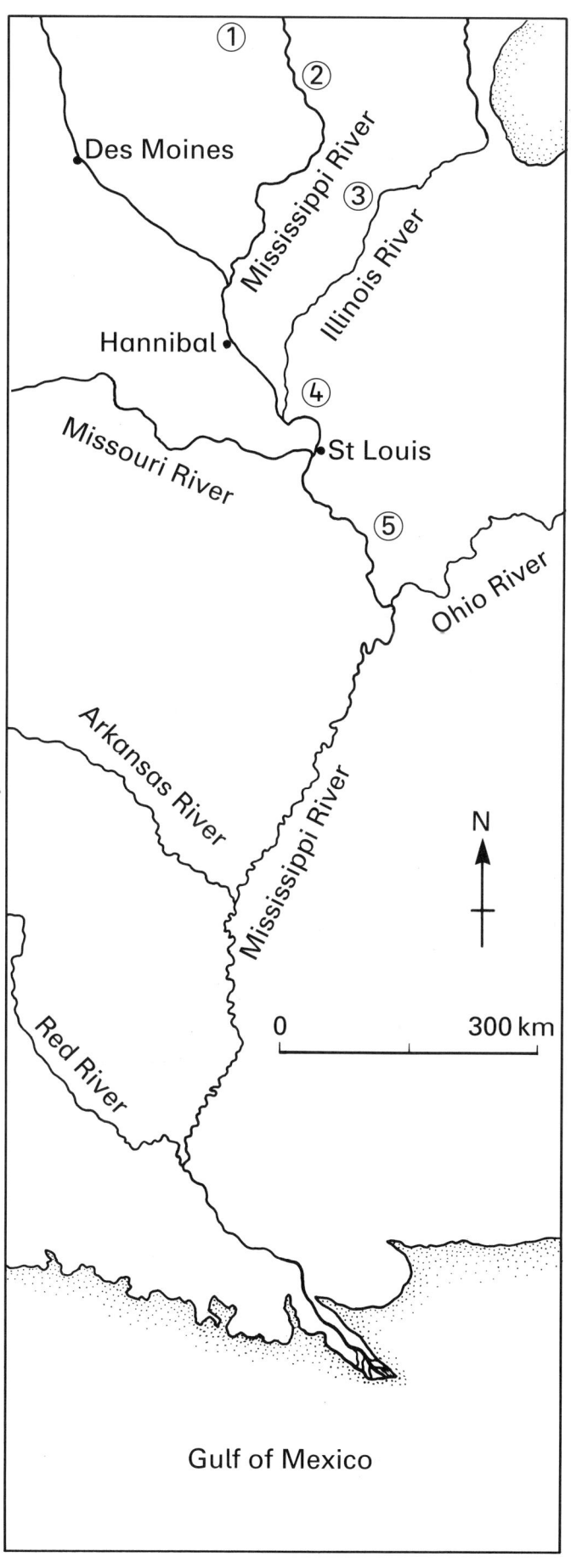

Controlling floods

1 Planting new trees in mountains

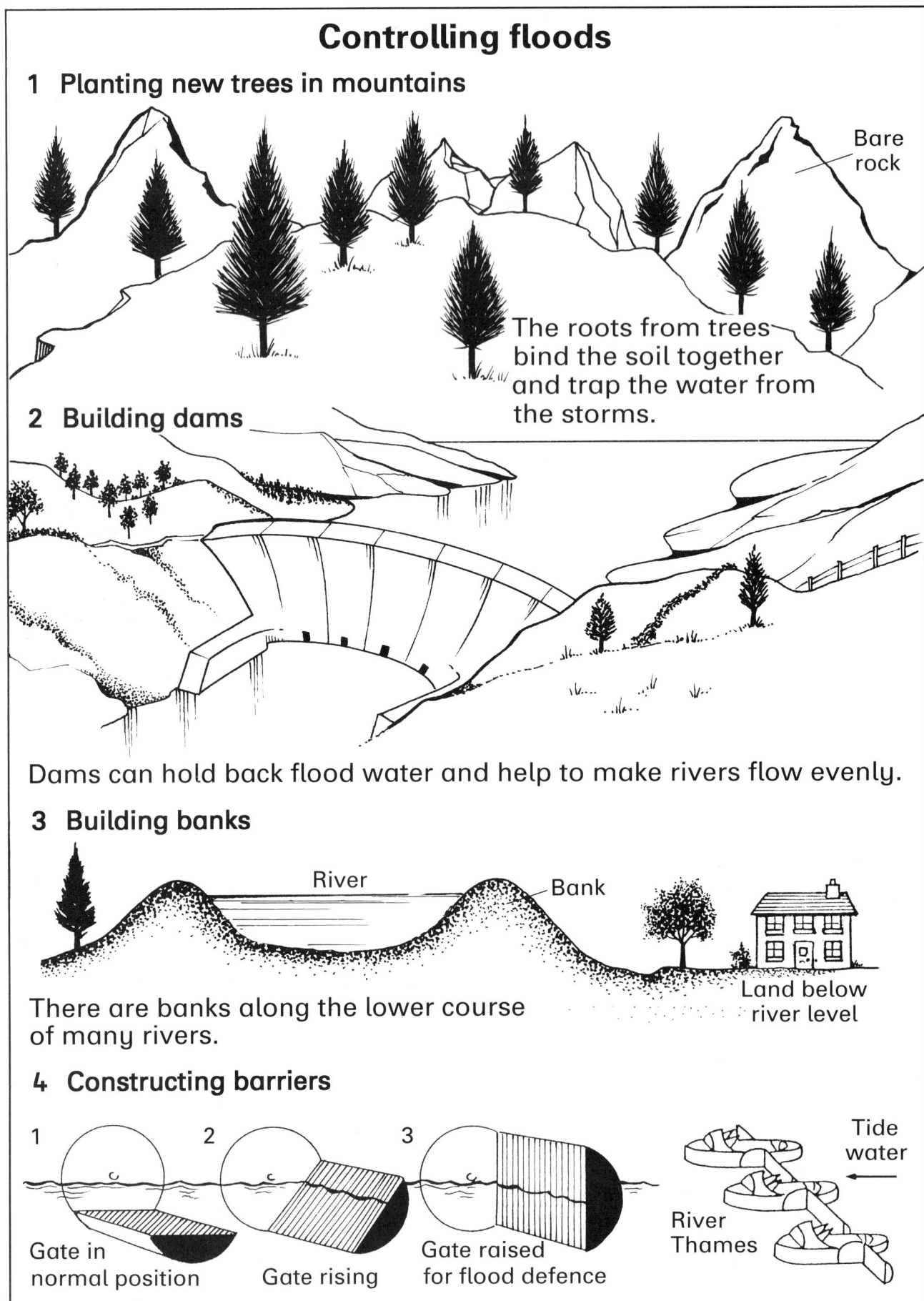

Bare rock

The roots from trees bind the soil together and trap the water from the storms.

2 Building dams

Dams can hold back flood water and help to make rivers flow evenly.

3 Building banks

River

Bank

Land below river level

There are banks along the lower course of many rivers.

4 Constructing barriers

1 Gate in normal position

2 Gate rising

3 Gate raised for flood defence

Tide water

River Thames

The Thames flood barrier stops seawater from flowing up the Thames and flooding London.

The water cycle

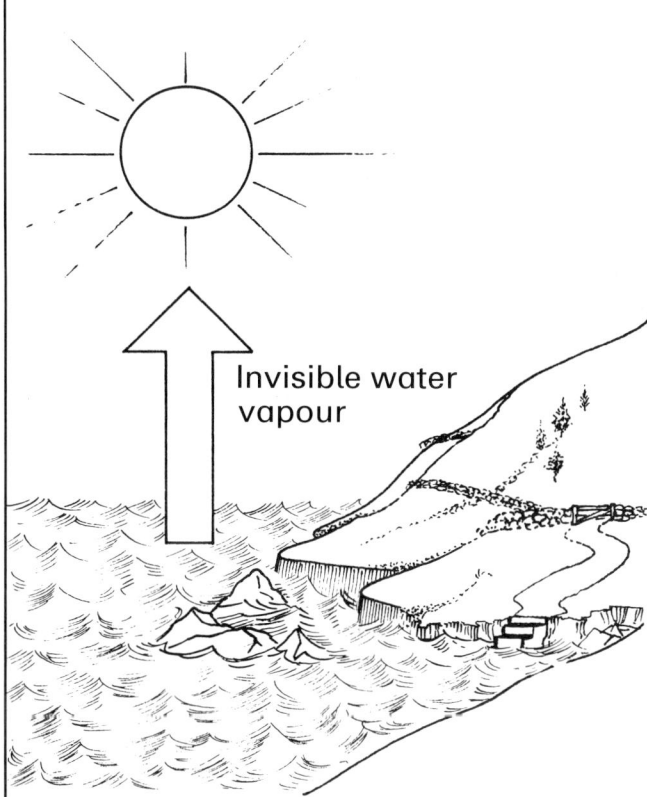

The sun warms the water in lakes and seas.

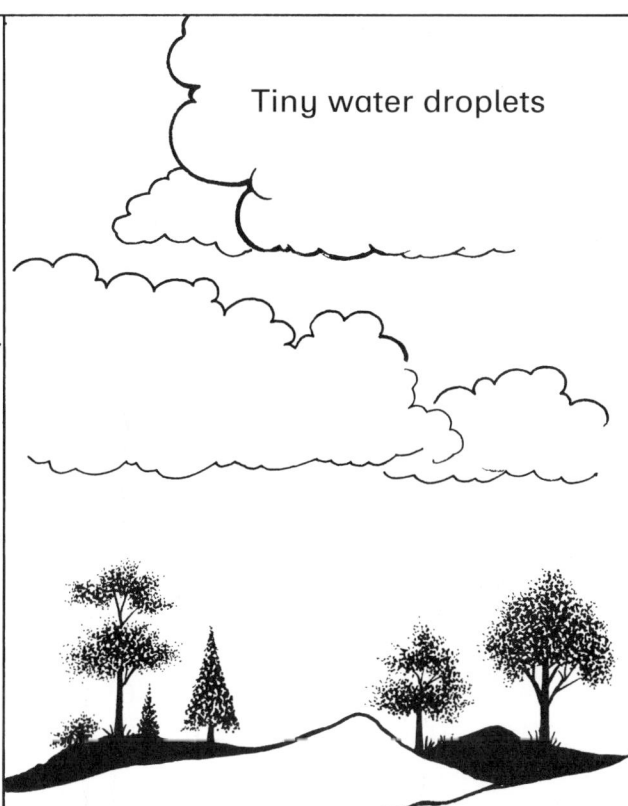

The water vapour cools to form clouds.

The water droplets get heavier and fall as rain.

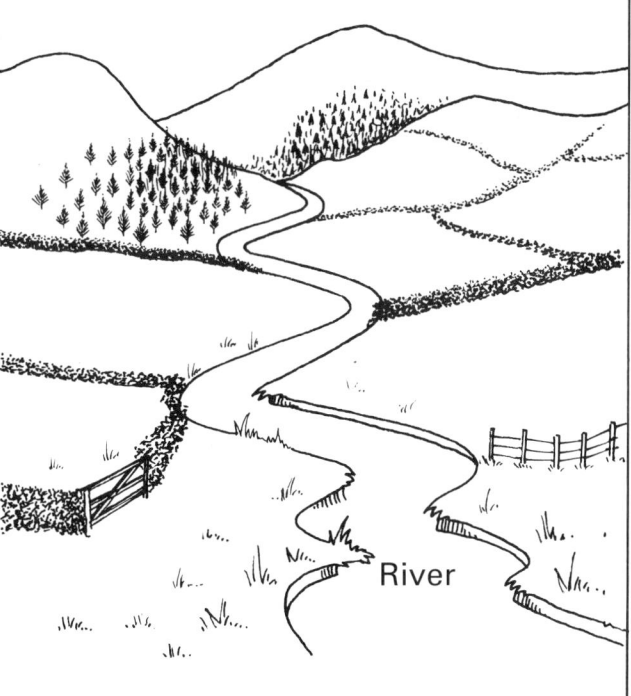

The water flows back to the sea.

Water supply system

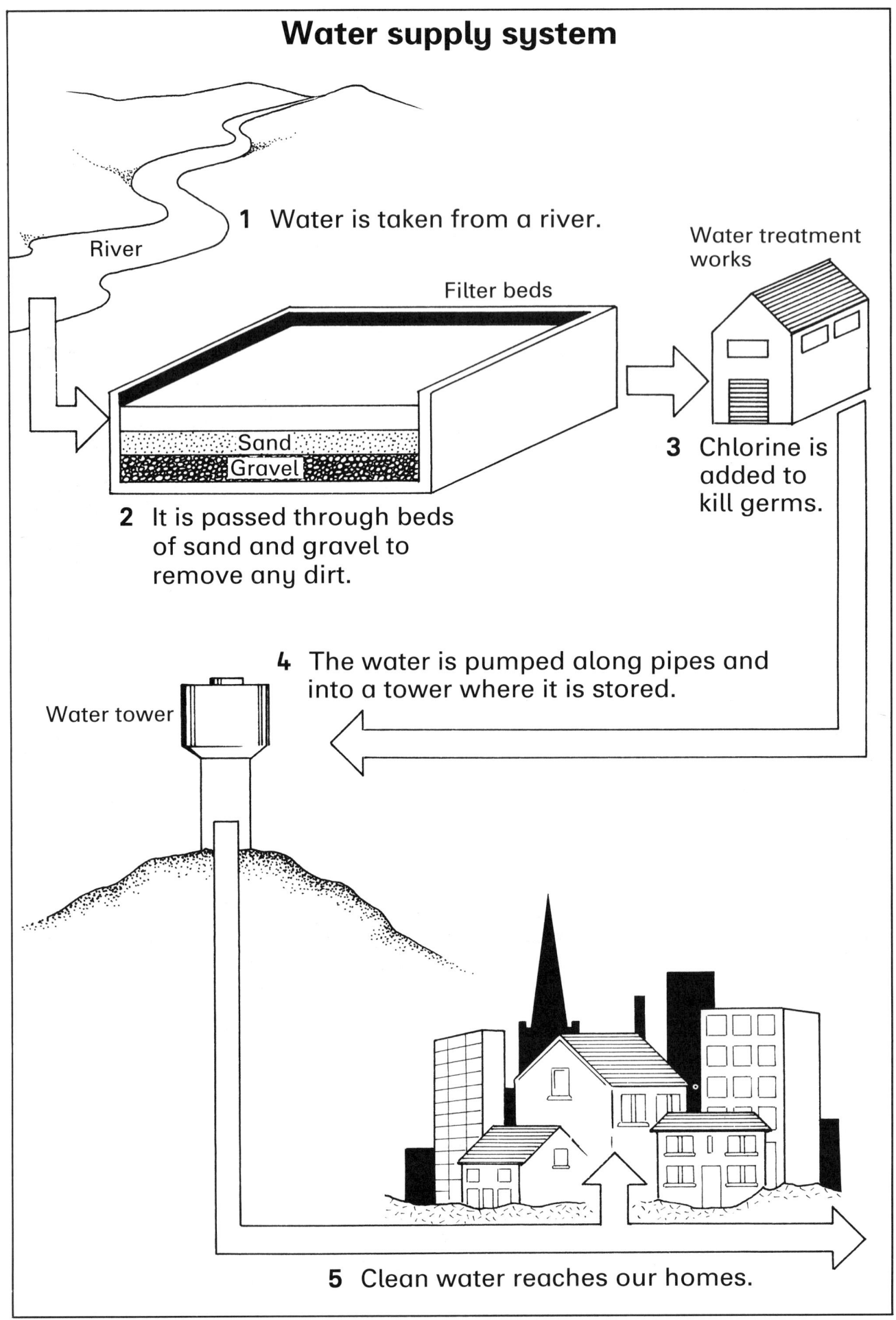

1 Water is taken from a river.

River

Water treatment works

Filter beds

Sand
Gravel

3 Chlorine is added to kill germs.

2 It is passed through beds of sand and gravel to remove any dirt.

4 The water is pumped along pipes and into a tower where it is stored.

Water tower

5 Clean water reaches our homes.

Water in the home

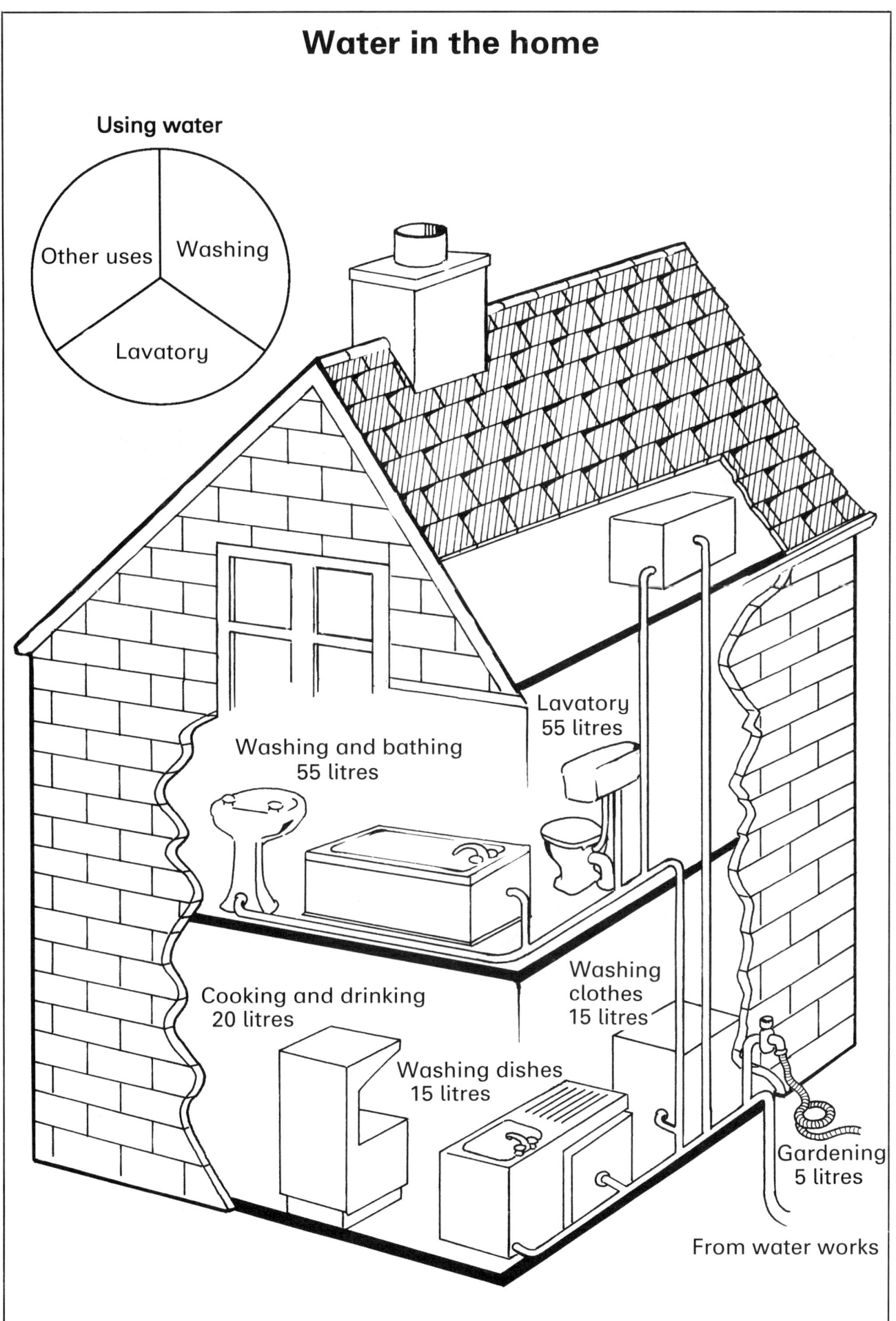

Using water

Other uses / Washing / Lavatory

Washing and bathing
55 litres

Lavatory
55 litres

Cooking and drinking
20 litres

Washing dishes
15 litres

Washing clothes
15 litres

Gardening
5 litres

From water works

Clouds

Cirrus (Ci)

Cirrus clouds are feathery. They are made of ice crystals high in the sky.

Cumulus (Cu)

Cumulus clouds form in heaps. They have flat bases. Big cumulus clouds bring showers.

Stratus (St)

Stratus clouds form a sheet across the sky causing rain or drizzle.

Cumulonimbus (Cn)

Cumulonimbus are tall storm clouds. They often bring thunder and lightening.

Clear sky	Some cloud	Half cloudy	Most cloudy	Sky covered

Wind speed

The Beaufort Scale measures the speed, or force, of the wind on a scale from 0–12.

0

Calm ———○ No wind

2

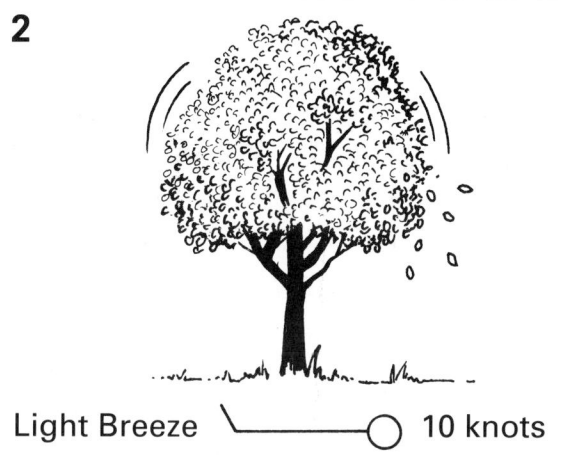

Light Breeze ＼—○ 10 knots

4

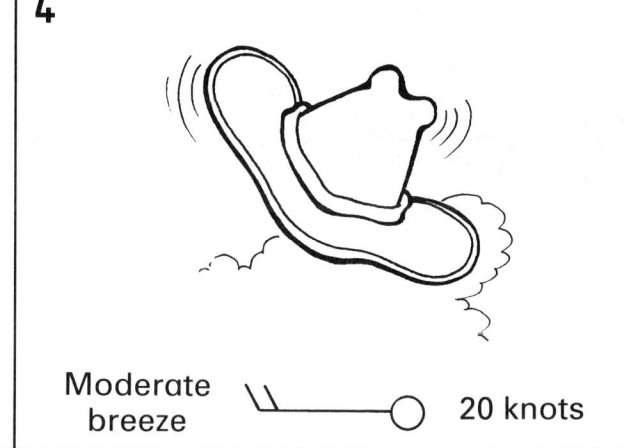

Moderate breeze ＼—○ 20 knots

6

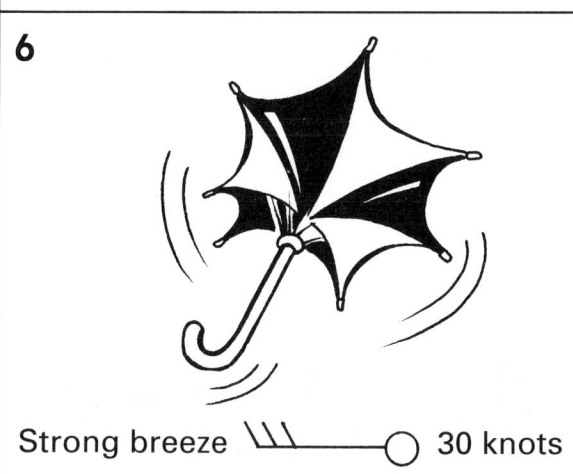

Strong breeze ＼＼—○ 30 knots

8

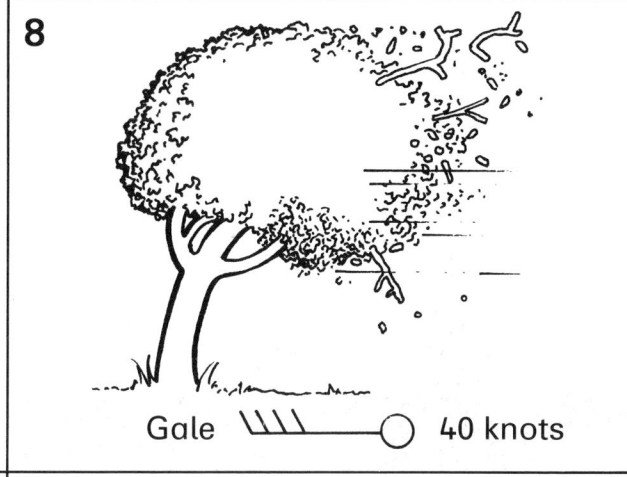

Gale ＼＼＼—○ 40 knots

10

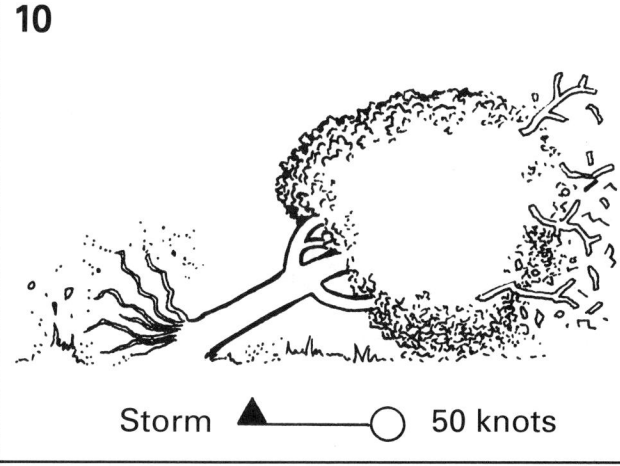

Storm ▲——○ 50 knots

12

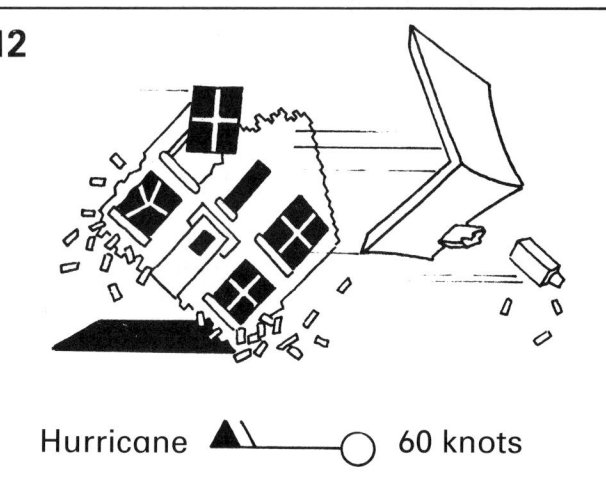

Hurricane ▲＼—○ 60 knots

Wind direction

Average wind direction in a three-week (21-day) period.

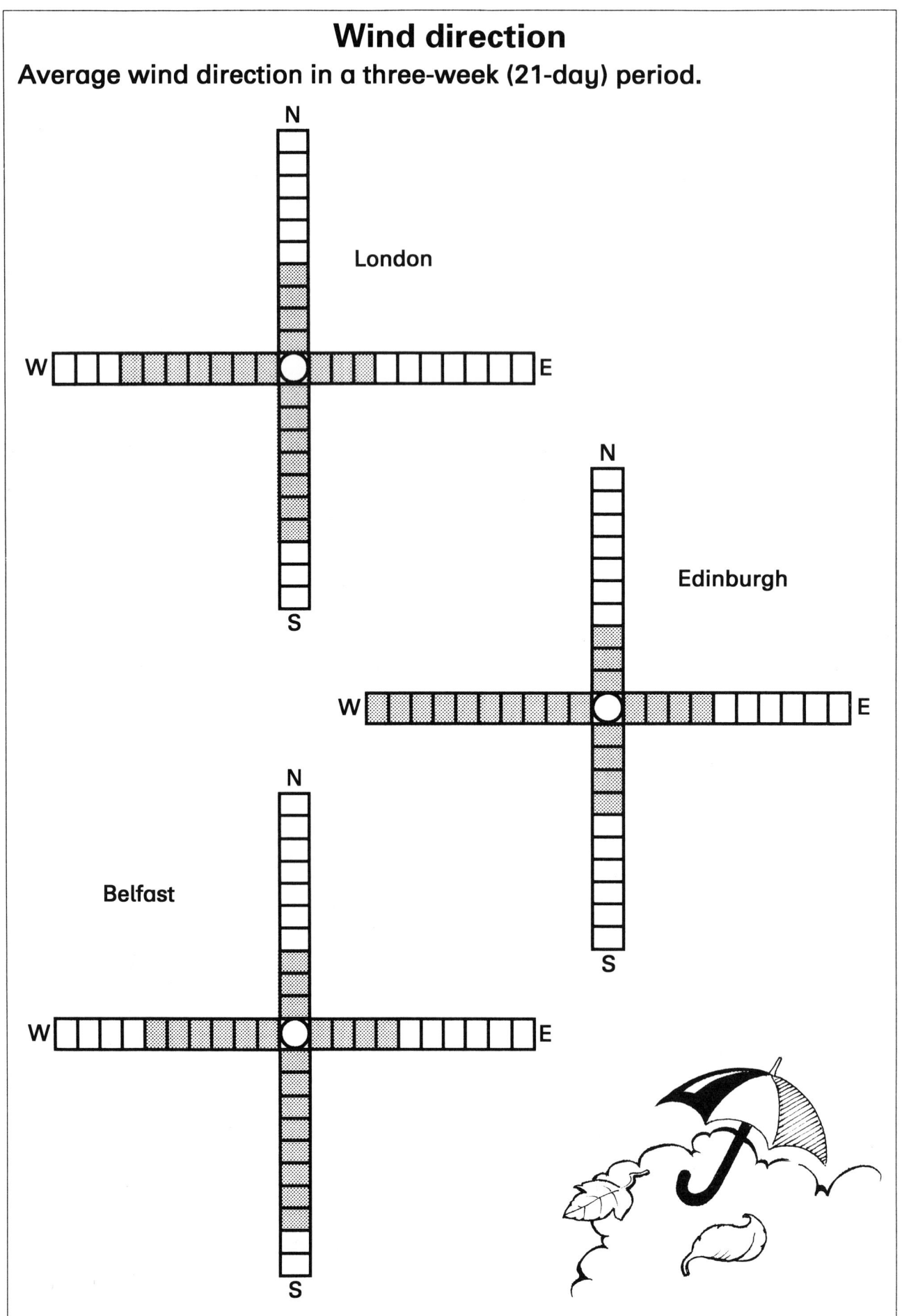

London

Edinburgh

Belfast

Types of air

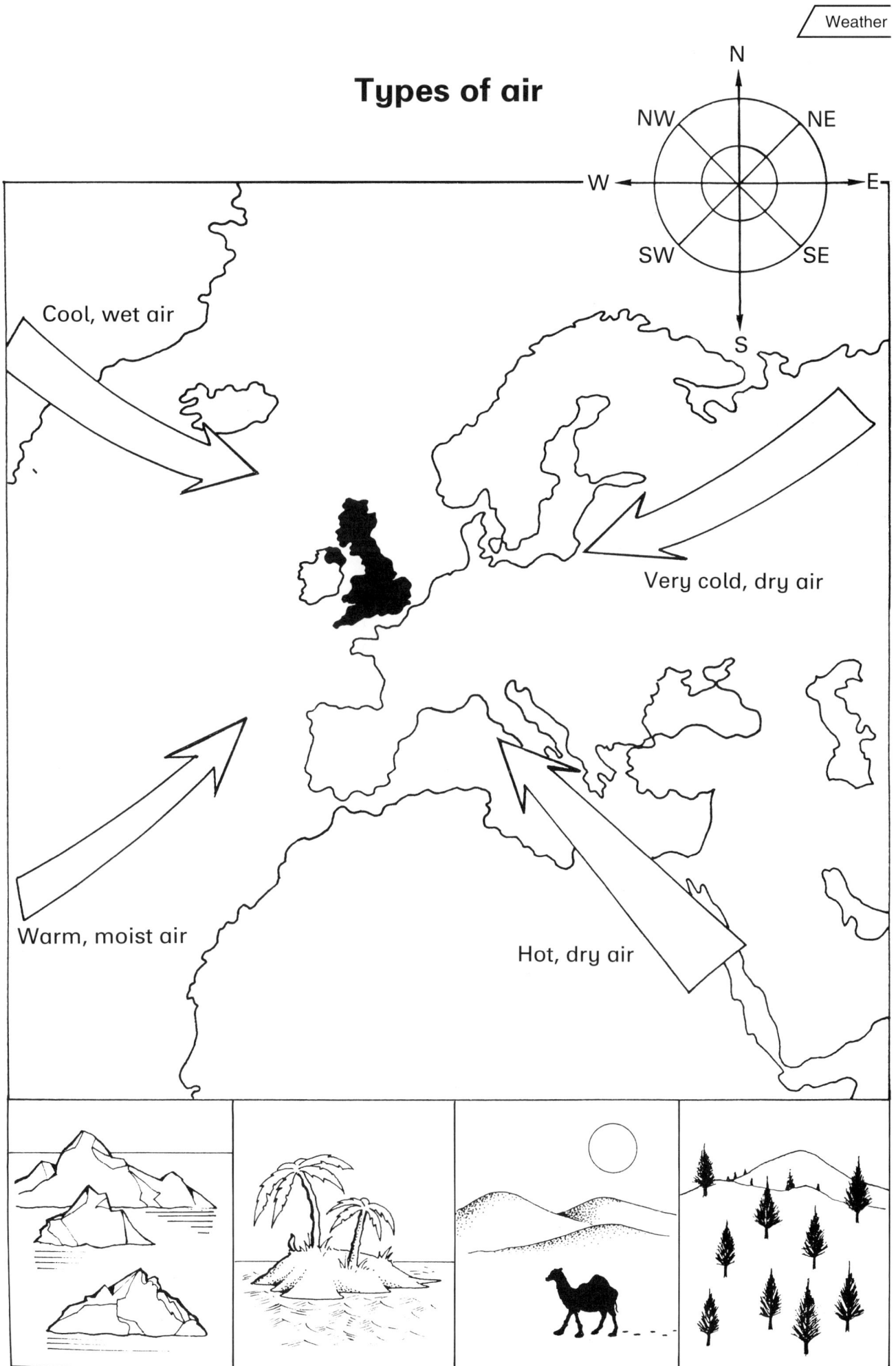

Cool, wet air

Very cold, dry air

Warm, moist air

Hot, dry air

N
NW   NE
W   E
SW   SE
S

Hurricanes

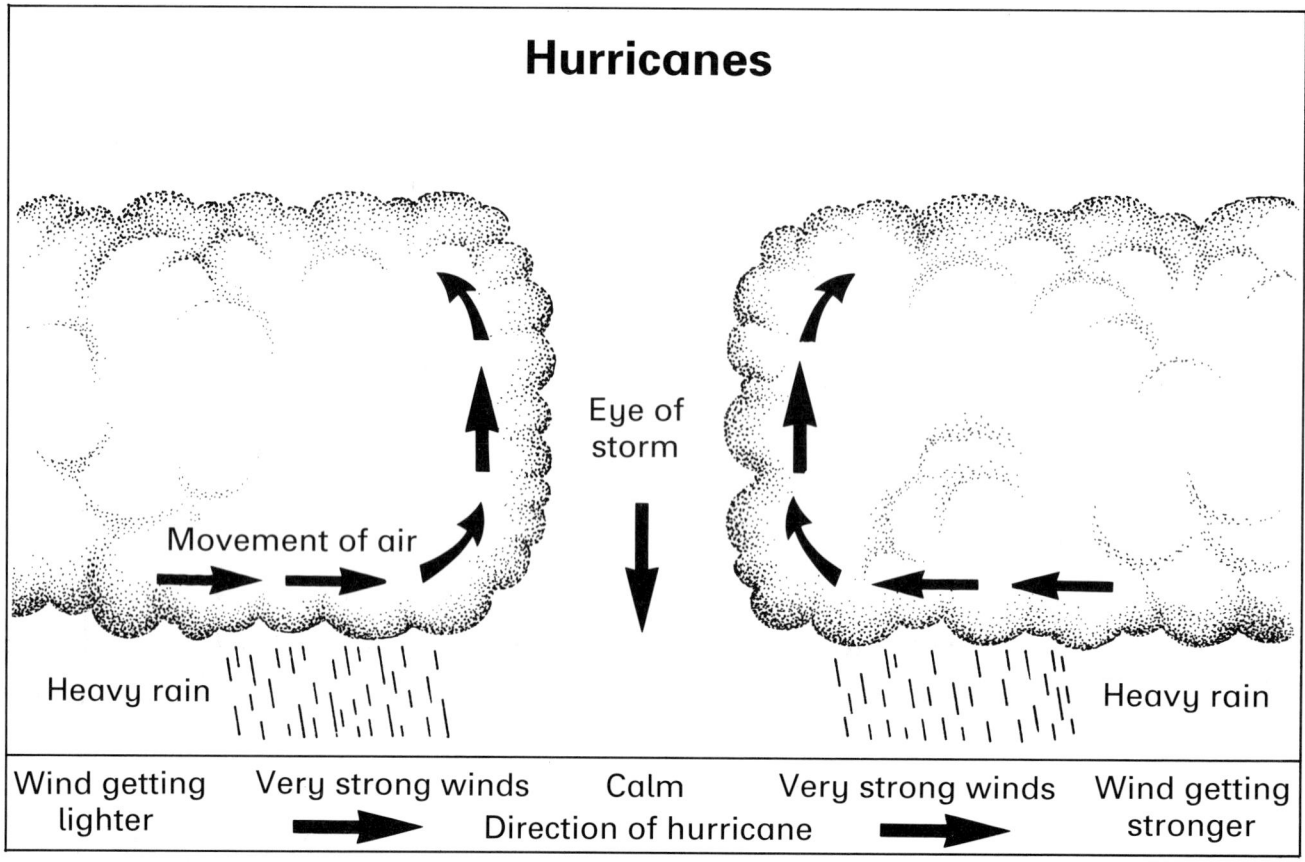

Wind getting lighter	Very strong winds	Calm	Very strong winds	Wind getting stronger

Direction of hurricane

Hurricanes are 500 km across and travel forwards at 25 kph.

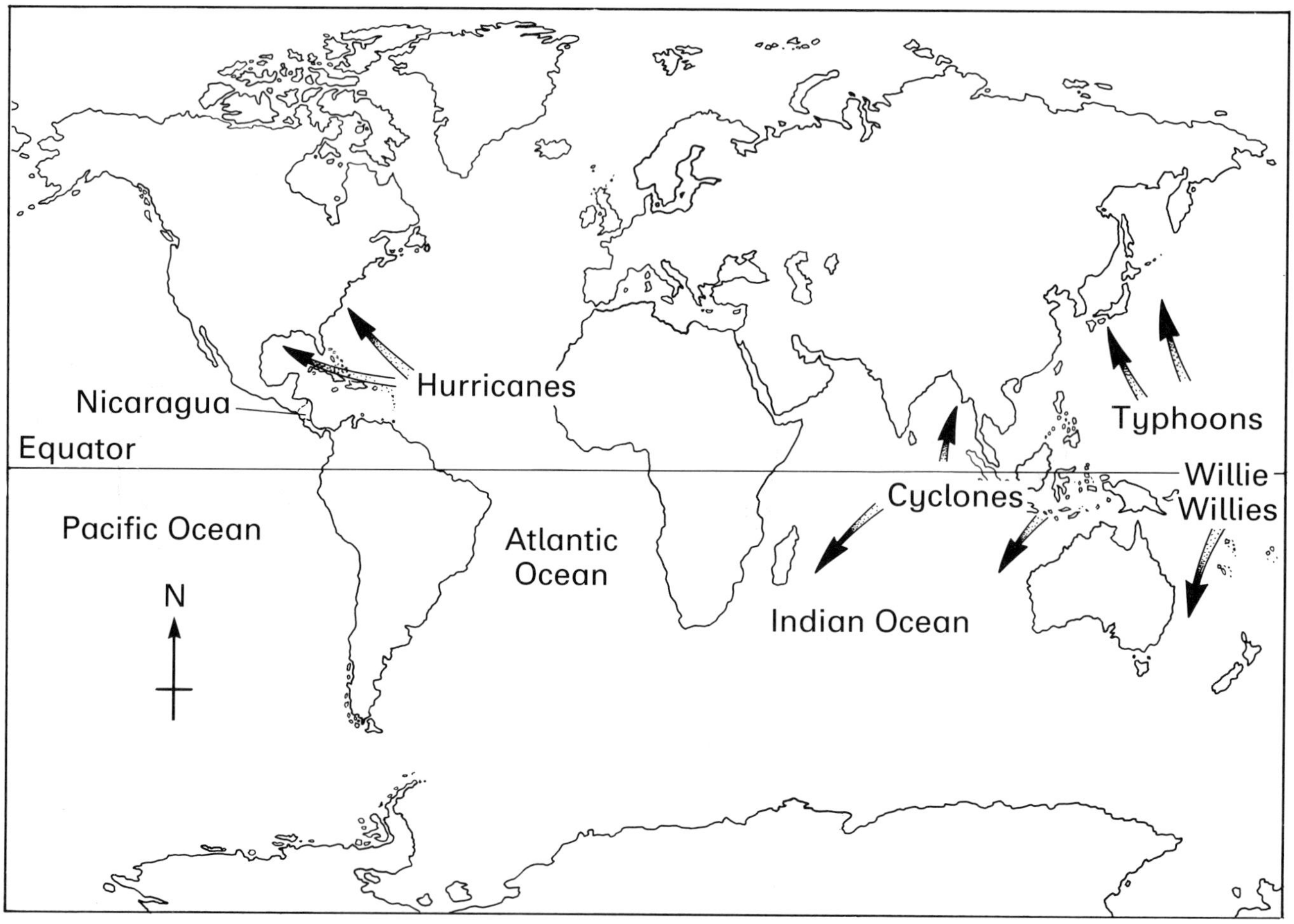

Hurricane Joan

In 1988 Hurricane Joan struck Bluefields on the coast of Nicaragua. Twenty people were killed.

Friday 21 October	Saturday 22 October
AFTERNOON	**NIGHT**

Friday 21 October

1.00 p.m. — Doors and windows nailed shut.

3.00 p.m. — Supplies of food, water and first aid kits organised.

5.00 p.m. — The storm is approaching. The wind speed is 125 kph.

7.00 p.m. — People take shelter in the church and concrete bunkers.

10.00 p.m. — Sea levels start to rise and the wind strengthens. Electricity supply fails.

12.00 midnight — Trees crash down in the street. As the sea level rises people move, roped together, to higher ground.

Saturday 22 October

1.00 a.m. — The church begins to fall down.

2.00 a.m. — The storm is at its worst. Winds reach 200 kph.

3.00 a.m. — The wind drops. This is the 'eye' of the storm.

5.00 a.m. — The wind starts blowing fiercely in the opposite direction.

7.00 a.m. — Heavy rain. The church roof is smashed.

9.00 a.m. — The storm has passed. People leave their shelters.

AFTERNOON / NIGHT — *NIGHT / MORNING*

Different climates 1

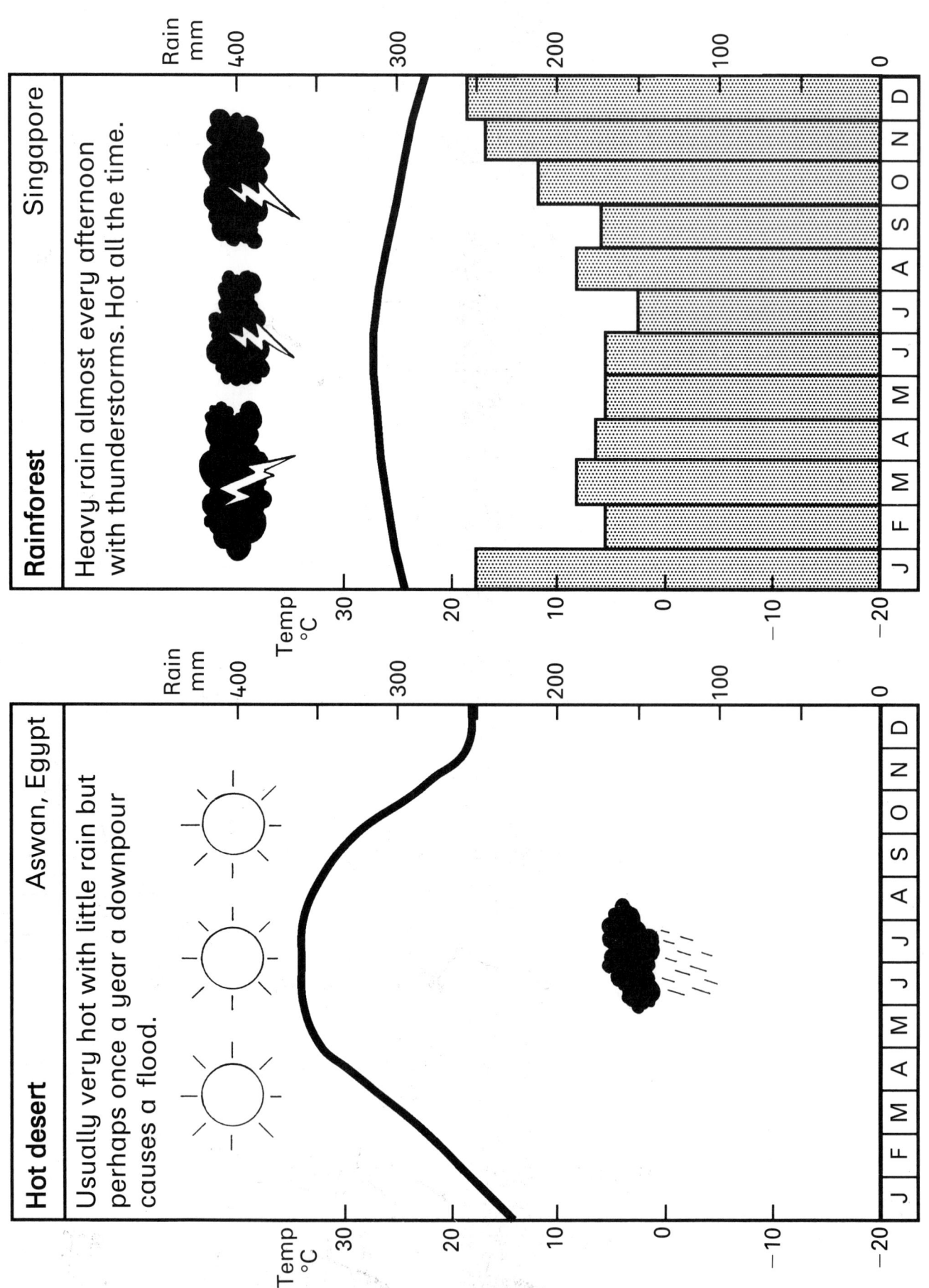

Hot desert — Aswan, Egypt

Usually very hot with little rain but perhaps once a year a downpour causes a flood.

Rainforest — Singapore

Heavy rain almost every afternoon with thunderstorms. Hot all the time.

Different climates 2

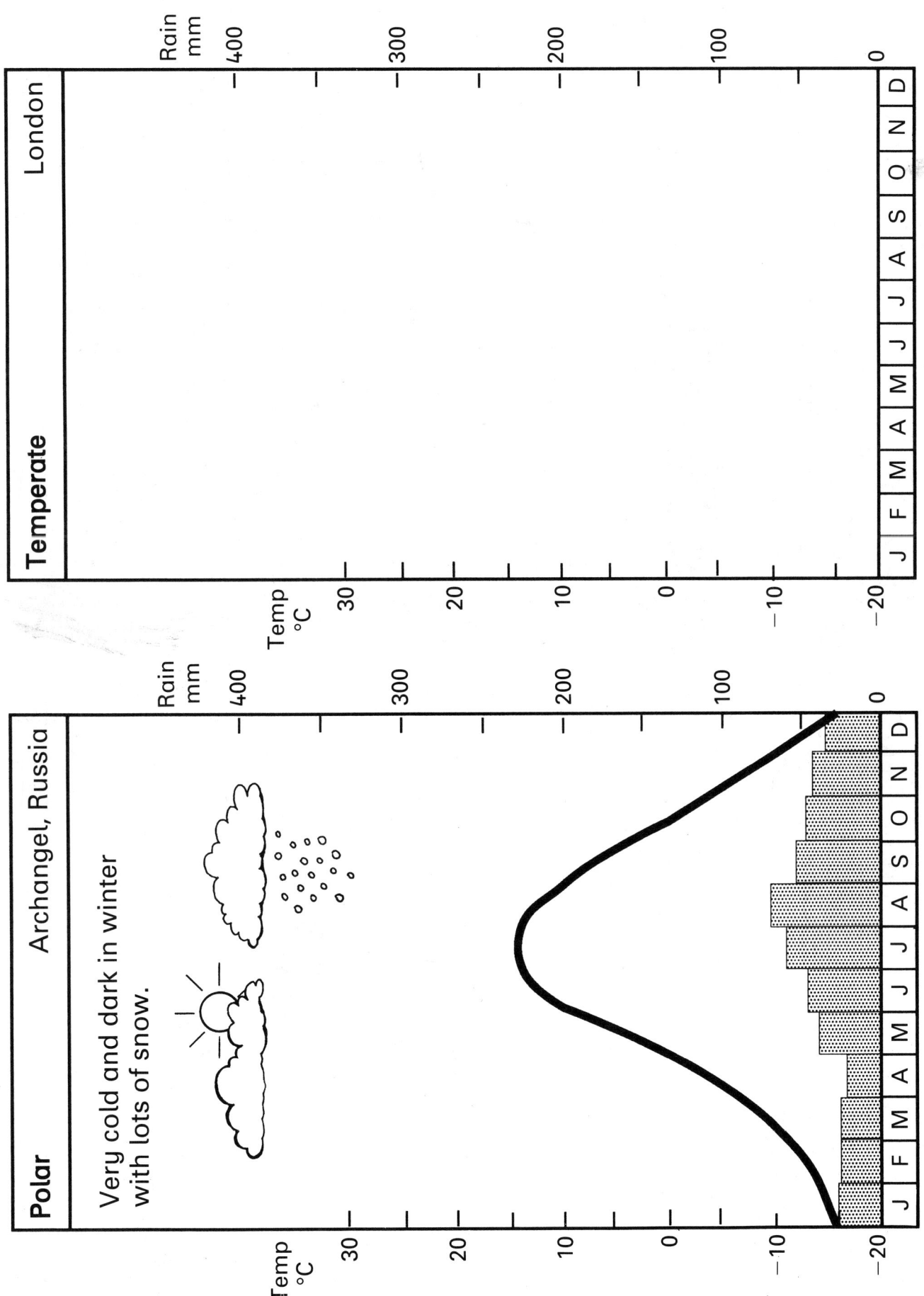

Temperate

London

Rain mm

400

300

200

100

0

J F M A M J J A S O N D

Temp °C

30

20

10

0

-10

-20

Polar

Archangel, Russia

Very cold and dark in winter with lots of snow.

Rain mm

400

300

200

100

0

J F M A M J J A S O N D

Temp °C

30

20

10

0

-10

-20

Copymaster 25

World climate

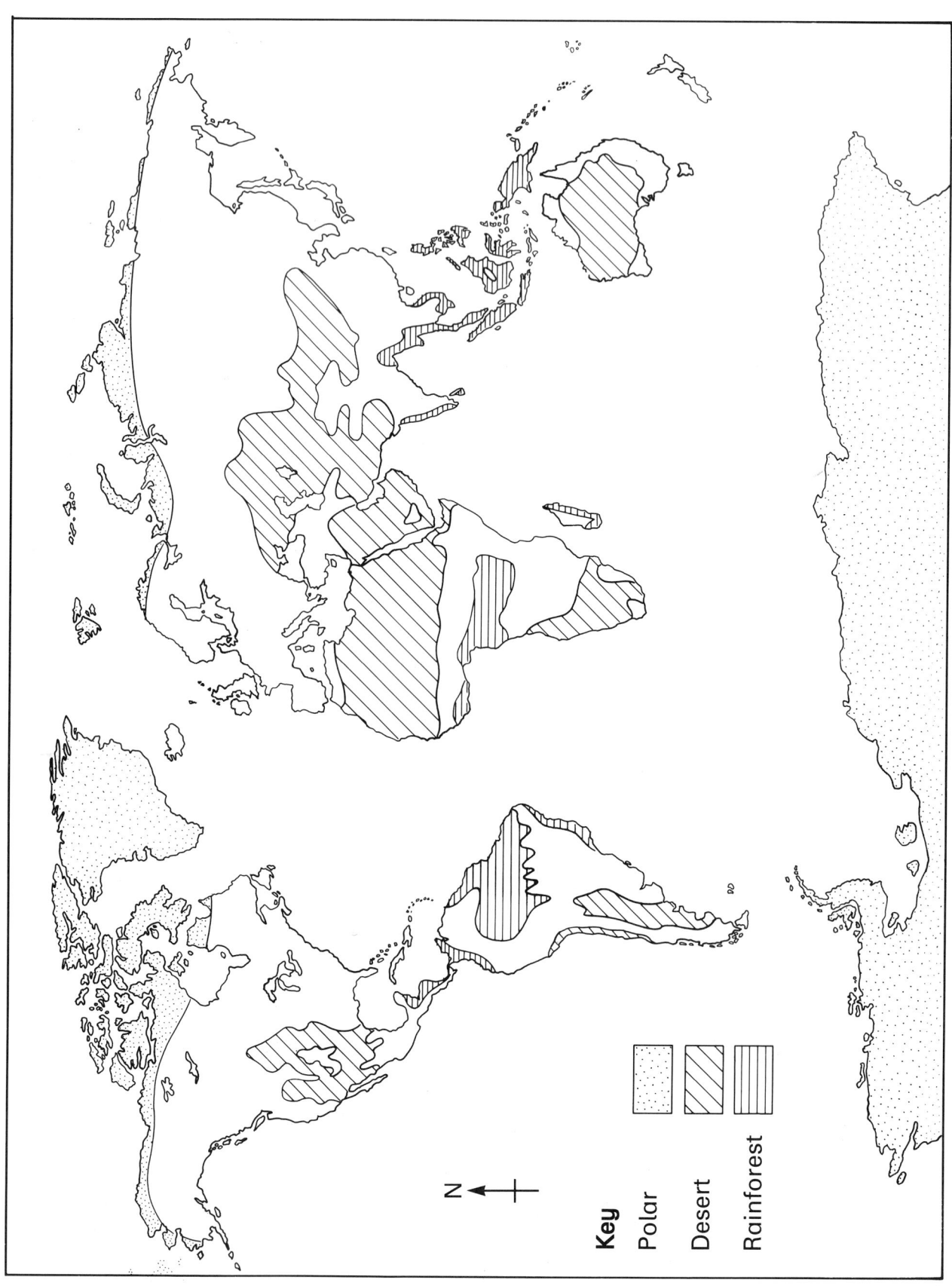

Key
Polar
Desert
Rainforest

N

The story of a volcano

Paricutin

Birth	**1 20 February 1943 (morning)**  Mr Pulido, a farmer, notices the ground is warm beneath his feet.	**2 20 February 1943 (afternoon)** 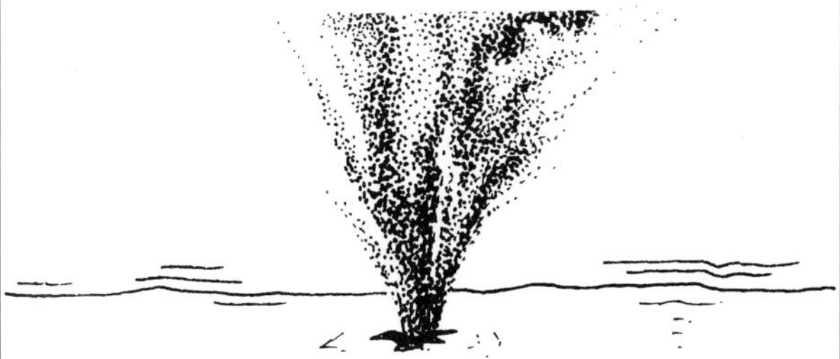 The earth begins to rumble and tremble and smoke rises from a hole in the ground.
Growth	**3 21 February 1943**  Rocks and ash make a hill 8 metres high.	**4 26 February 1943** Fold  The volcano has now covered many fields and is 150 metres high.
Old Age	**5 30 September 1943**  Paricutin is now 400 metres high. The nearby village, Tancitaro, is buried by rock and ash.	**6 4 March 1952** Fold 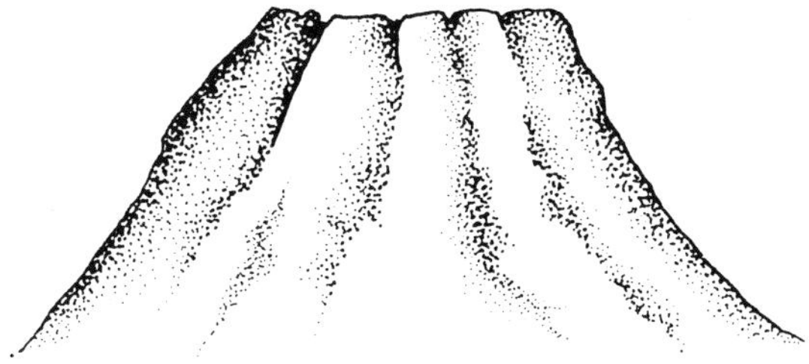 Eruptions stop. Paricutin has stayed dormant (sleeping) ever since.

Flap

Copymaster 27

Mount Etna

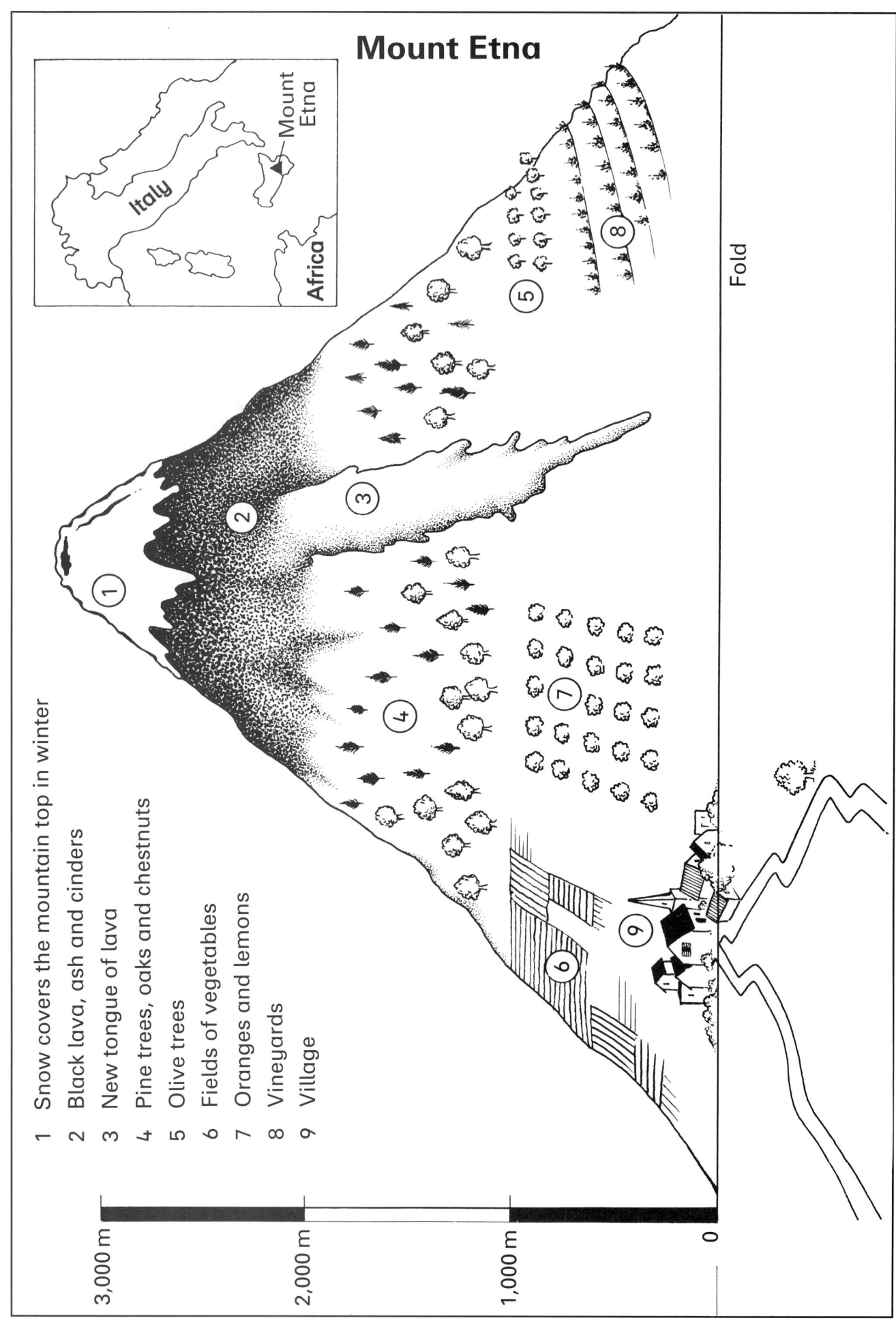

1 Snow covers the mountain top in winter
2 Black lava, ash and cinders
3 New tongue of lava
4 Pine trees, oaks and chestnuts
5 Olive trees
6 Fields of vegetables
7 Oranges and lemons
8 Vineyards
9 Village

Italy

Mount Etna

Africa

Fold

3,000 m

2,000 m

1,000 m

0

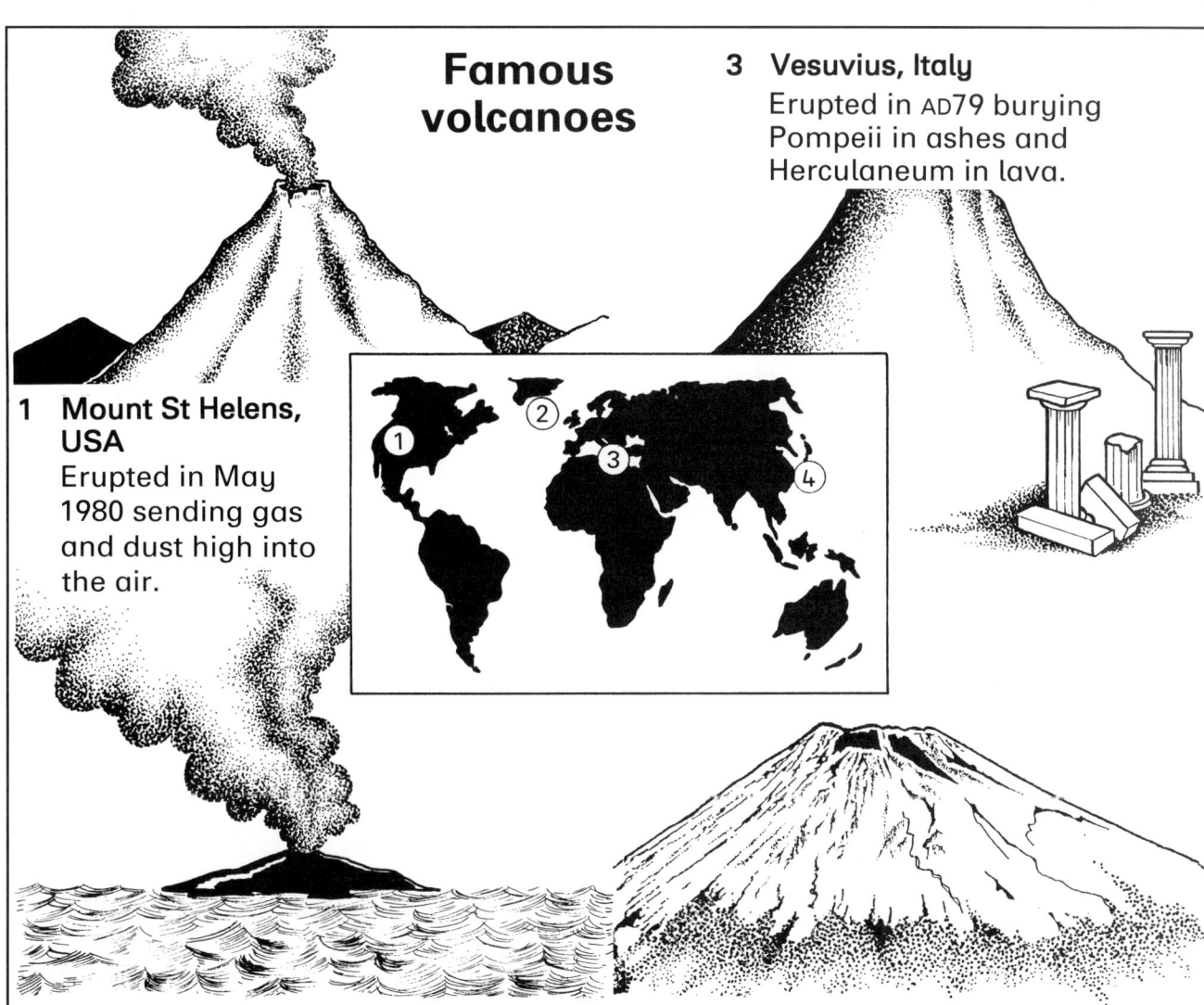

Famous volcanoes

3 Vesuvius, Italy
Erupted in AD79 burying Pompeii in ashes and Herculaneum in lava.

1 Mount St Helens, USA
Erupted in May 1980 sending gas and dust high into the air.

2 Surtsey, Iceland
An undersea volcano formed in 1963.

4 Mount Fujiyama, Japan
A dormant volcano and holy mountain.

Volcano	Place	Why is it famous?
Krakatoa	Indonesia	Exploded in 1883 causing a huge tidal wave.
Mauna Loa	Hawaii, Pacific Ocean	The largest active volcano in the world. Erupts every 3–4 years.
Mount Kilamanjaro	Tanzania	The highest mountain in Africa. Now extinct.
Mount Erebus	Antarctica	The only active volcano in Antarctica.
Tristan da Cuhna	South Atlantic Ocean	Believed to be extinct but erupted in 1961.

Copymaster 29

Earthquake model

Leninakan, Armenia, December 1988

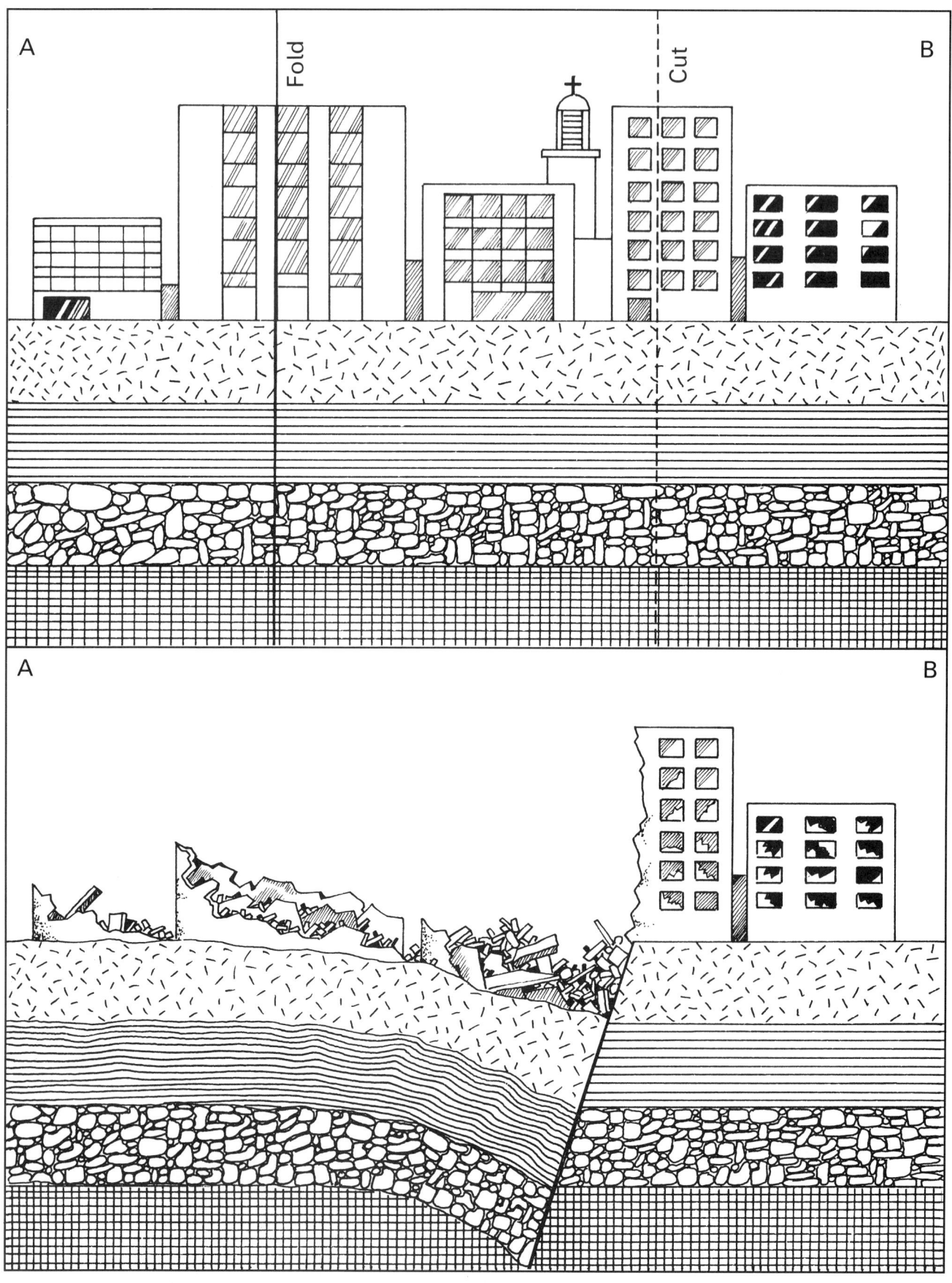

Measuring earthquakes

The Mercalli scale measures the effect of an earthquake on people and buildings.

1–2	Vibrations felt by people sitting or lying down.	
3–4	Windows and doors rattle. Hanging objects swing.	
5–6	Doors swing open. Furniture moves. Windows break.	
7–8	Walls crack. Chimneys fall down. Difficult to stand up.	
9–10	Houses fall down. Dams damaged. Landslides.	
11–12	Ground cracks. Buildings destroyed. Very serious damage.	

Earthquake disasters

Tidal wave hits Japan

EASTERN EUROPE ROCKED BY MASSIVE QUAKE

BRITAIN SENDS FOOD AND MEDICINES

SCIENTISTS FEAR RISING DEATH TOLL

LARGE DAMS CAN TRIGGER EARTHQUAKES

Earthquakes leave thousands homeless

Survivors found alive after 5 days

Earthquake causes millions of pounds of damage

MORE TREMORS EXPECTED

SOME SERIOUS EARTHQUAKES

Place	Country	Date	Dead
Naples	Italy	1980	5,000
Mexico City	Mexico	1985	10,000
Leninakan	Armenia	1988	25,000
Caspian Sea	Iran	1990	50,000
Khilari	India	1993	25,000

How rocks are formed

Igneous rocks come from inside the earth. (Igneous means made by fire.)

Pumice

Granite

Ash and rock

Volcano

Liquid rock

Sedimentary rocks are made from sediment on the sea bed.

Limestone

Sandstone

Rivers carry grains to the sea

Dead sea creatures

Stones

Gravel

Sea

Sand

Silt

Metamorphic rocks have been changed in the earth by heat and pressure (squeezing).

Slate

Marble

Layers of rock folded and squeezed

Copymaster 33

Useful rocks

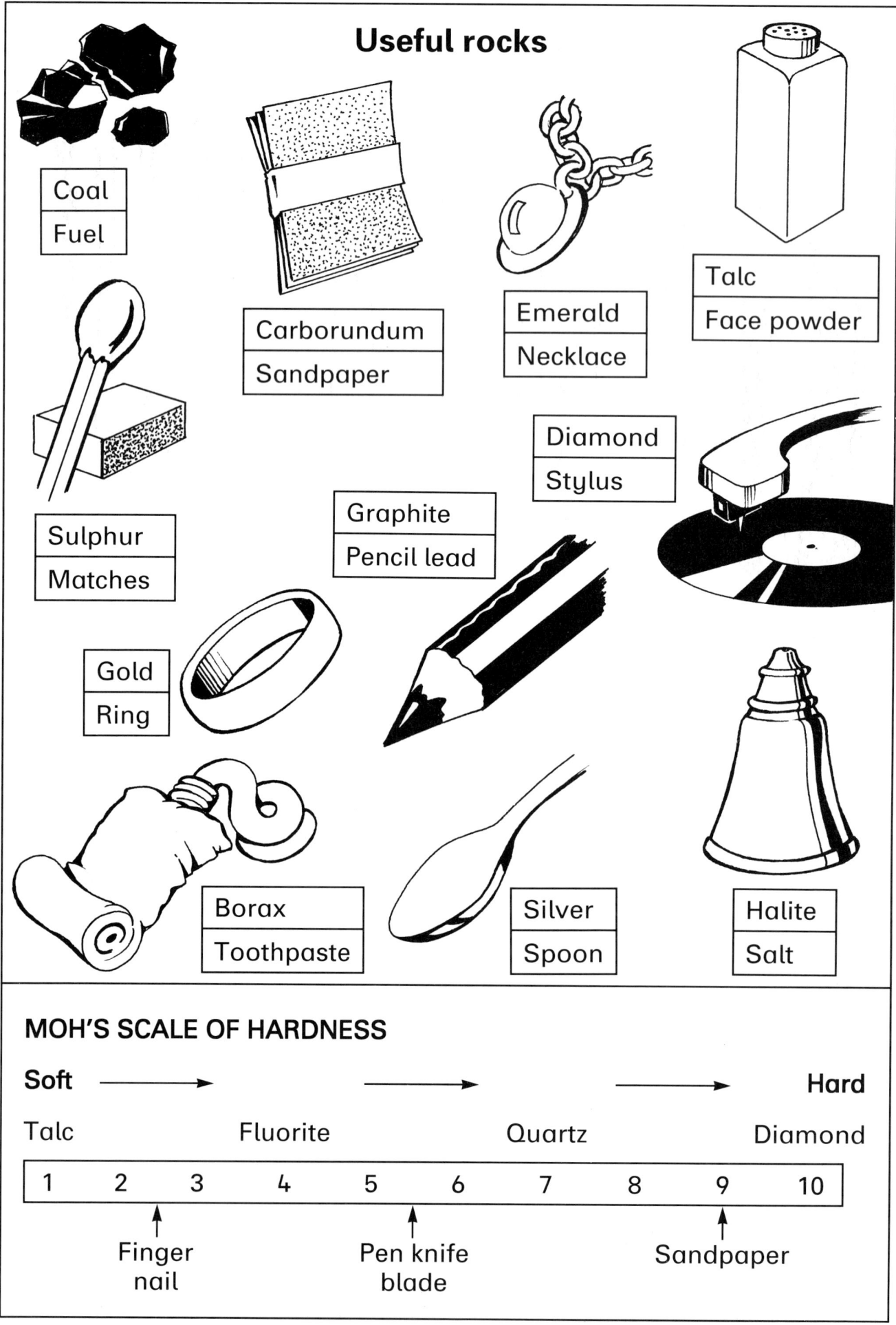

Coal
Fuel

Carborundum
Sandpaper

Emerald
Necklace

Talc
Face powder

Sulphur
Matches

Diamond
Stylus

Graphite
Pencil lead

Gold
Ring

Borax
Toothpaste

Silver
Spoon

Halite
Salt

MOH'S SCALE OF HARDNESS

Soft ⟶ ⟶ ⟶ **Hard**

Talc   Fluorite   Quartz   Diamond

1	2	3	4	5	6	7	8	9	10

Finger
nail

Pen knife
blade

Sandpaper

Old and new rocks

Time	Period	Life forms	
100 million years ago	Cretaceous Chalk	Mammals	Oak trees
200 million years ago	Triassic Sandstone	Dinosaurs	Conifer trees
300 million years ago	Carboniferous Coal	Insects	Ferns
400 million years ago	Silurian Shale	Fish	Seaweed

Copymaster 35

Soil formation

Weathering

 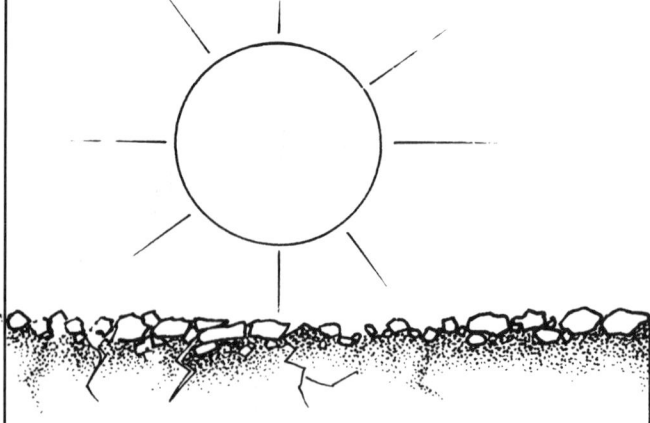

Rain gets into cracks in rocks. The rock cracks when the water freezes.	The rock crumbles in the heat of the sun.

Action of plants

Plant roots break up pieces of rock.	Leaves and roots rot making more soil.

Action of animals

Animal droppings and dead creatures build up the soil.	Worms and insects turn over the soil and keep it healthy.

Creatures in the soil

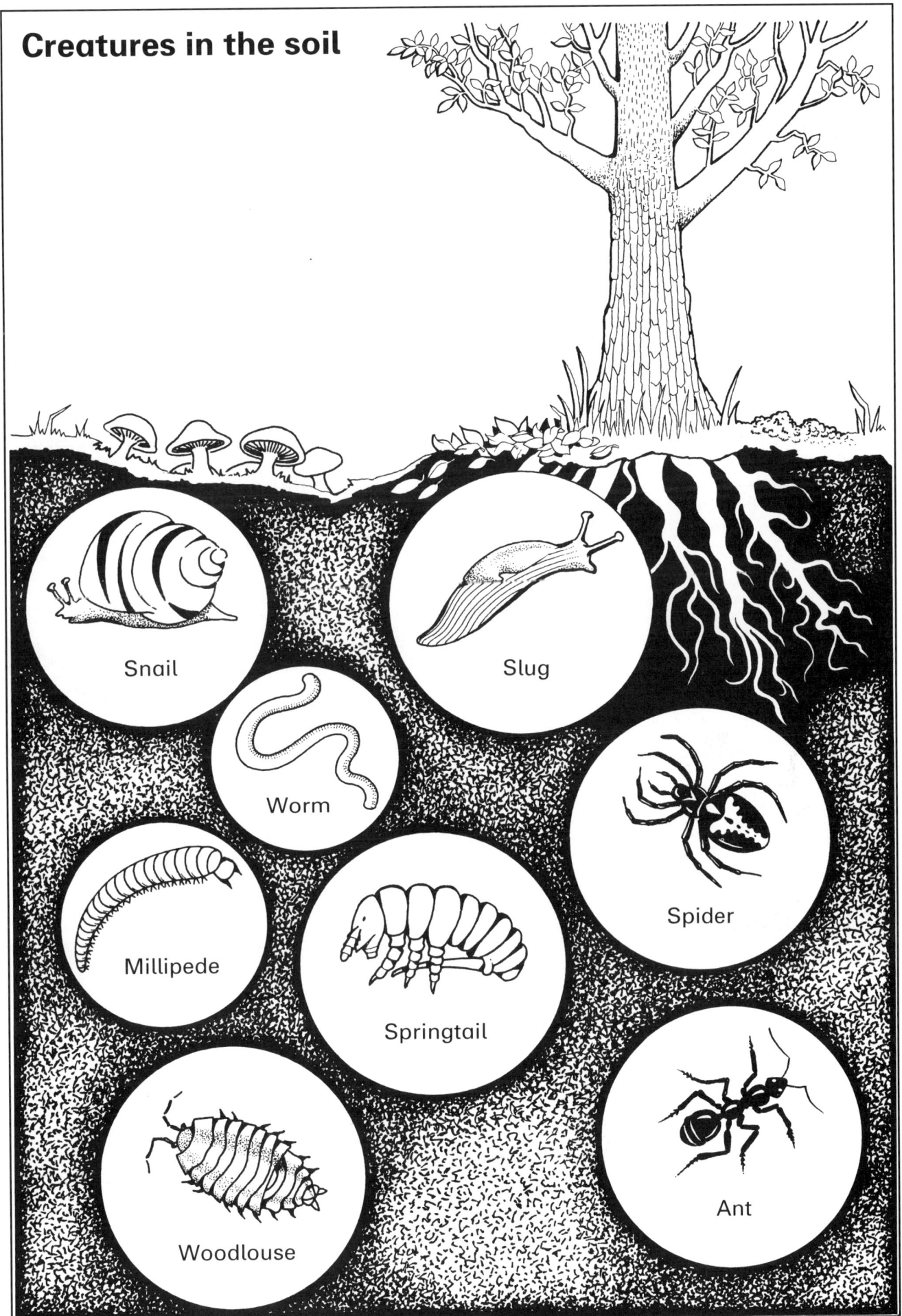

Snail

Slug

Worm

Millipede

Spider

Springtail

Woodlouse

Ant

Soil profile

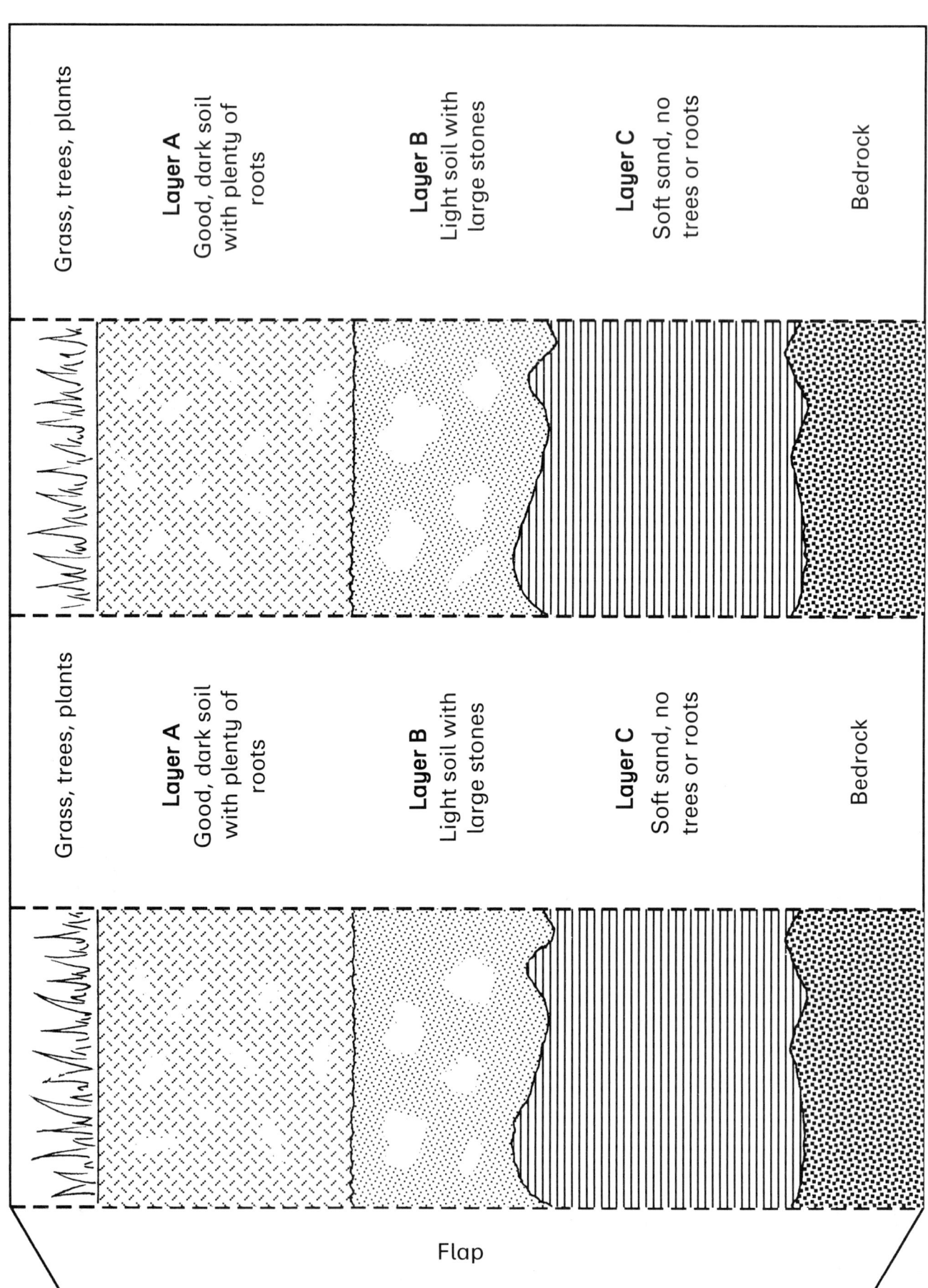

Grass, trees, plants

Layer A
Good, dark soil with plenty of roots

Layer B
Light soil with large stones

Layer C
Soft sand, no trees or roots

Bedrock

Grass, trees, plants

Layer A
Good, dark soil with plenty of roots

Layer B
Light soil with large stones

Layer C
Soft sand, no trees or roots

Bedrock

Flap

Copymaster 38

Soil at risk

In some parts of the USA the soil has been used so much it is now exhausted.

As trees are cleared in the Himalayas storms wash the soil away and cause floods downstream.

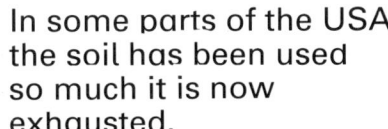

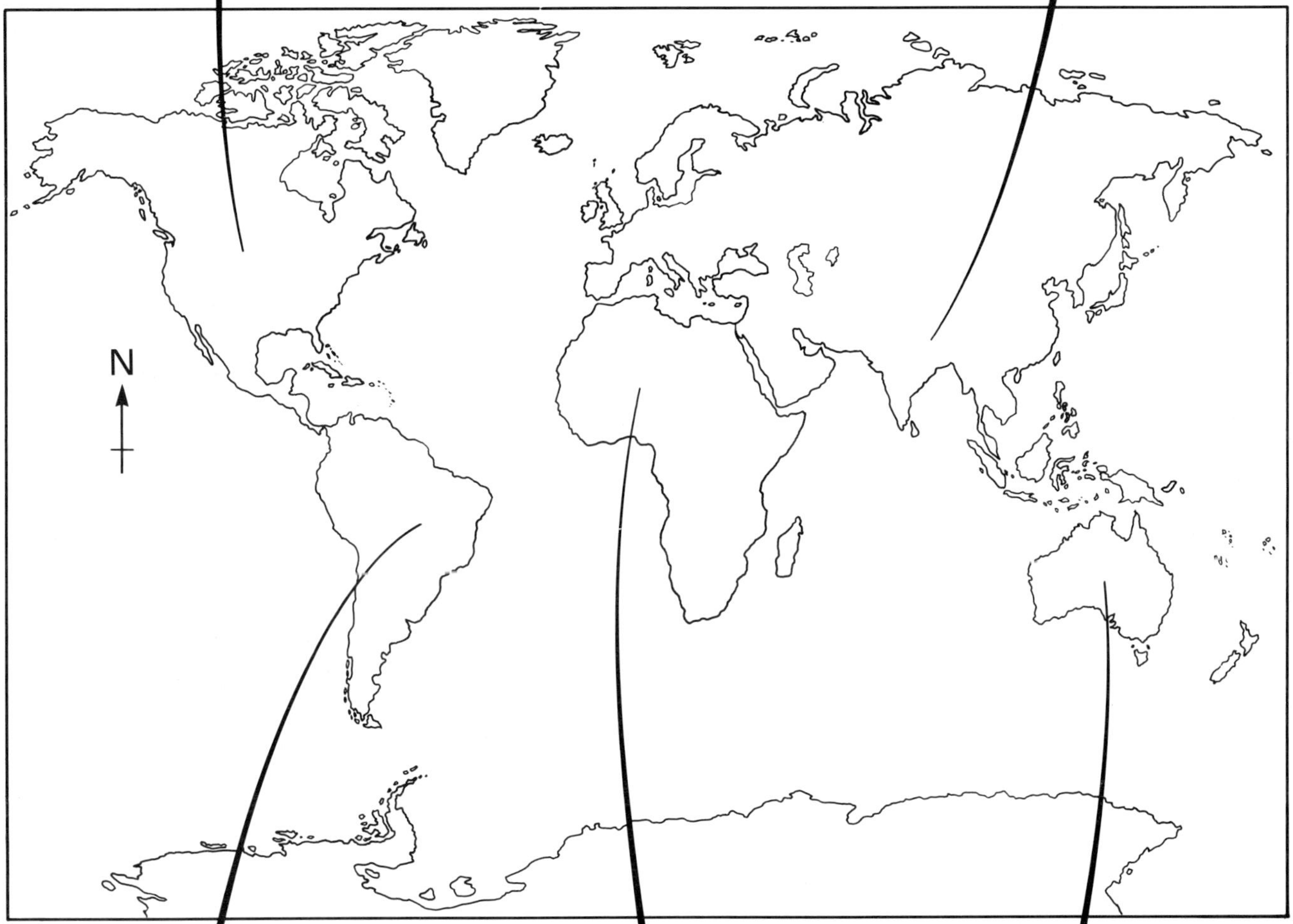

In South America the rainforest is being cleared for farming and the soil then washes away.

The Sahara Desert is spreading southwards as too many animals feed on the land.

Three-quarters of the land in Australia is at risk from blowing away.

Looking after the soil

Planting trees

Building terraces

Keeping fewer animals

Planting shelter belts

House types

Detached

Semi-detached

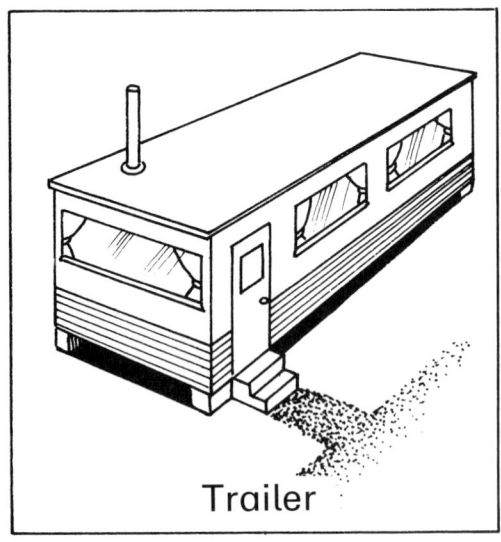

Trailer

Terrace

Bungalow

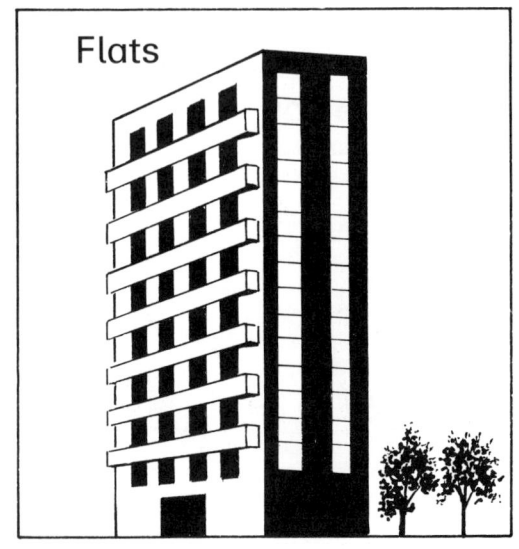

Flats

House plans

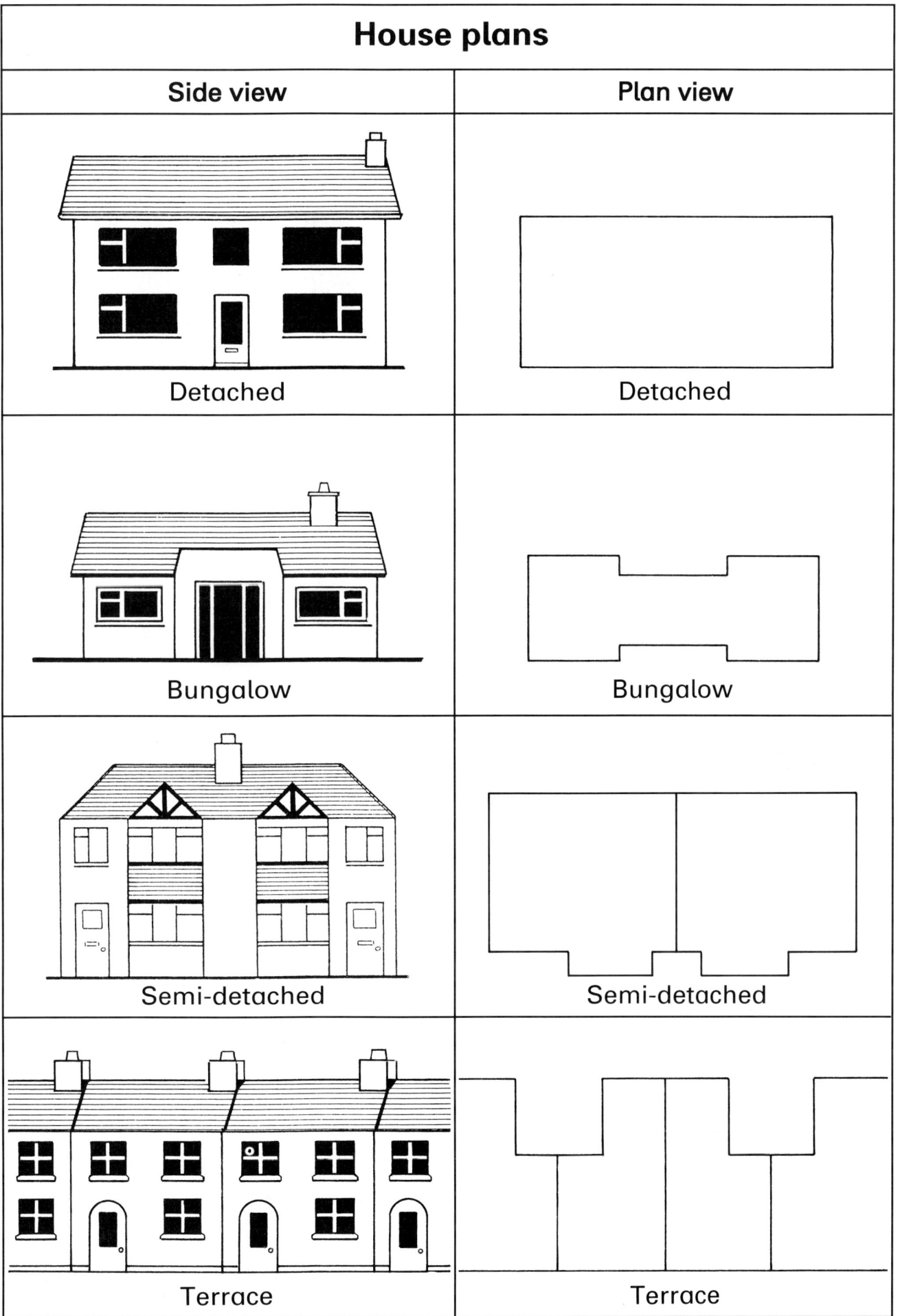

Side view	Plan view
Detached	Detached
Bungalow	Bungalow
Semi-detached	Semi-detached
Terrace	Terrace

Houses in towns

Elizabethan 1600
- Wood frame
- Jetty (overhang)

Georgian 1750
- Tall windows
- Pillars round porch

Victorian villa 1870
- Unbalanced plan
- Many patterns and decorations

Inter-war 1930
- Bay windows
- Fake half-timbers

Post-war 1960
- Large 'picture' windows
- Plain with few decorations

1600
1650
1700
1750
1800
1850
1900
1950
2000

Homes around the world

Temperate climate

Fire keeps house warm

Large windows let in sunlight

Brick walls keep room dry

Brick house, United Kingdom

Rainforest climate

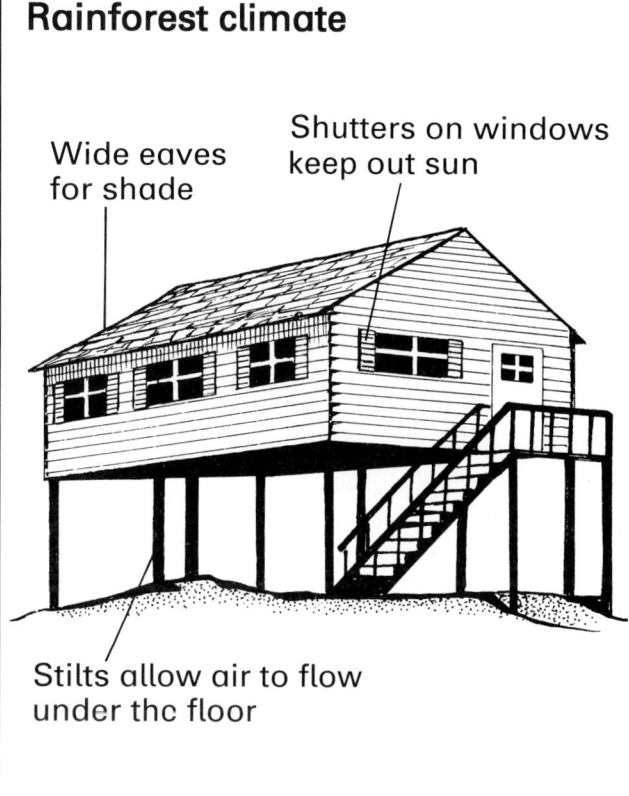

Wide eaves for shade

Shutters on windows keep out sun

Stilts allow air to flow under the floor

Wood house, Australia

Mountain climate

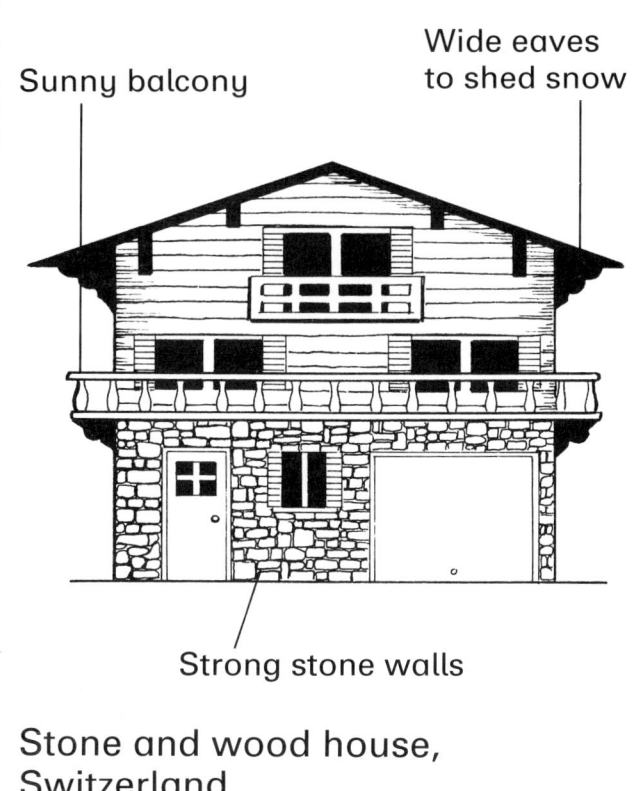

Sunny balcony

Wide eaves to shed snow

Strong stone walls

Stone and wood house, Switzerland

Desert climate

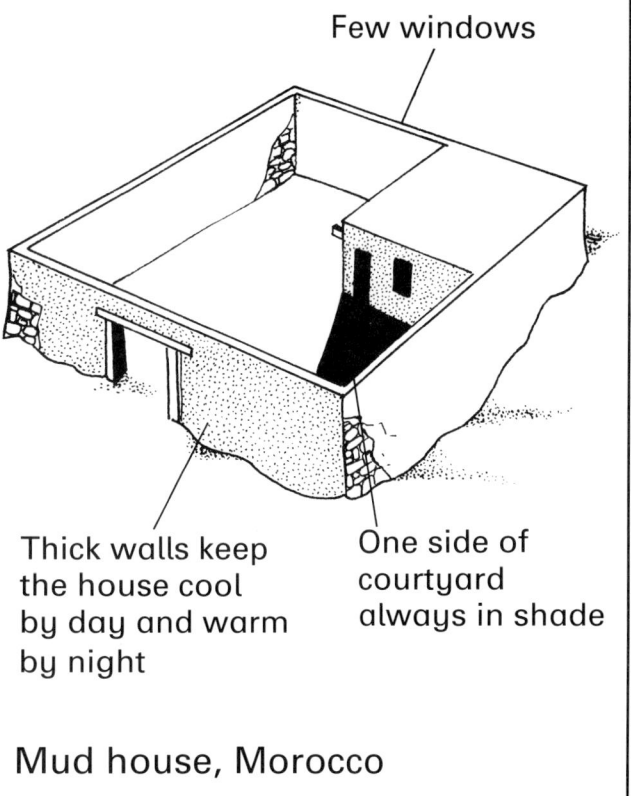

Few windows

Thick walls keep the house cool by day and warm by night

One side of courtyard always in shade

Mud house, Morocco

Copymaster 43

Traditional homes

Ice
In the Arctic the Inuit used to make house of blocks of ice as there were no other building materials.

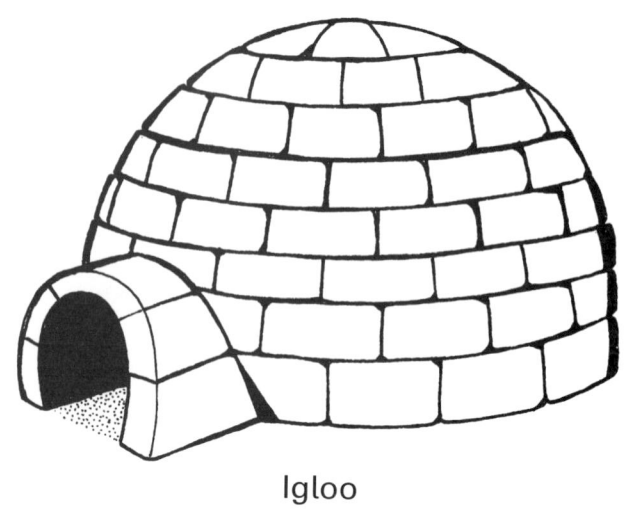

Igloo

Wood
In Northern Europe people built houses of wood because there were so many trees.

Log cabin

Cloth
In deserts people needed to move around with their animals. They used tents which could be packed away and carried from place to place.

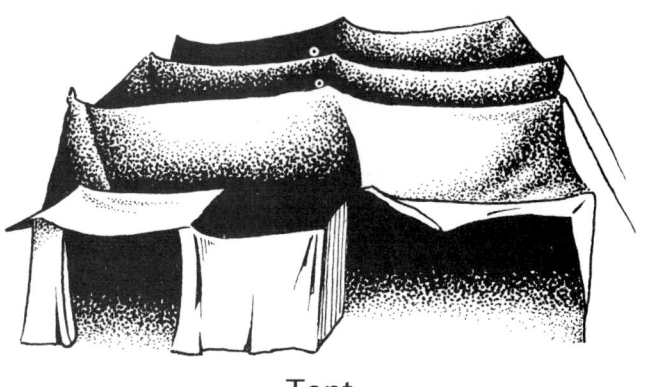

Tent

Under the street

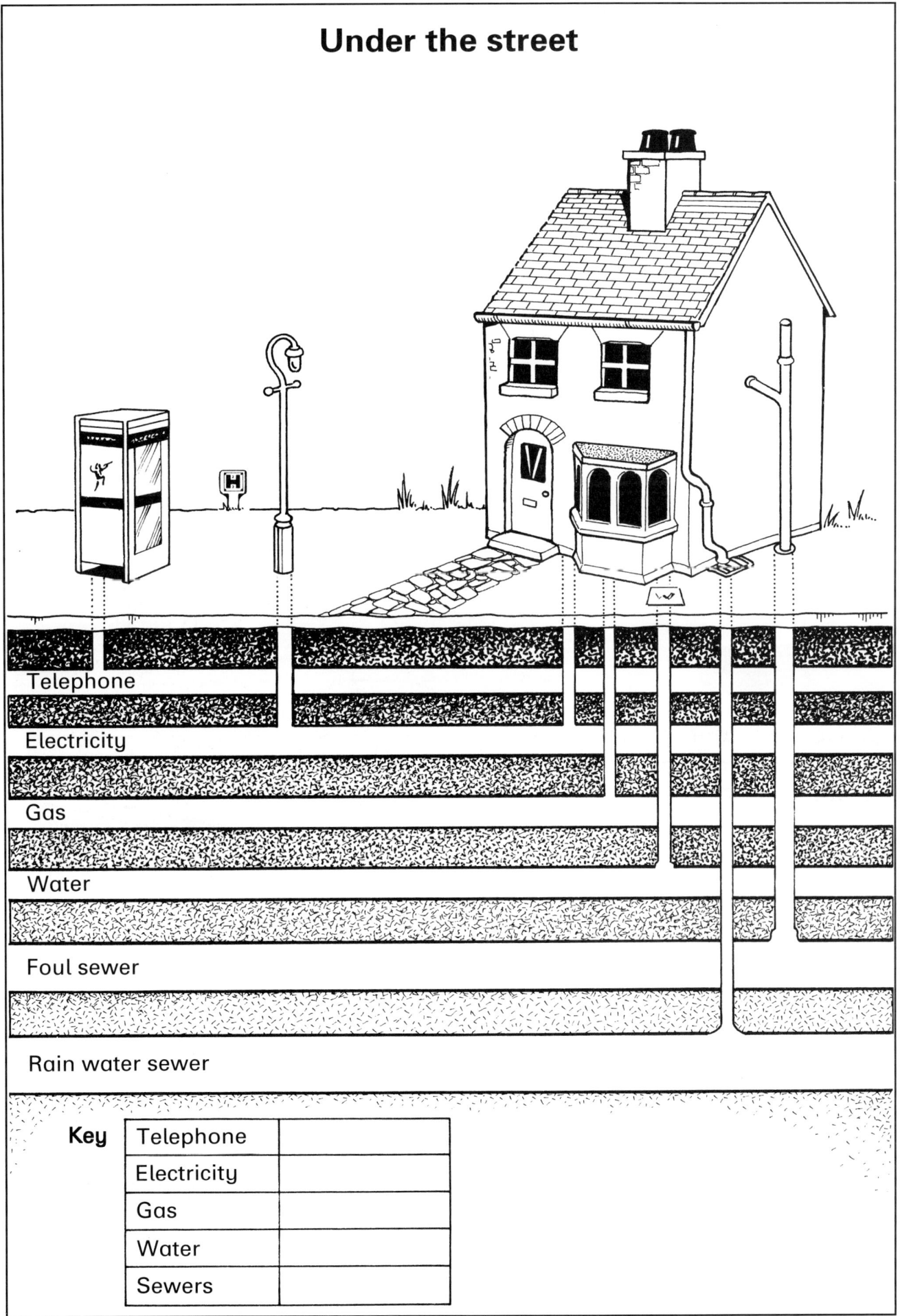

Telephone

Electricity

Gas

Water

Foul sewer

Rain water sewer

Key	Telephone	
	Electricity	
	Gas	
	Water	
	Sewers	

Street furniture

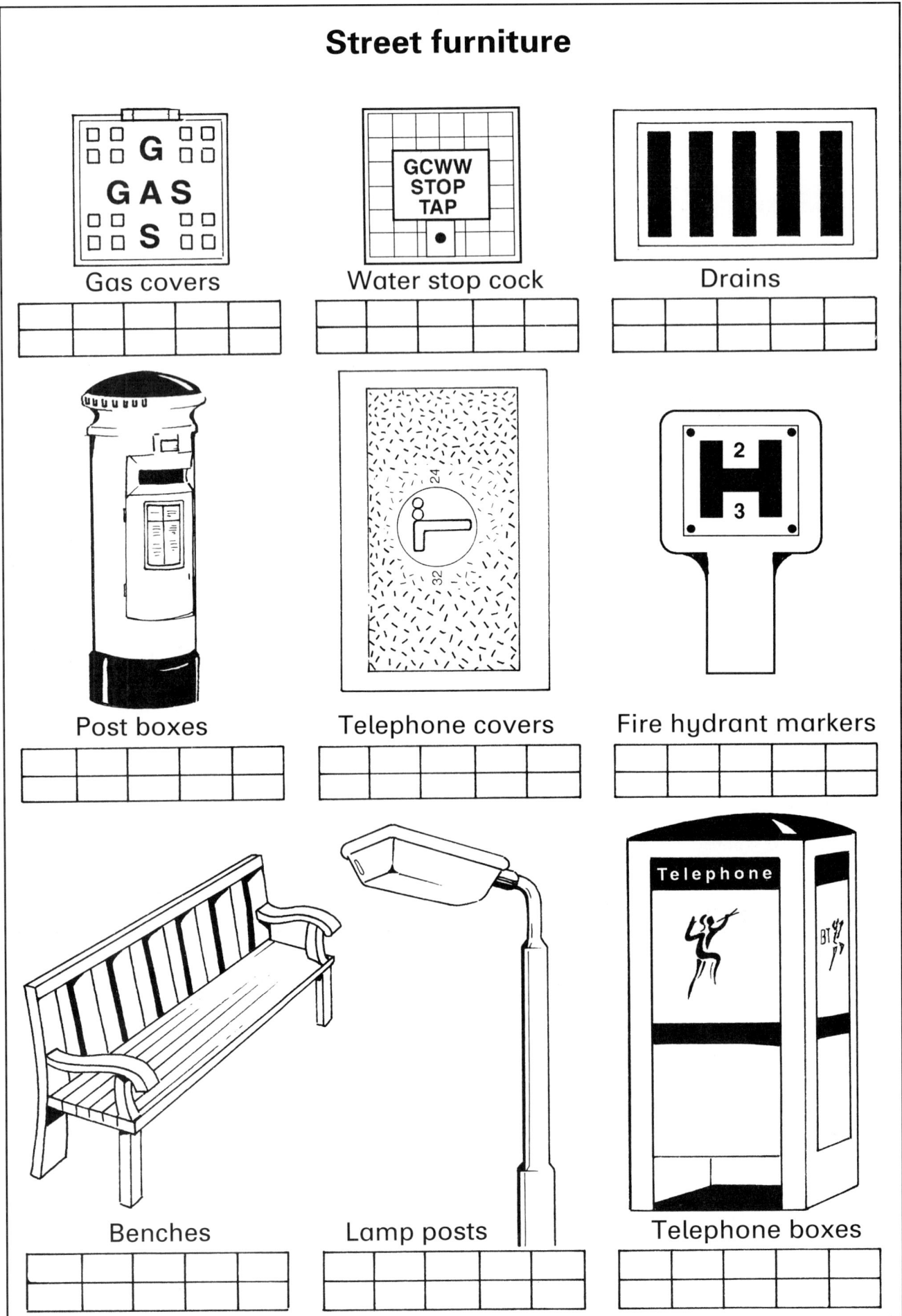

Gas covers

Water stop cock

Drains

Post boxes

Telephone covers

Fire hydrant markers

Benches

Lamp posts

Telephone boxes

Towns in Scotland

Glasgow

Stirling

Grangemouth

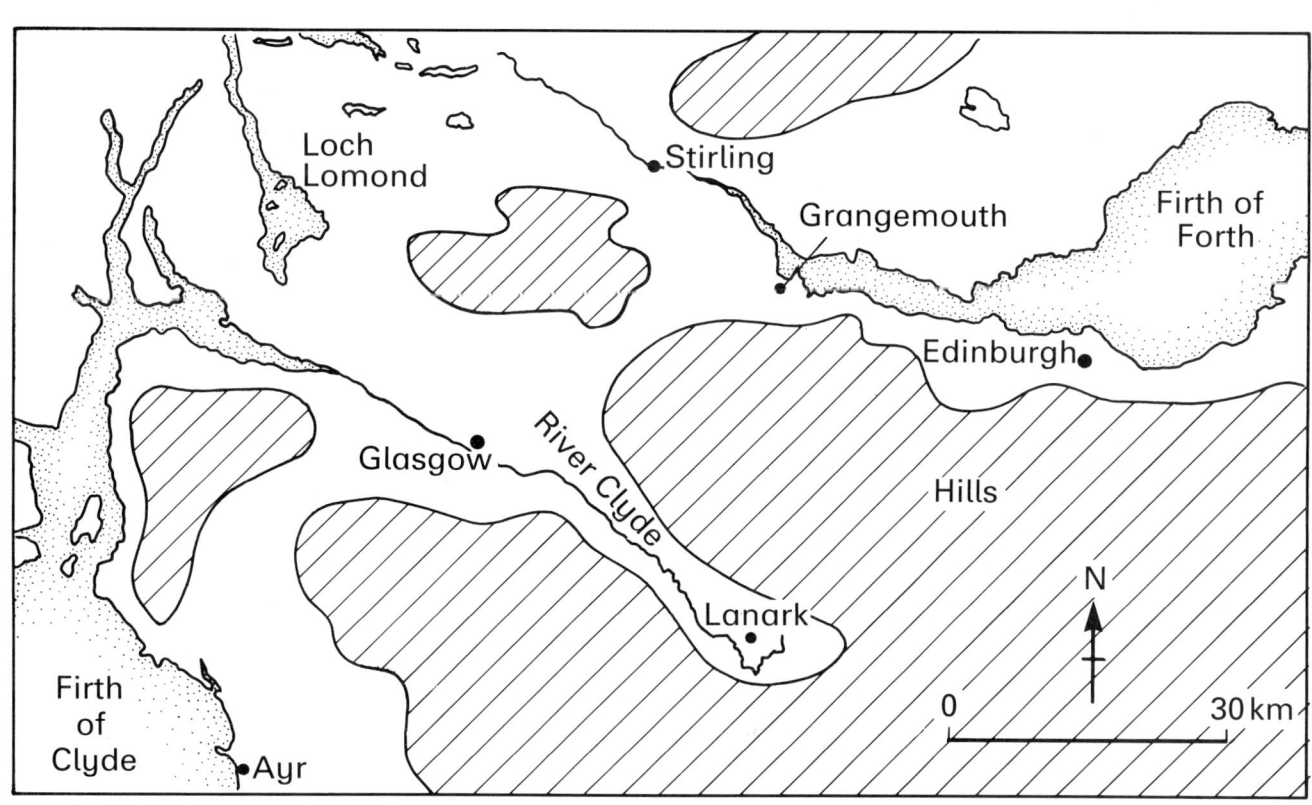

Port

Crossing point

Factories

Ayr

Lanark

Edinburgh

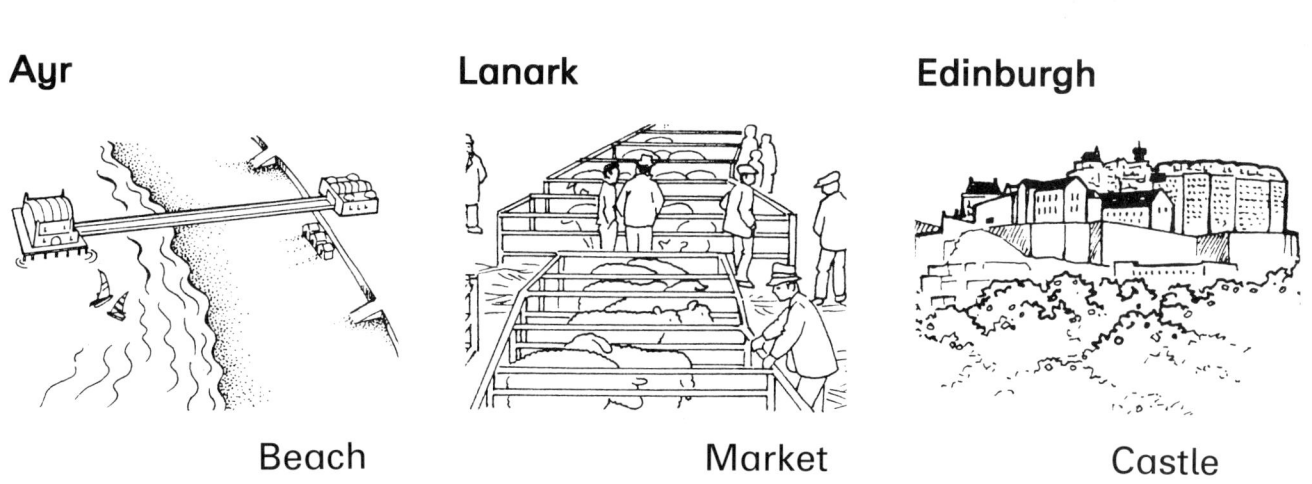

Beach

Market

Castle

Places in London

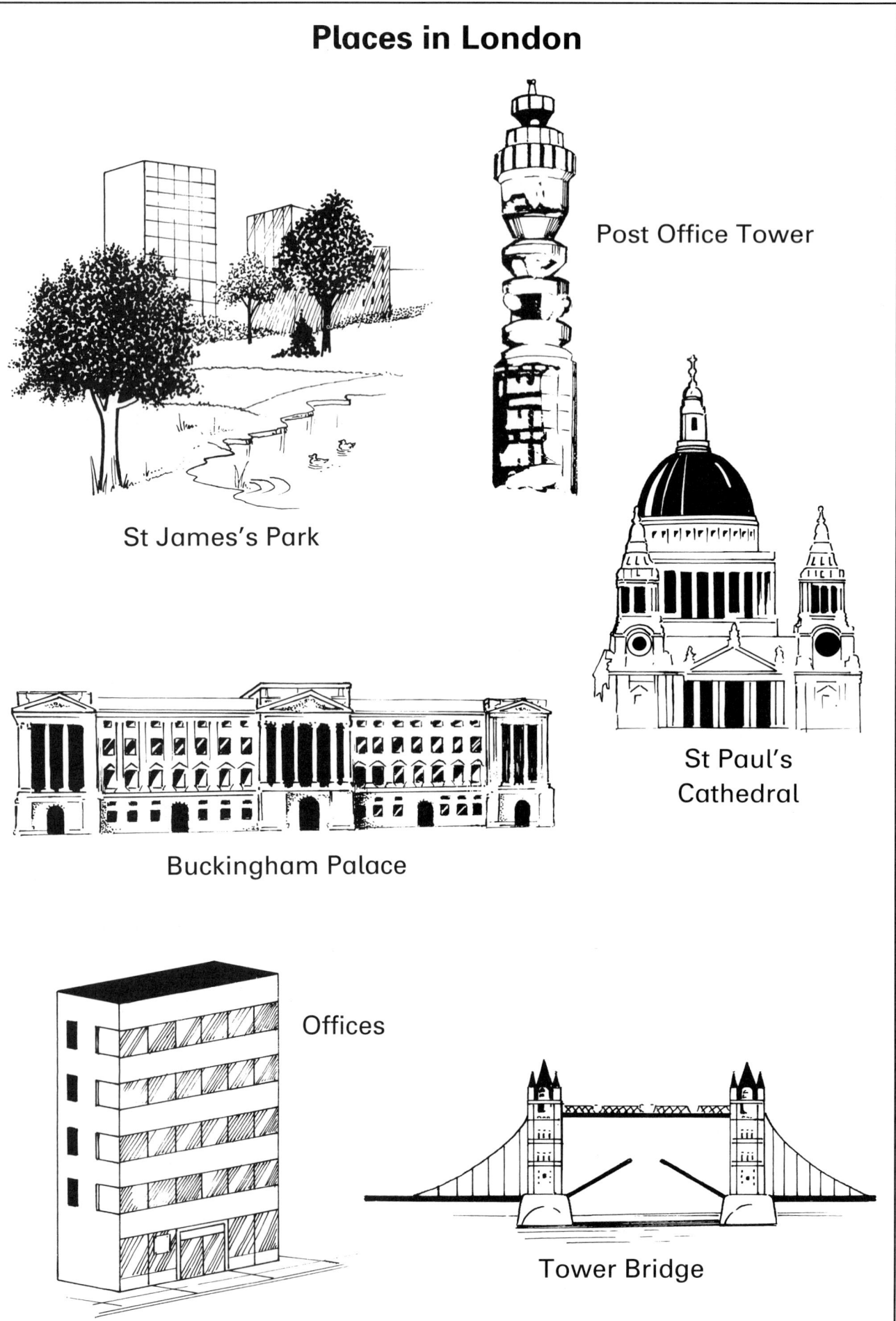

Post Office Tower

St James's Park

St Paul's Cathedral

Buckingham Palace

Offices

Tower Bridge

Places in Nairobi

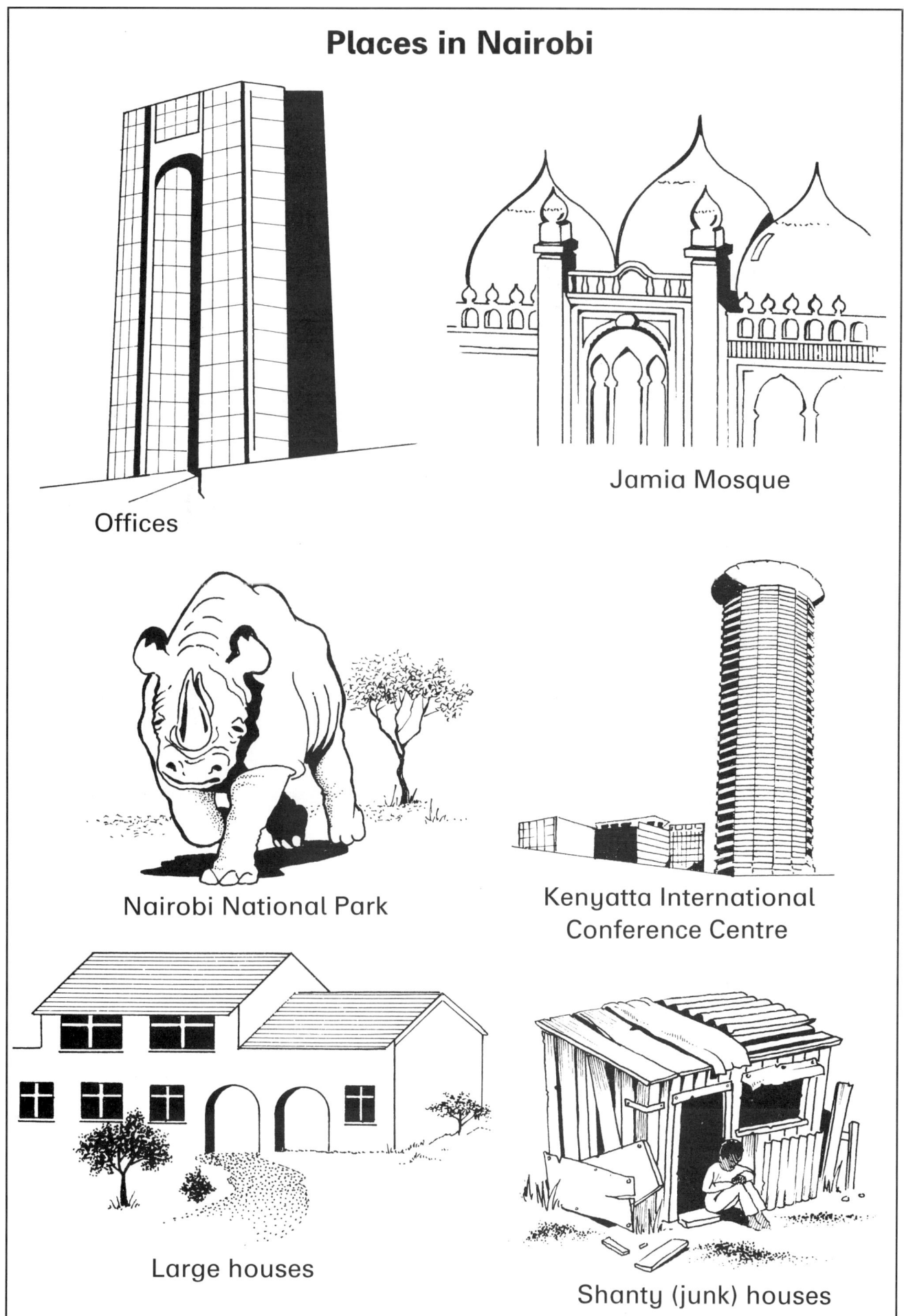

Offices

Jamia Mosque

Nairobi National Park

Kenyatta International
Conference Centre

Large houses

Shanty (junk) houses

Transport in Nairobi

Business people often travel by car or taxi.

People crowd into small buses called matatu. The conductor holds up the number of the bus.

Wooden hand carts carry large loads.

Tourists start their safaris (visits to game parks) in Nairobi.

Moving to Nairobi

We left our village because there was no work.

I wanted to earn more money.

All our crops died in the drought.

There's running water and electricity in Nairobi.

I didn't want to spend my life working in the fields.

There's a hospital in Nairobi.

There's nothing to do in the countryside.

I wanted to be in an exciting place with lots of other people.

Great cities

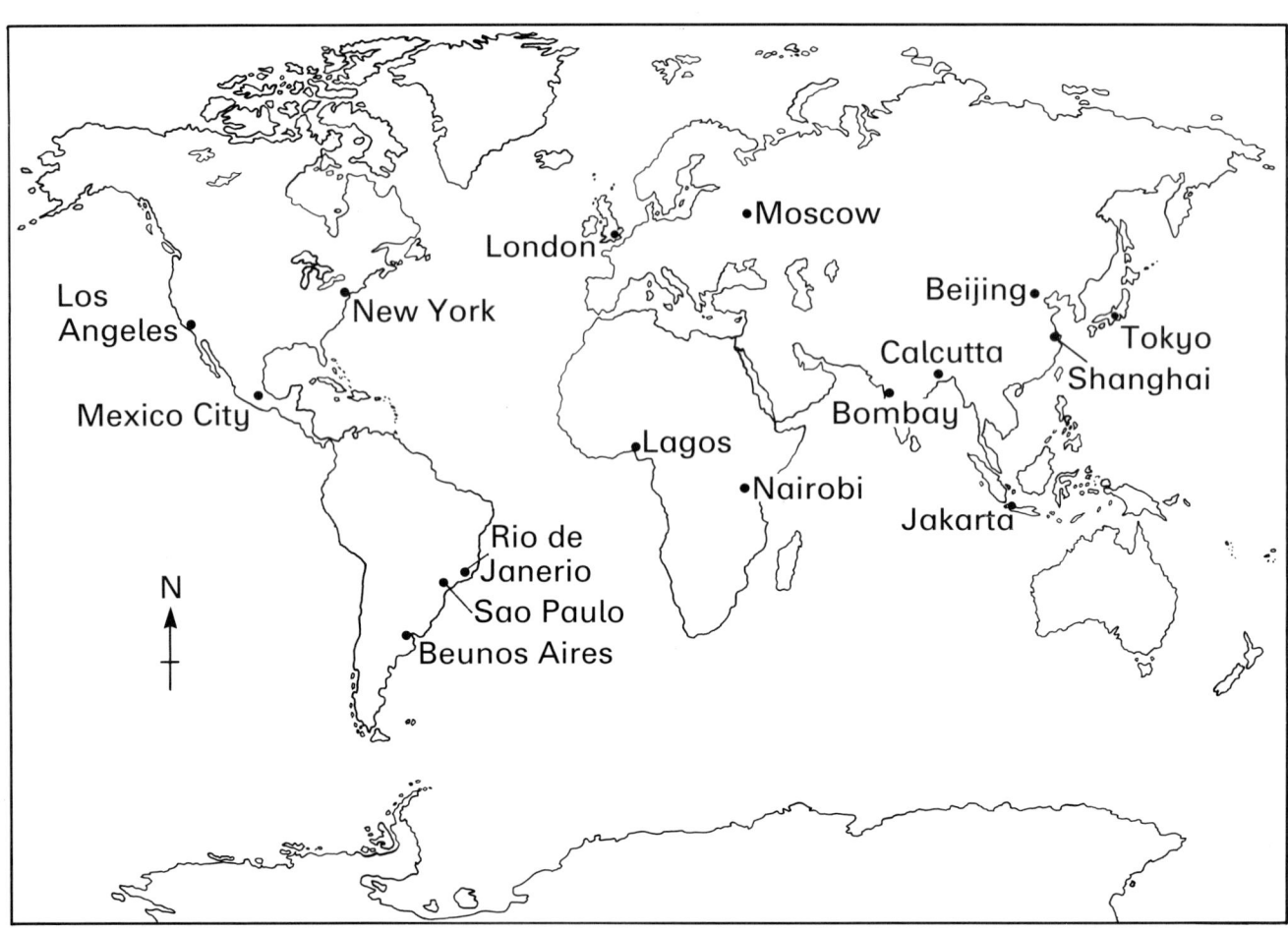

Expected population in the year 2000

City	Population (millions)	Graph
New York	17	
Mexico	26	
Sao Paulo	22	
London	10	
Nairobi	5	
Moscow	5	
Bombay	15	
Tokyo	15	

0 2 4 6 8 10 12 14 16 18 20 22 24

Millions

Famous buildings

1 Statue of Liberty

New York

2 Eiffel Tower

Paris

3 Kremlin

Moscow

4 Imperial Palace

Beijing

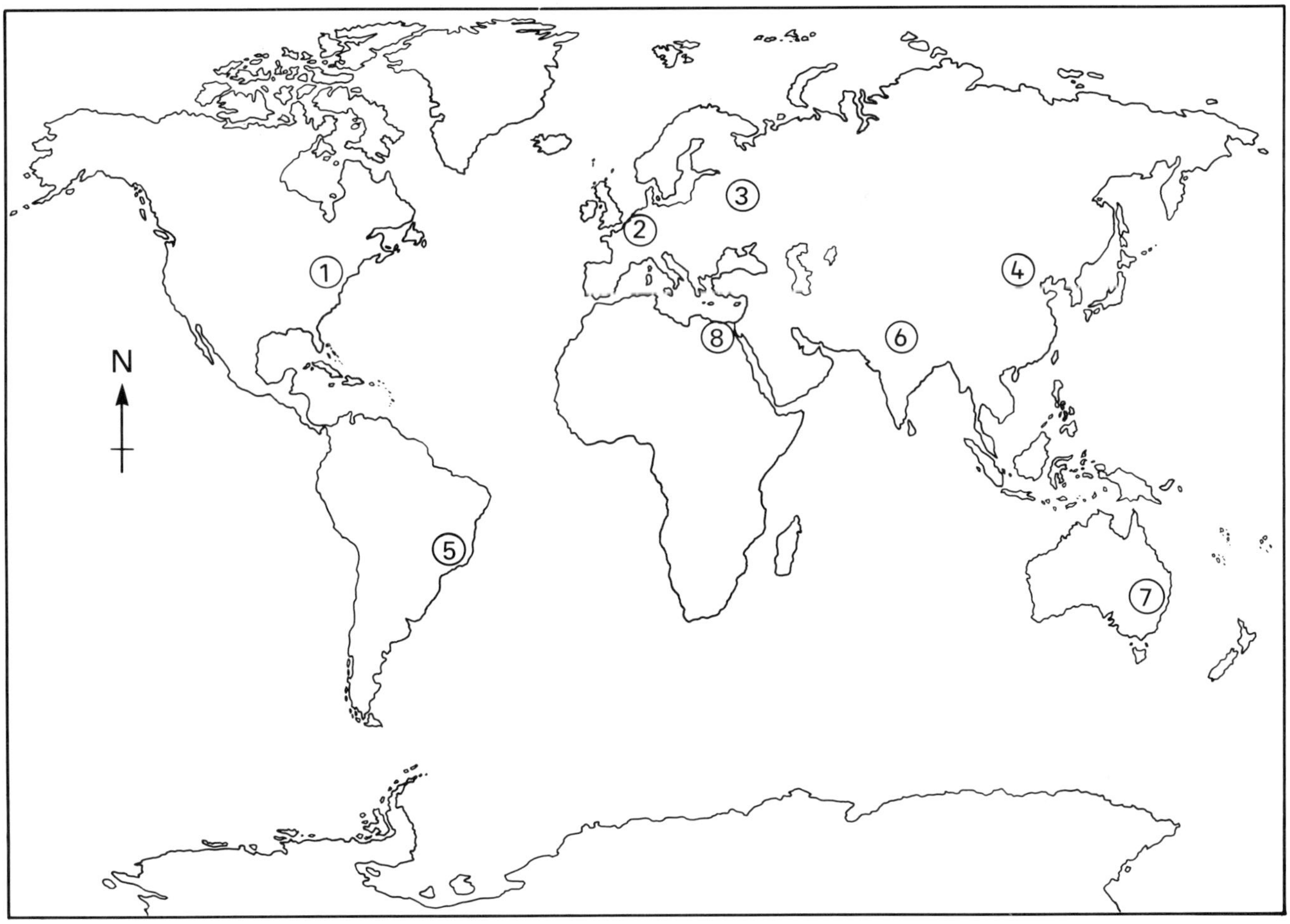

N
↑

5 Statue of Christ

Rio de Janerio

6 Taj Mahal

Agra

7 Opera House

Sydney

8 Pyramids

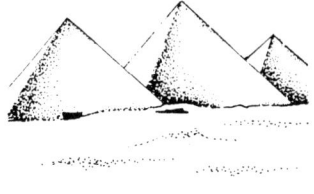

Cairo

Copymaster 53

Road signs

Warning signs

Roundabout

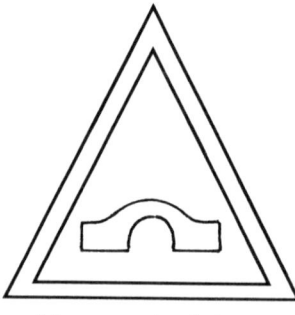
Hump bridge

School

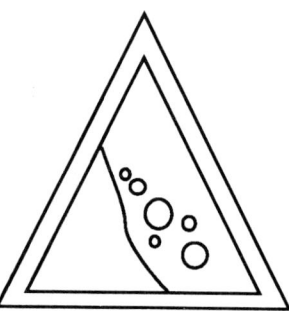
Falling rocks

Slippery road

Accident

Signs giving orders

No right turn

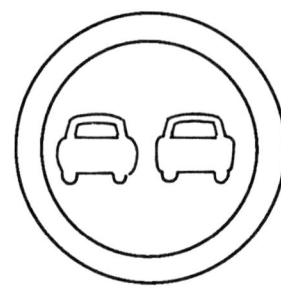
No overtaking

No cycling

Information signs

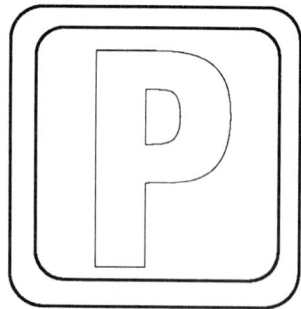
Parking place

One-way street

Hospital

Travelling by rail

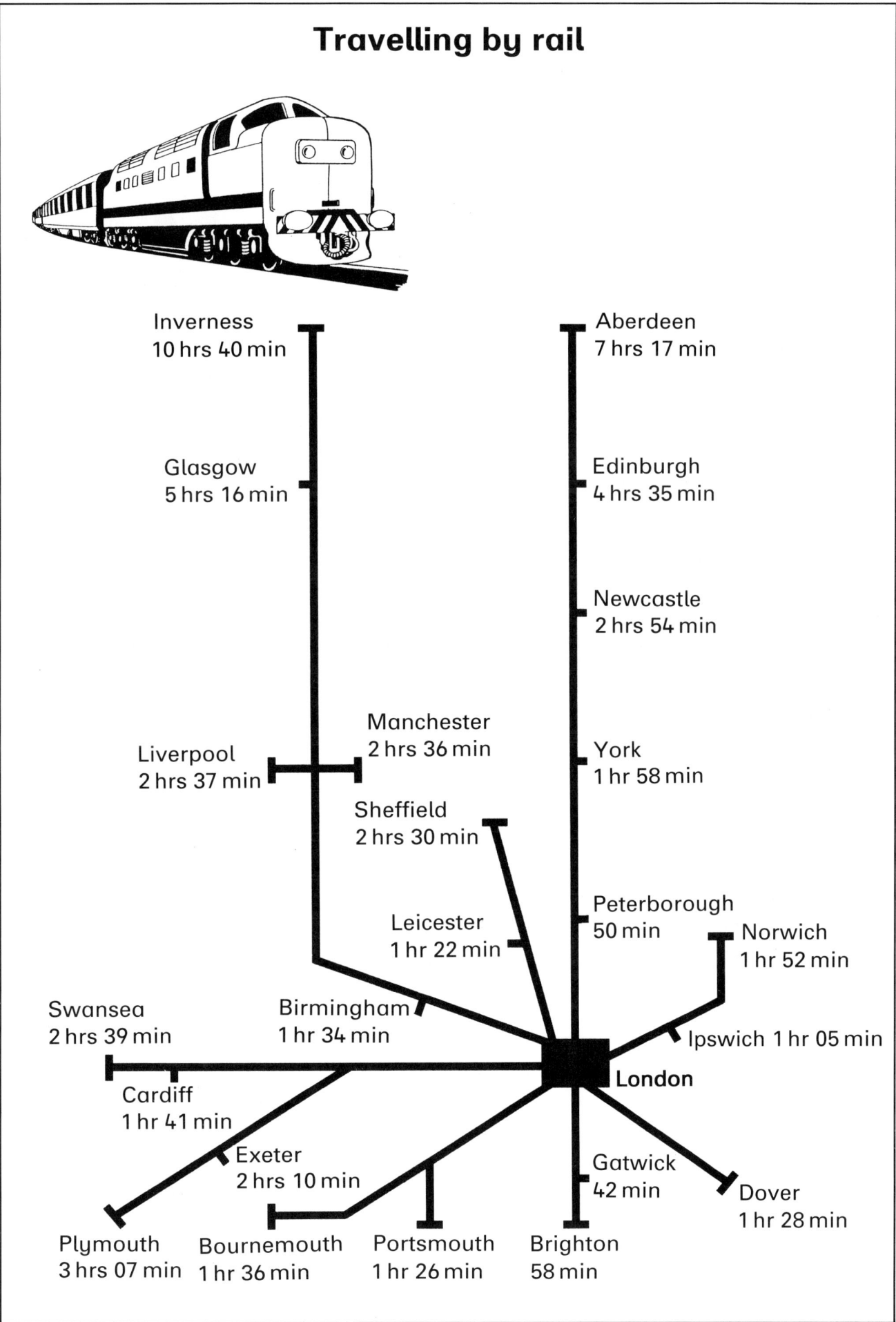

Inverness
10 hrs 40 min

Aberdeen
7 hrs 17 min

Glasgow
5 hrs 16 min

Edinburgh
4 hrs 35 min

Newcastle
2 hrs 54 min

Manchester
2 hrs 36 min

Liverpool
2 hrs 37 min

York
1 hr 58 min

Sheffield
2 hrs 30 min

Leicester
1 hr 22 min

Peterborough
50 min

Norwich
1 hr 52 min

Swansea
2 hrs 39 min

Birmingham
1 hr 34 min

Ipswich 1 hr 05 min

London

Cardiff
1 hr 41 min

Exeter
2 hrs 10 min

Gatwick
42 min

Dover
1 hr 28 min

Plymouth
3 hrs 07 min

Bournemouth
1 hr 36 min

Portsmouth
1 hr 26 min

Brighton
58 min

Ferry routes

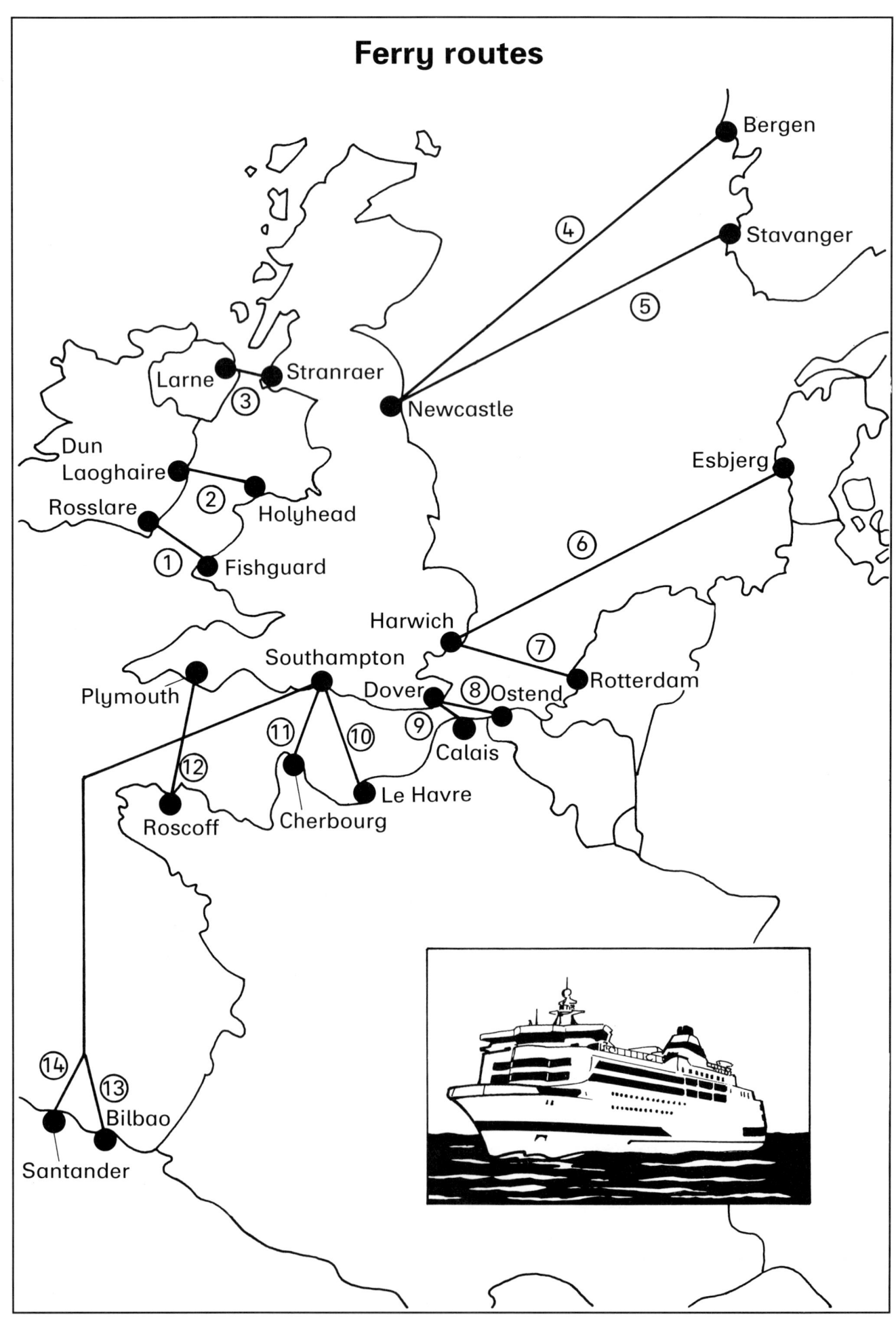

Crossing the world

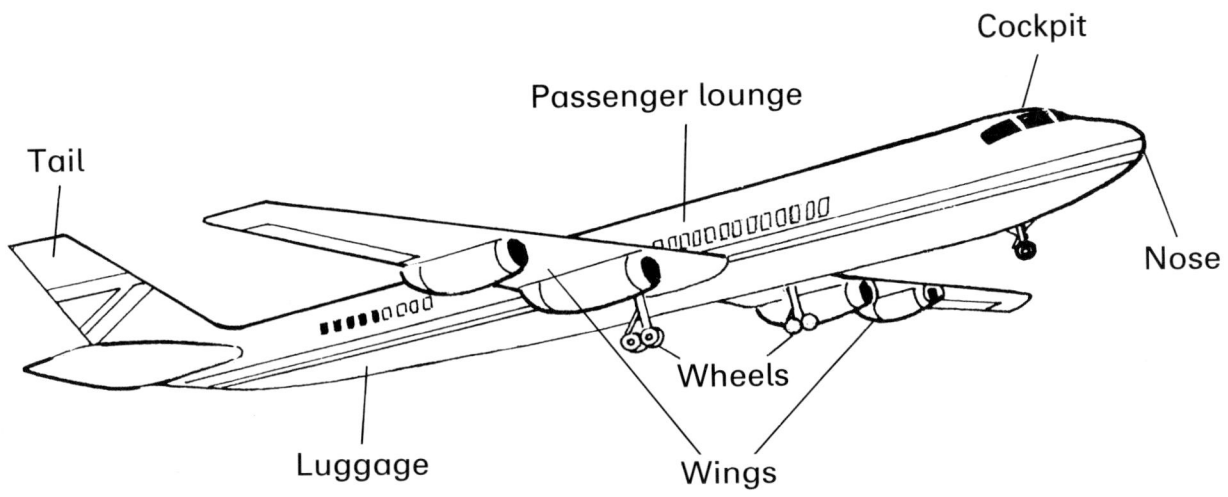

Tail

Passenger lounge

Cockpit

Nose

Wheels

Luggage

Wings

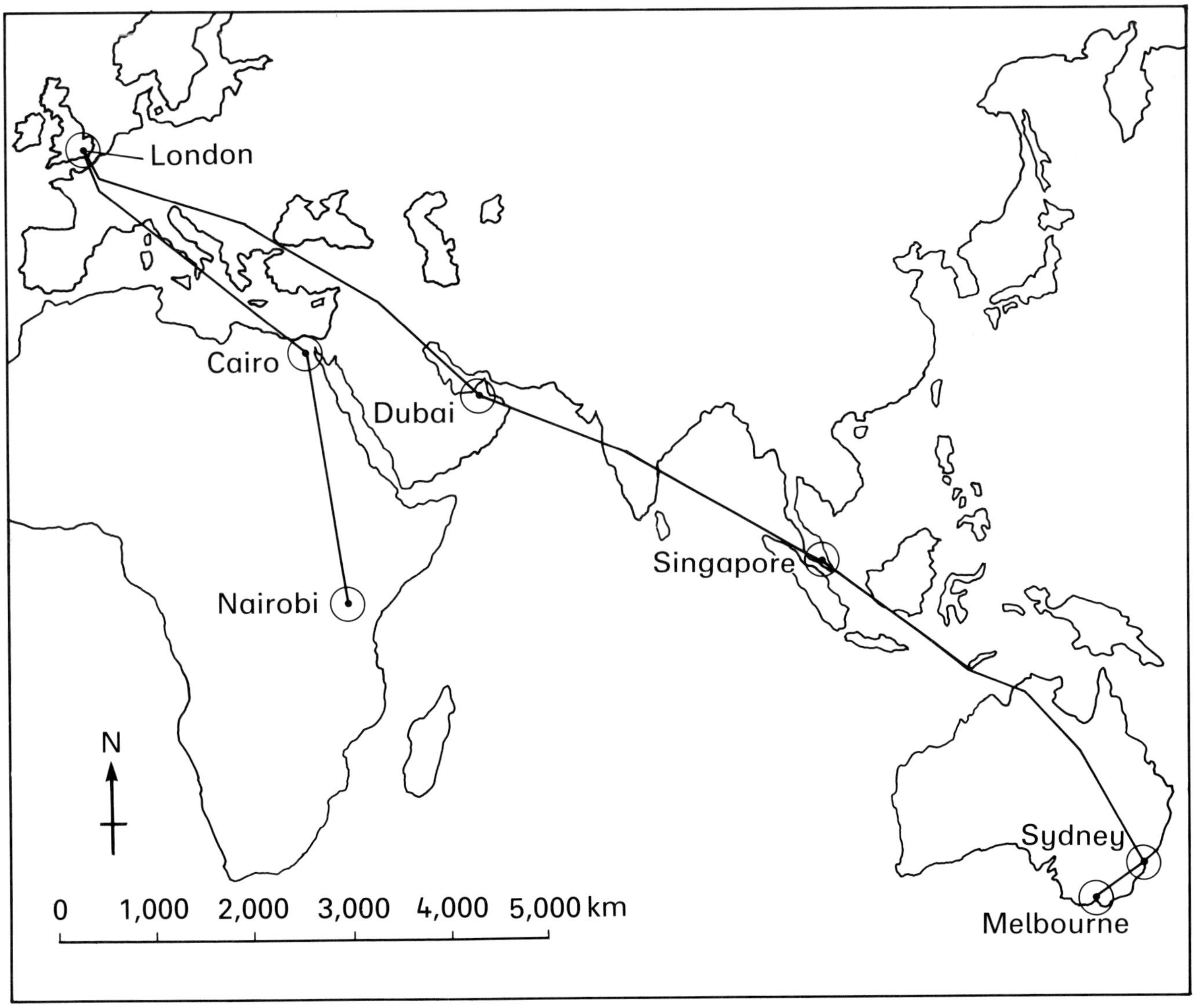

London

Cairo

Dubai

Nairobi

Singapore

Sydney

Melbourne

N

0   1,000   2,000   3,000   4,000   5,000 km

Copymaster 57

Crossing obstacles

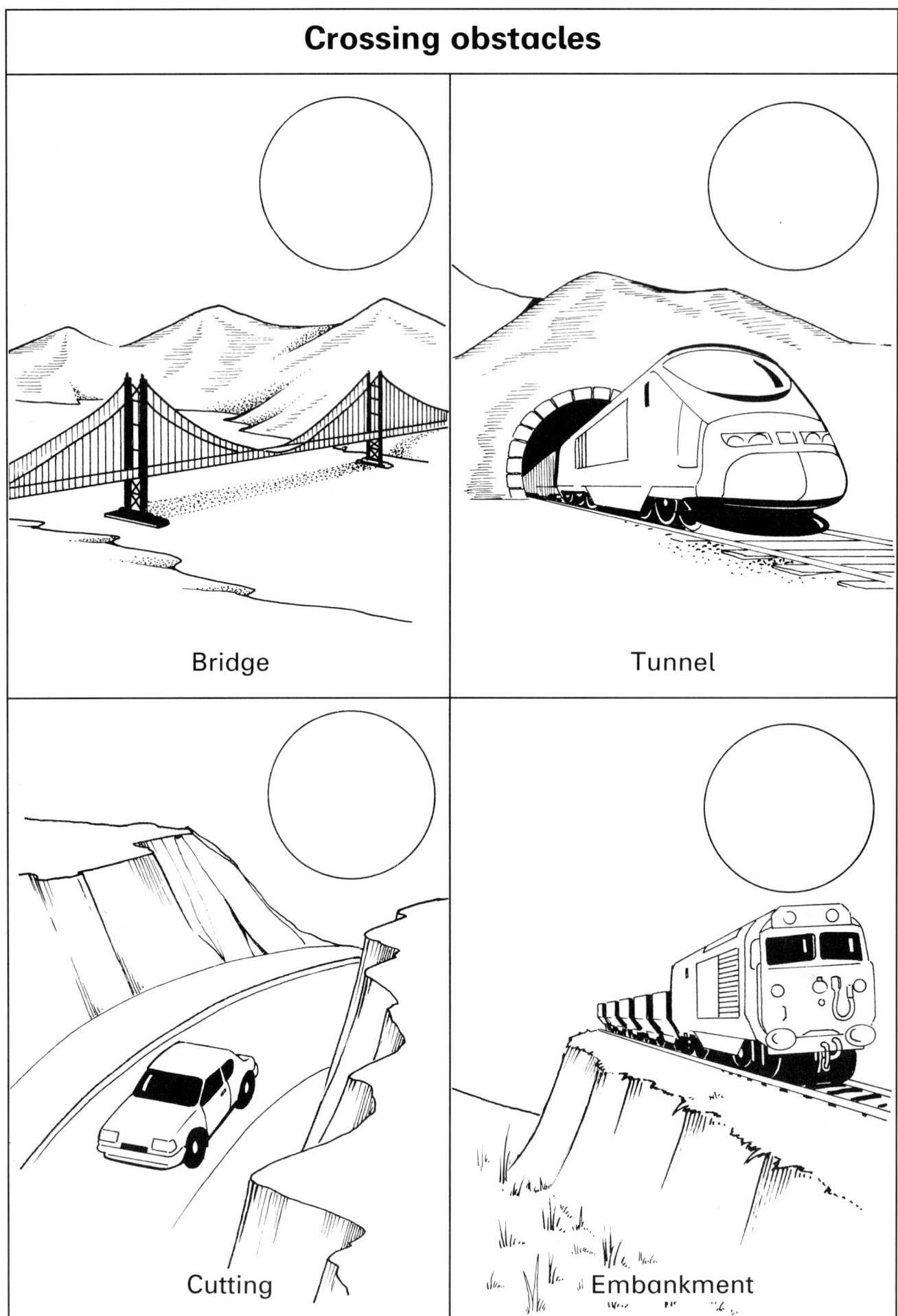

Bridge

Tunnel

Cutting

Embankment

Bridges and tunnels

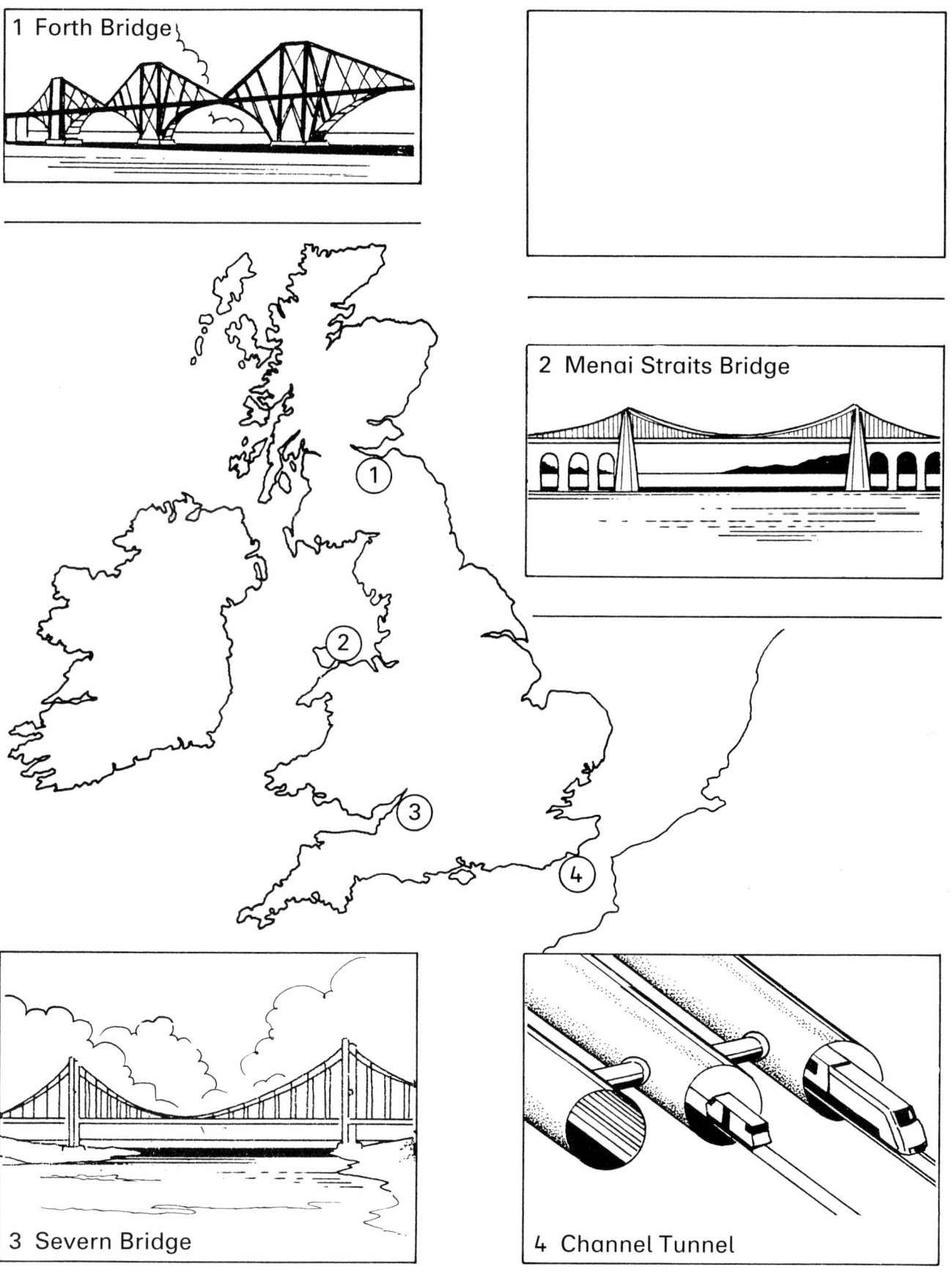

1 Forth Bridge

2 Menai Straits Bridge

3 Severn Bridge

4 Channel Tunnel

Types of transport

Advantages	ROAD	Disadvantages
• Travel when you want • Goes from door to door • Easy to use		• Traffic jams • Exhaust fumes cause pollution • Risk of accidents
Advantages	RAIL	**Disadvantages**
• Comfortable • Fast and safe • Travels to city centre		• Expensive • Poor service for villages • People have to carry luggage
Advantages	SEA	**Disadvantages**
• Interesting way to travel • Relax on the boat • Enjoy the view		• Slow • Not many sailings • Links only a few places
Advantages	AIR	**Disadvantages**
• Very fast • Exciting • Can cross seas and mountains		• Noise from airports • Expensive • Extra charge for heavy luggage

Transport problems

Oil tanker accident in Shetland

TRAINS DELAYED BY SNOW AND ICE

AIRCRAFT TOO NOISY SAY LOCAL RESIDENTS

Car fumes and hot weather cause London smog

Park and ride scheme helps traffic in city centre

Hundreds will lose jobs if ferry closes

Road works cause motorway delay

Accident causes ten mile traffic jam on M25

Protests over new road route

NEW BYPASS FOR VILLAGE

Bigger planes could save space in crowded skies

ROAD TRAFFIC COULD DOUBLE IN 30 YEARS

RAILWAYS NEED MORE MONEY FOR REPAIRS

Sheep farming in the Lake District

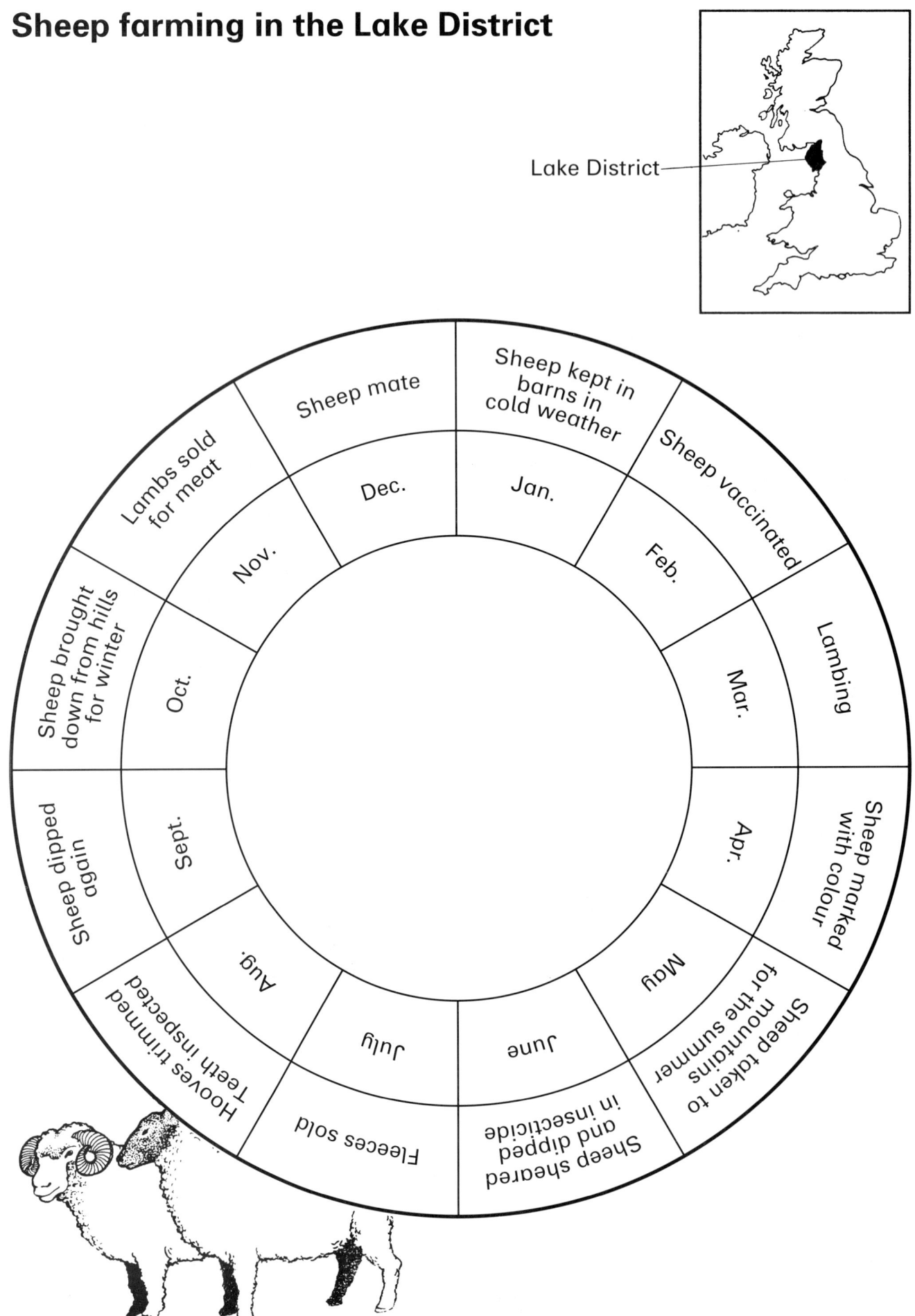

Lake District

Sheep mate

Sheep kept in barns in cold weather

Sheep vaccinated

Lambs sold for meat

Dec.

Jan.

Feb.

Nov.

Lambing

Sheep brought down from hills for winter

Oct.

Mar.

Sheep marked with colour

Sheep dipped again

Sept.

Apr.

Hooves trimmed Teeth inspected

Aug.

May

Sheep taken to mountains for the summer

Fleeces sold

July

June

Sheep sheared and dipped in insecticide

A crop farm in Kent

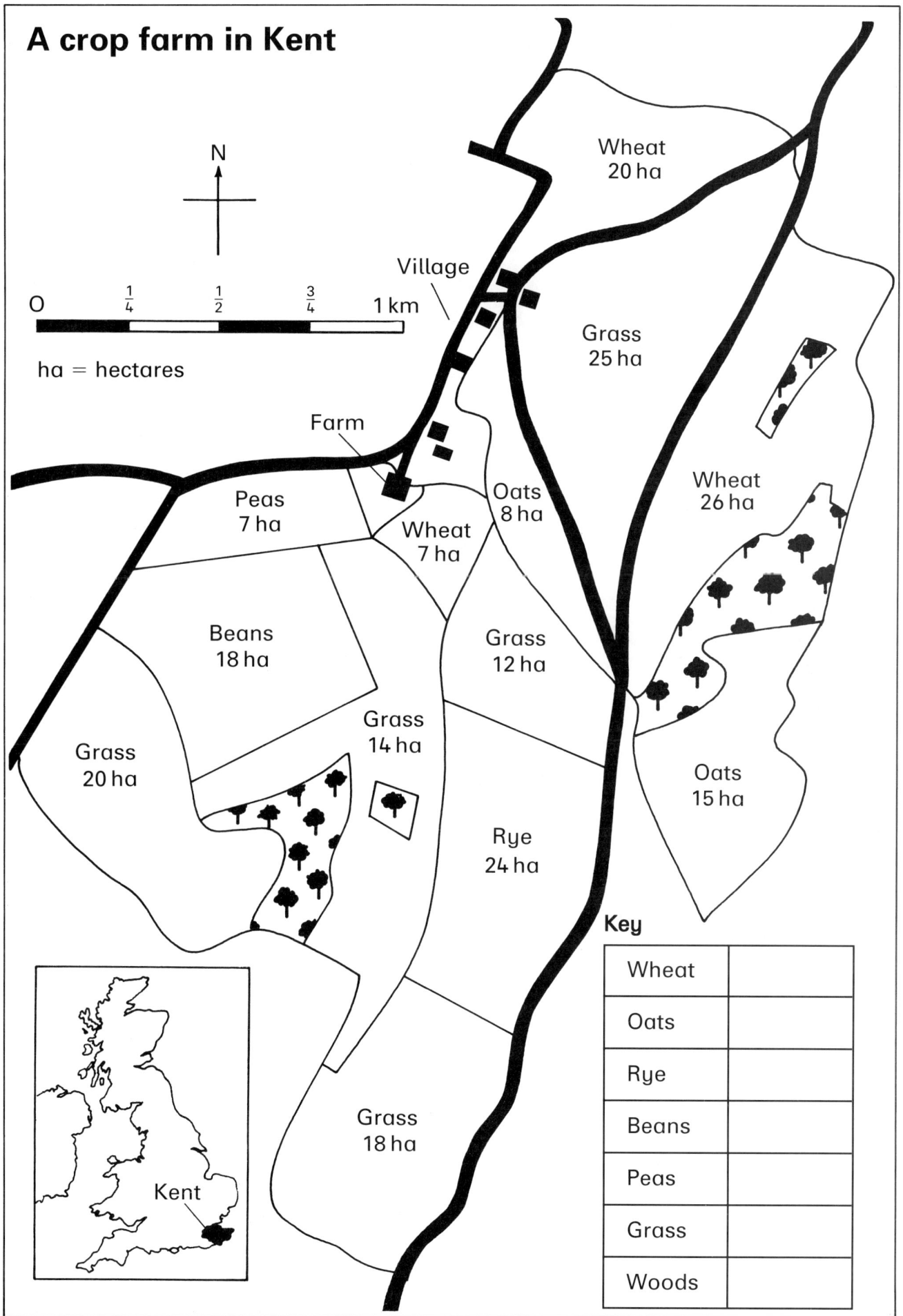

N

ha = hectares

O $\frac{1}{4}$ $\frac{1}{2}$ $\frac{3}{4}$ 1 km

Village

Farm

Wheat
20 ha

Grass
25 ha

Wheat
26 ha

Peas
7 ha

Oats
8 ha

Wheat
7 ha

Grass
12 ha

Oats
15 ha

Beans
18 ha

Grass
14 ha

Grass
20 ha

Rye
24 ha

Grass
18 ha

Kent

Key

Wheat	
Oats	
Rye	
Beans	
Peas	
Grass	
Woods	

Copymaster 63

Farm products

Inputs

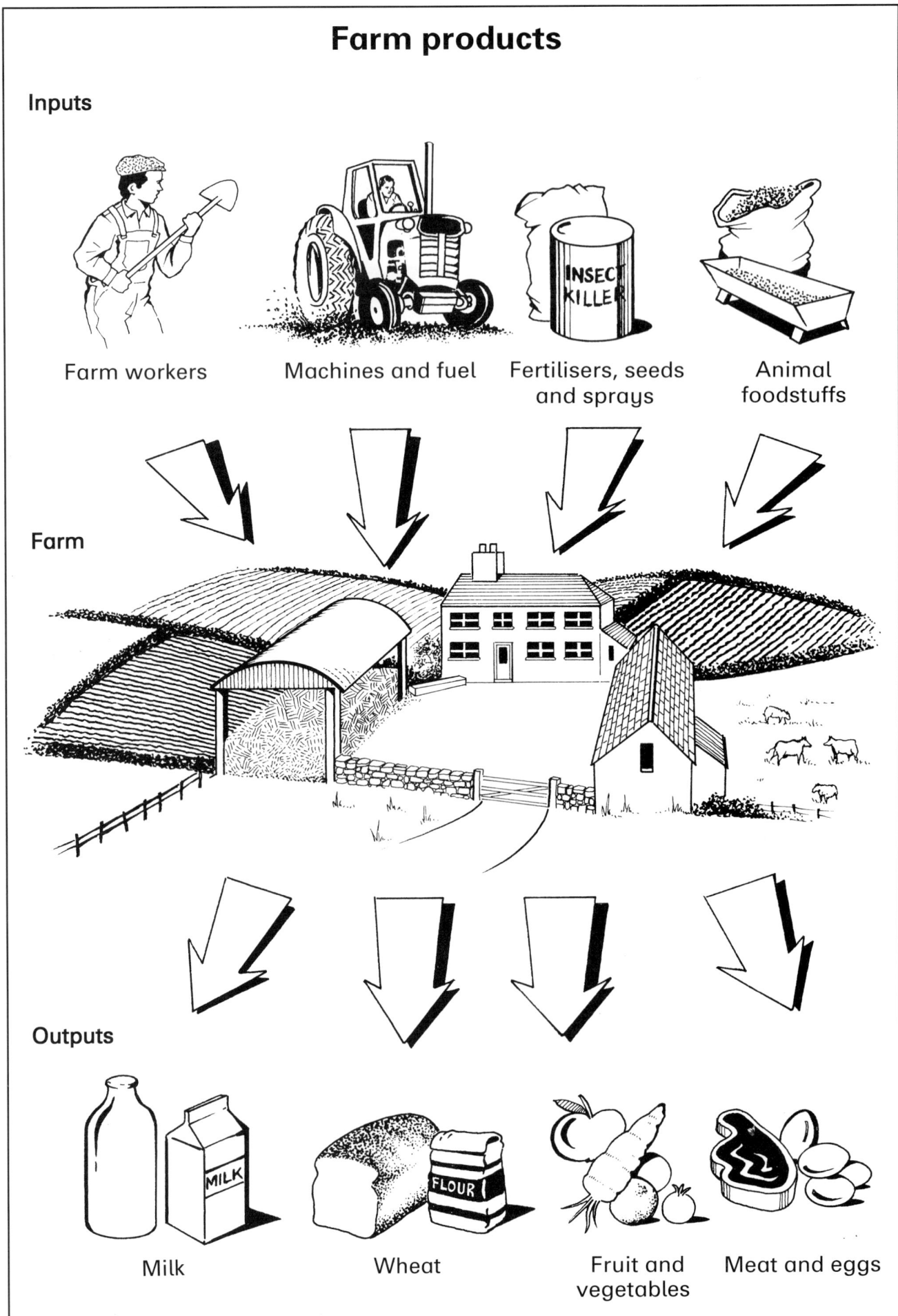

Farm workers

Machines and fuel

Fertilisers, seeds and sprays

Animal foodstuffs

Farm

Outputs

Milk

Wheat

Fruit and vegetables

Meat and eggs

Growing rice

1 The seeds are planted in special beds.

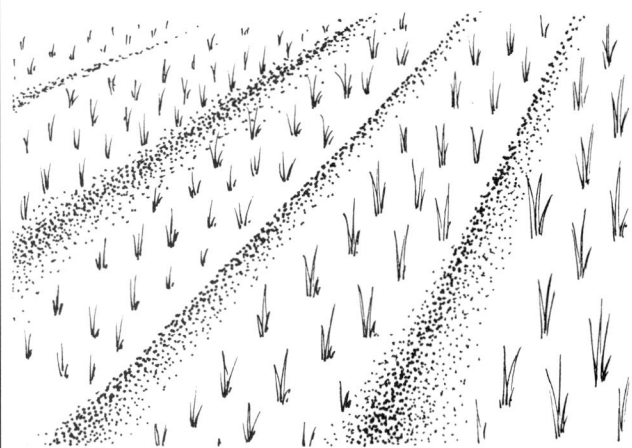

2 The plants stay in the beds for three months as they grow.

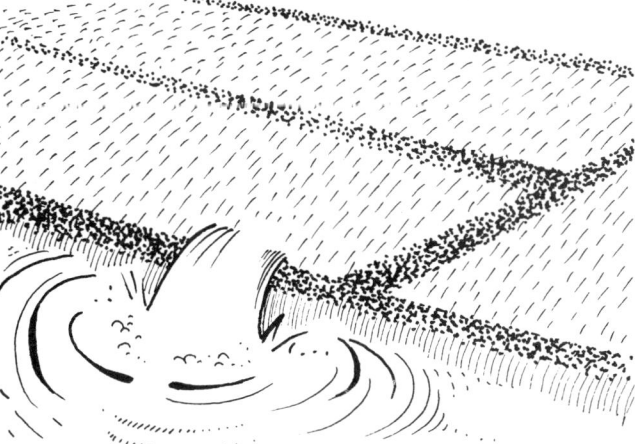

3 The fields are flooded with water.

4 The rice plants are put out in rows in the flooded fields.

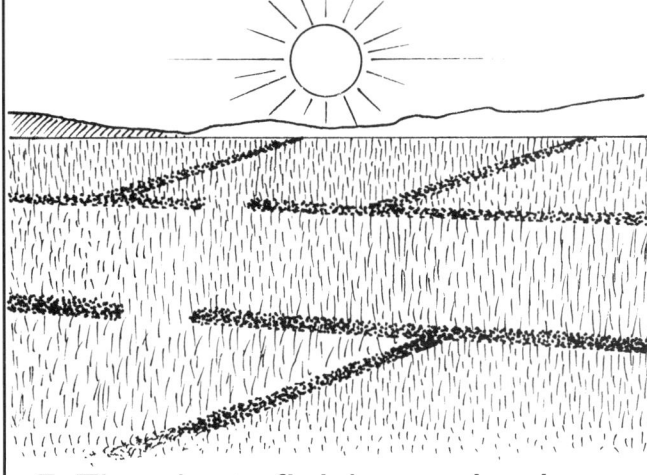

5 The plants finish growing in dry, hot weather.

6 The rice is harvested.

Oranges from Israel

20 January
The oranges are picked in Israel.

21 January
They are loaded onto a ship at the docks at Tel Aviv.

24 January
Gales in the Bay of Biscay cause a delay.

30 January
The oranges are sold in a supermarket.

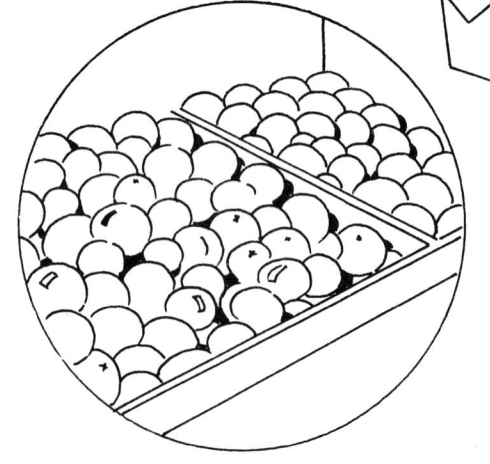

28 January
The oranges are unloaded and taken to a warehouse.

Food from around the world

CEREALS

Wheat

Wheat is used for bread, cakes and biscuits.

Main producers: Russia, USA, China

Rice

Rice is the chief food in Southern Asia.

Main producers: China, India, Indonesia

FRUIT

Bananas

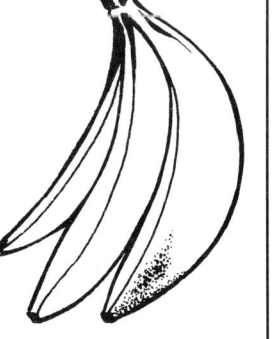

Grown on plantations for sale to other countries.

Main producers: Brazil, India, Indonesia, Caribbean Islands

Oranges

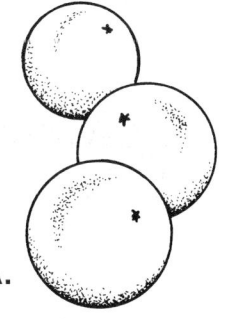

Grown in orchards in southern Europe and parts of the USA.

Main producers: USA, Spain, Italy, Israel

DRINKS

Tea

Tea comes from the dried leaves of a bush.

Main producers: China, India, Sri Lanka, Kenya

Coffee

Coffee is made from the beans (seeds) of the coffee tree.

Main producers: Brazil, Colombia, Kenya, Uganda

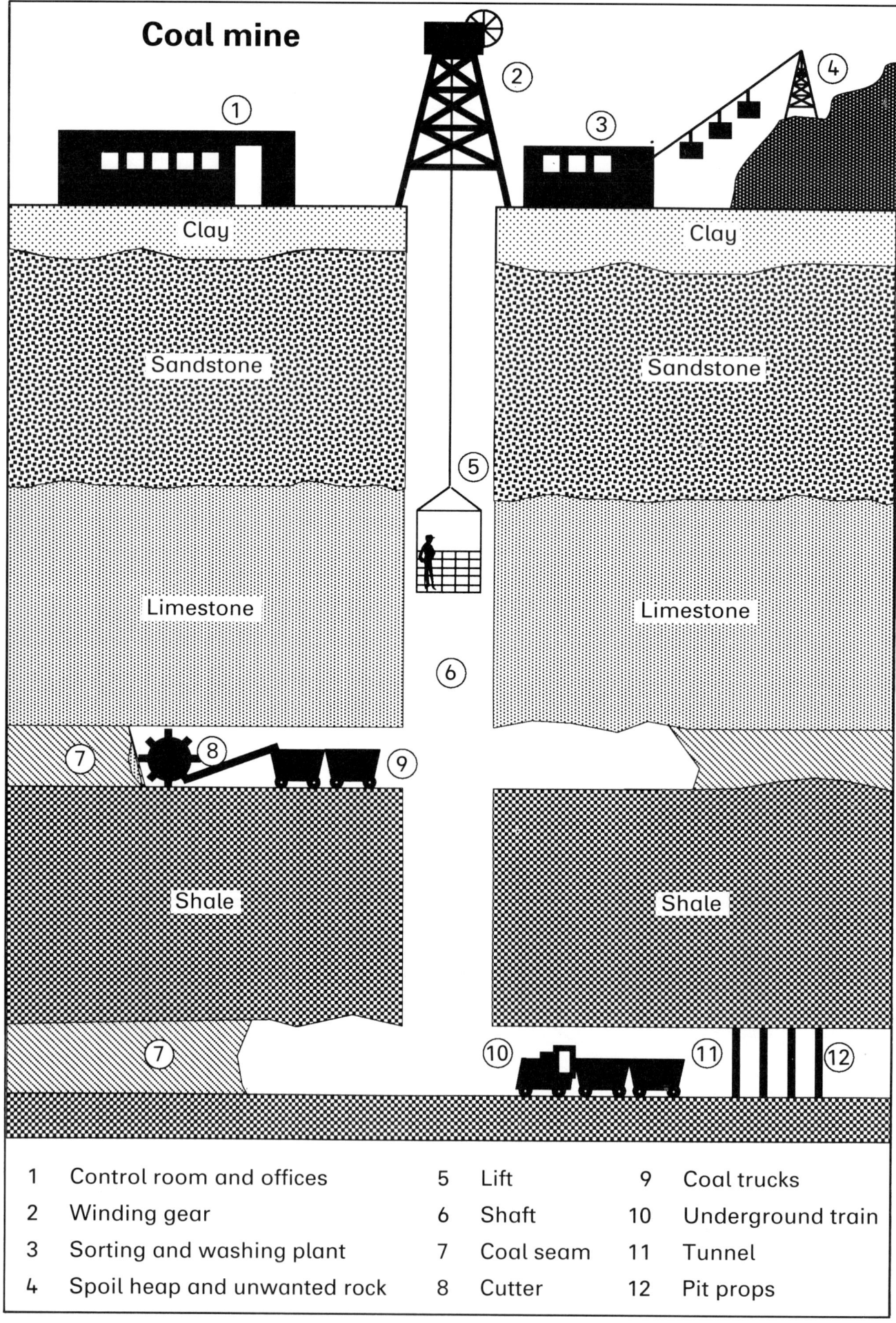

Coal mine

Clay

Sandstone

Limestone

Shale

Clay

Sandstone

Limestone

Shale

1	Control room and offices	5	Lift	9	Coal trucks
2	Winding gear	6	Shaft	10	Underground train
3	Sorting and washing plant	7	Coal seam	11	Tunnel
4	Spoil heap and unwanted rock	8	Cutter	12	Pit props

Copymaster 68

North Sea oil rig

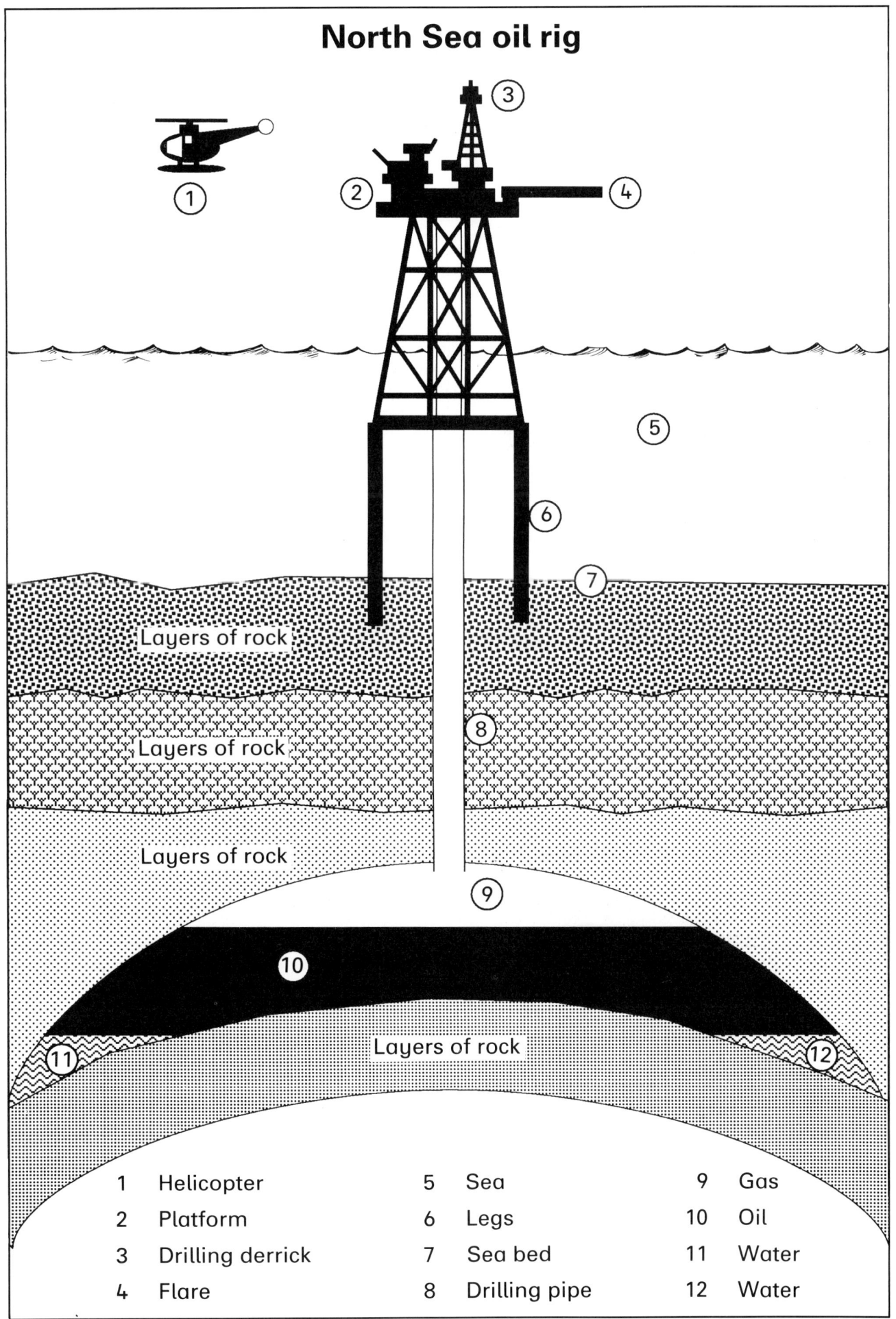

Layers of rock

Layers of rock

Layers of rock

Layers of rock

1	Helicopter	5	Sea	9	Gas
2	Platform	6	Legs	10	Oil
3	Drilling derrick	7	Sea bed	11	Water
4	Flare	8	Drilling pipe	12	Water

Stone quarry

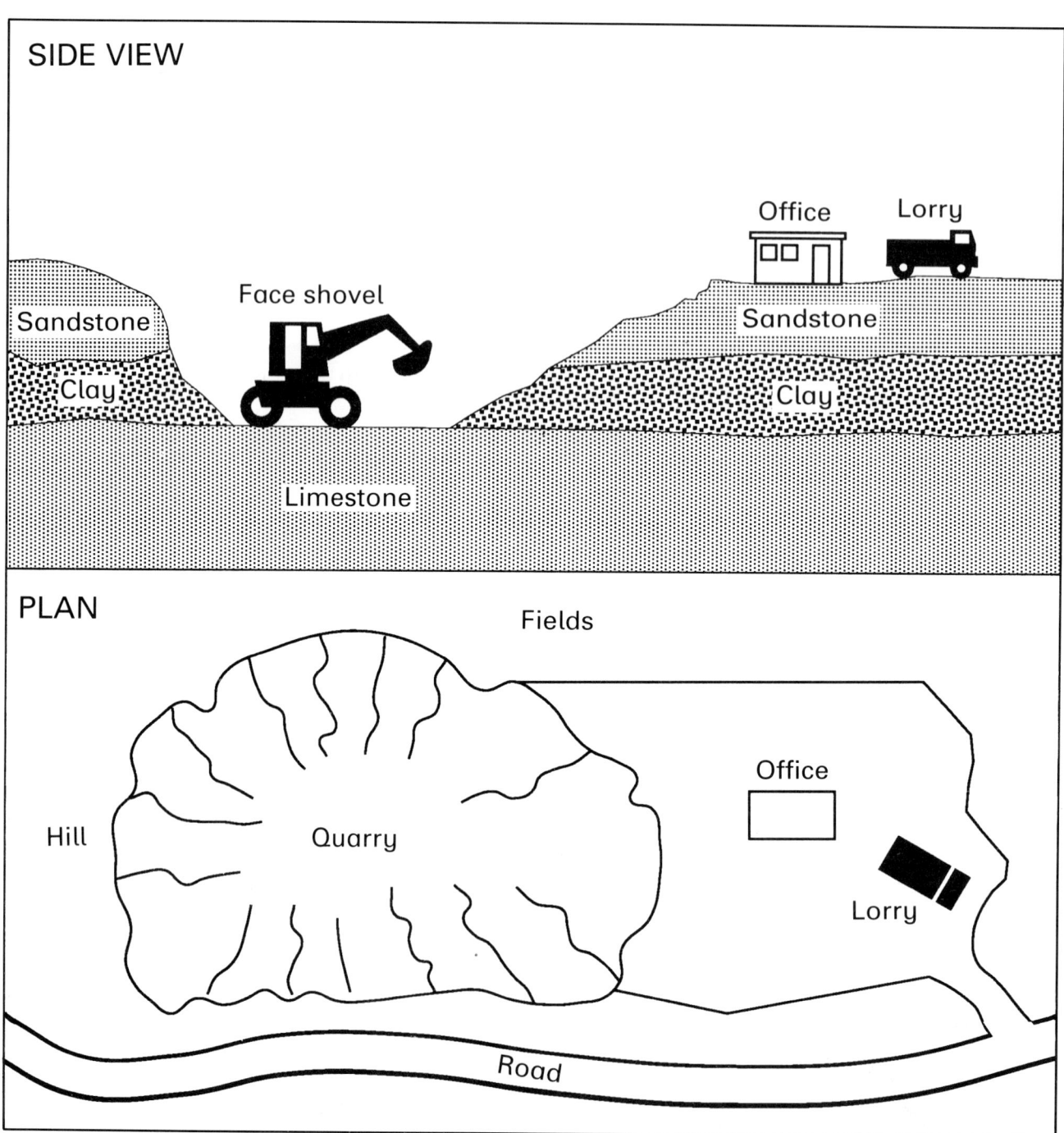

SIDE VIEW

Office   Lorry

Sandstone

Face shovel

Sandstone

Clay   Clay

Limestone

PLAN

Fields

Office

Hill   Quarry

Lorry

Road

FACT FILE
Resources from quarries

Energy	Metals	Building materials
Coal Fuel for nuclear power stations	Iron ore Copper ore Bauxite (for aluminium)	Building stone Sand and gravel Clay for bricks Limestone for cement Slate for roofs

Copymaster 70

Resources worldwide

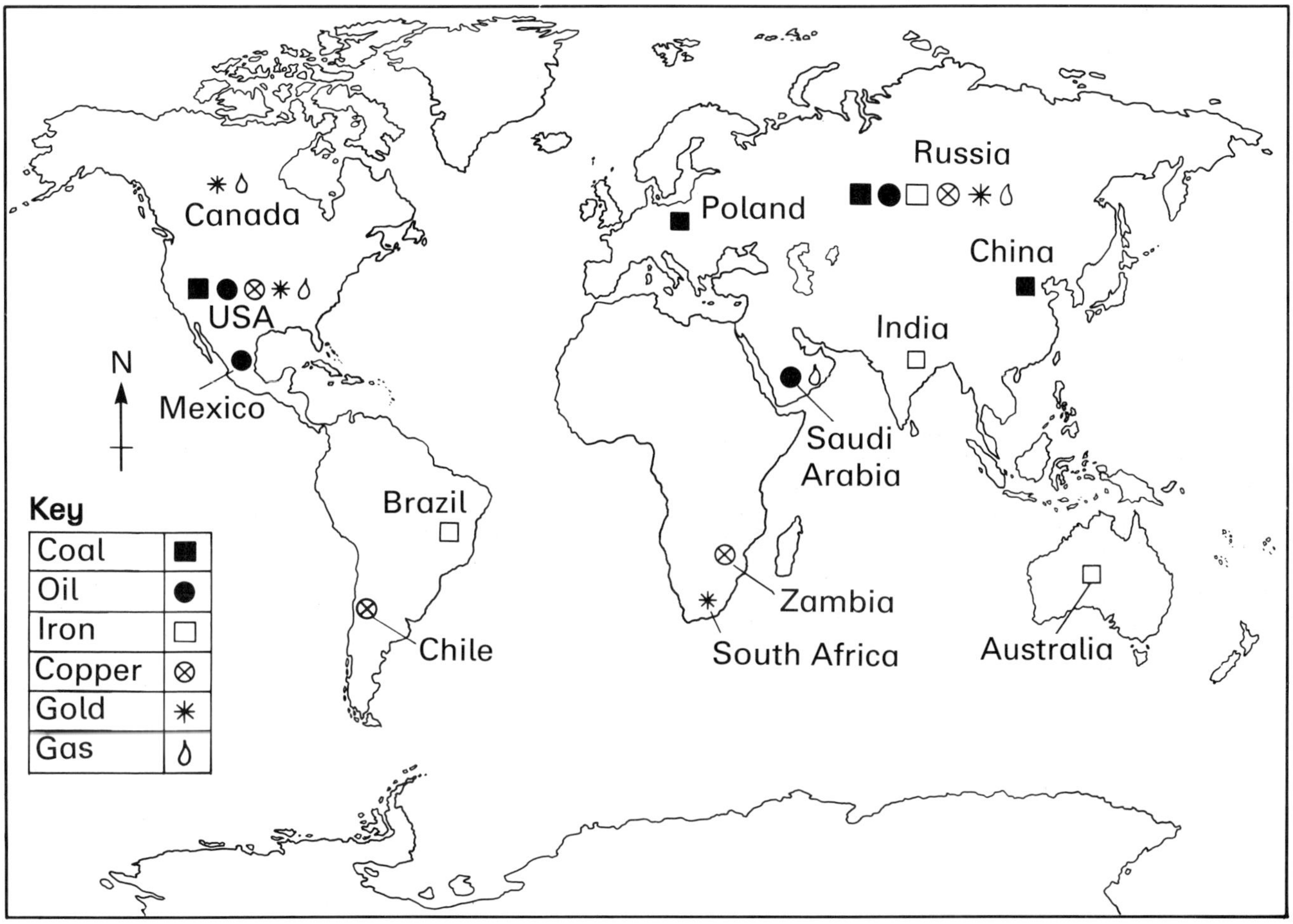

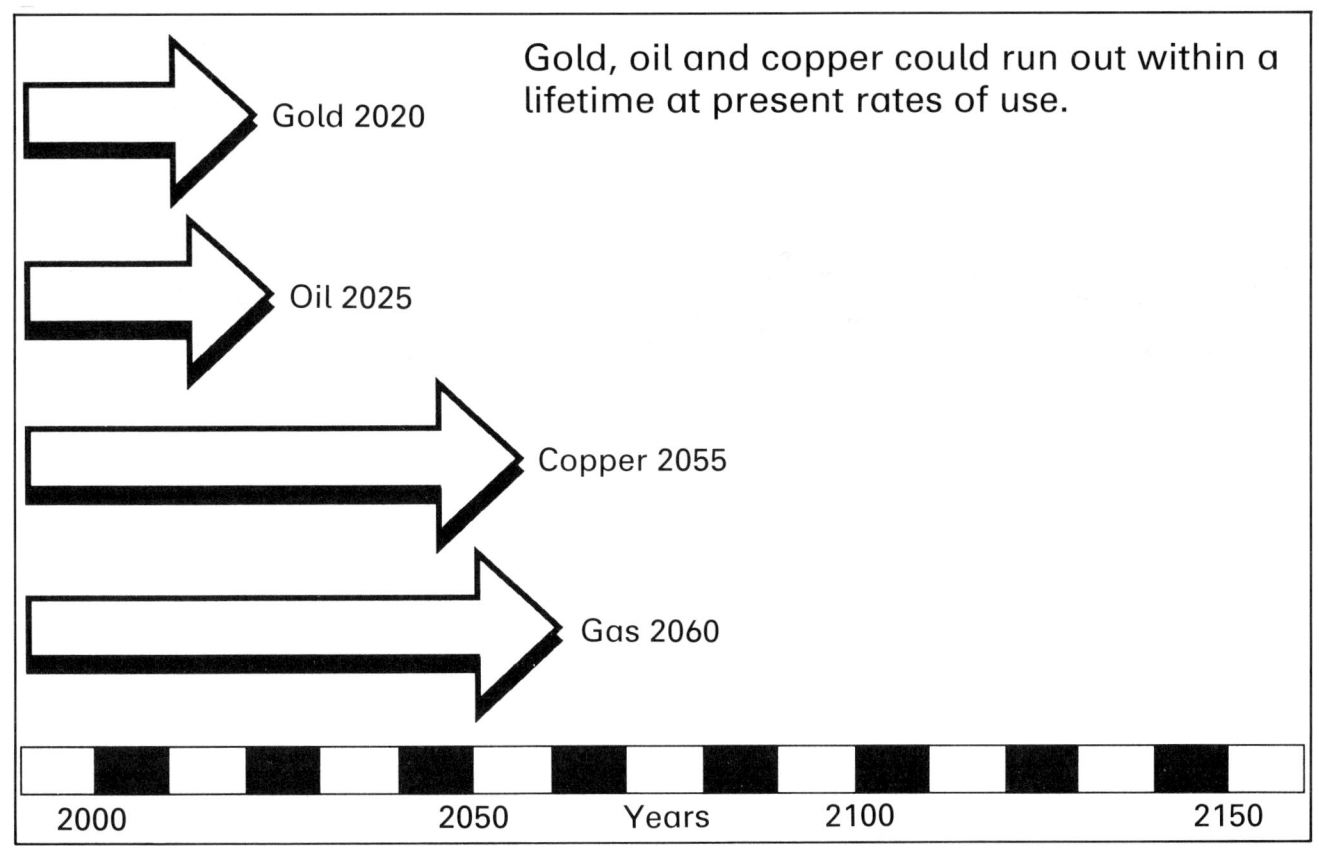

Key

Coal	■
Oil	●
Iron	□
Copper	⊗
Gold	✳
Gas	◊

Gold, oil and copper could run out within a lifetime at present rates of use.

Gold 2020

Oil 2025

Copper 2055

Gas 2060

| 2000 | 2050 | Years | 2100 | 2150 |

Forestry

SOFTWOOD

Fir

Pine

Fact file

- Trees grow in northern forests
- Used for wood pulp
- Main forests:
  Canada
  Scandinavia
  Russia
  USA

Flap

HARDWOOD

Teak

Mahogany

Fact file

- Trees grow in rainforests
- Used for house building
- Main forests:
  Central America
  Brazil
  West Africa
  SE Asia

Flap

Food from the sea

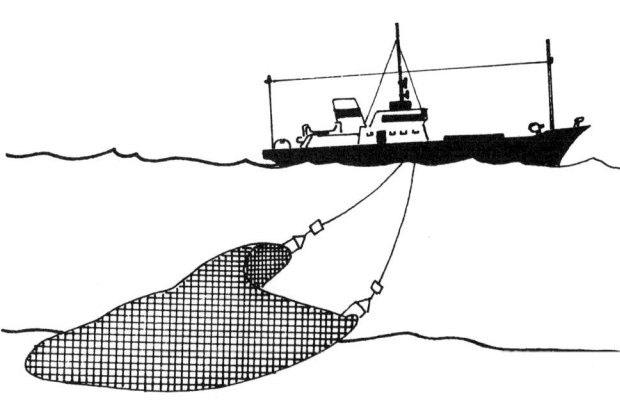

A **trawl net** drags along the sea bed and scoops up fish.

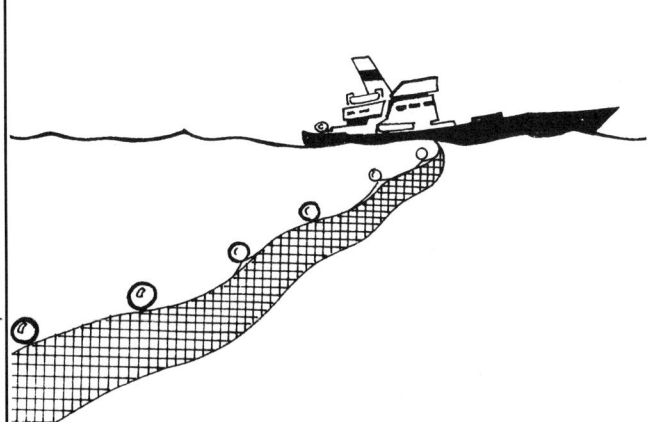

A **drift net** hangs like a curtain. The fish swim into the net and get stuck in the holes.

Shark

Whale

Seal

Herring

Dolphin

Octopus

Crab

Plaice

Making paper in the USA

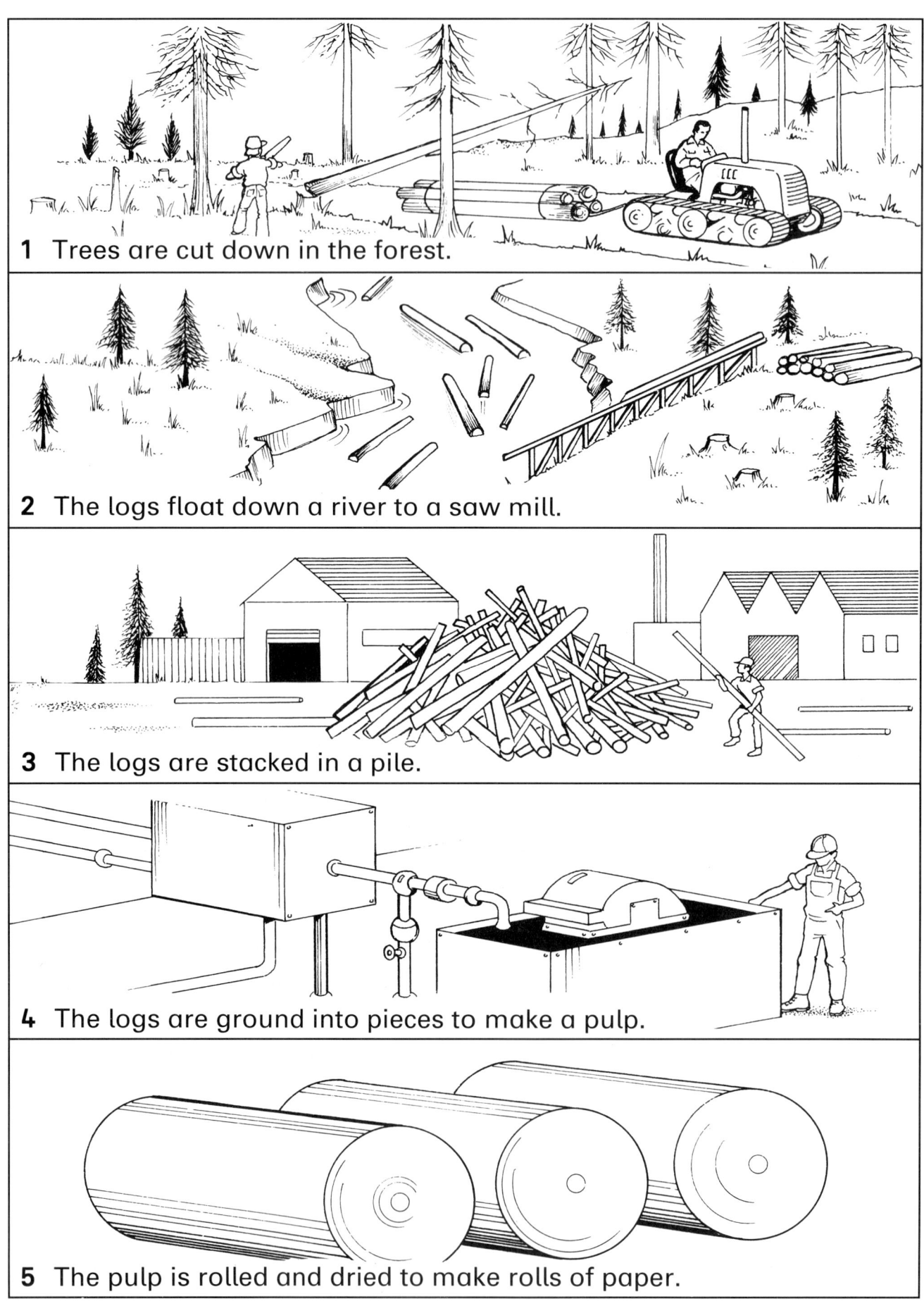

1 Trees are cut down in the forest.

2 The logs float down a river to a saw mill.

3 The logs are stacked in a pile.

4 The logs are ground into pieces to make a pulp.

5 The pulp is rolled and dried to make rolls of paper.

Making pencils in Keswick

Graphite (pencil lead) comes from Sri Lanka, China and Korea.

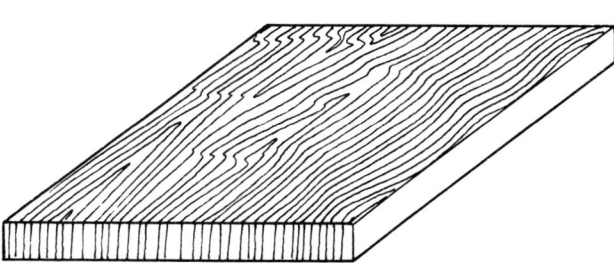

Slats (thin blocks) of cedar wood come from California, USA.

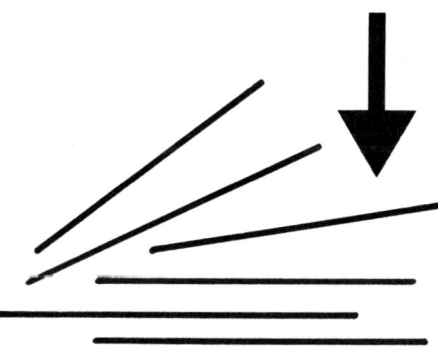

The graphite it pressed into thin strips.

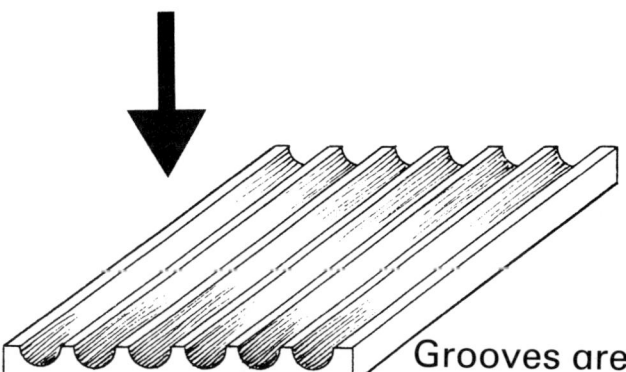

Grooves are cut in the slats.

The graphite strips are dropped into the grooves. A cover slat is then glued onto the top.

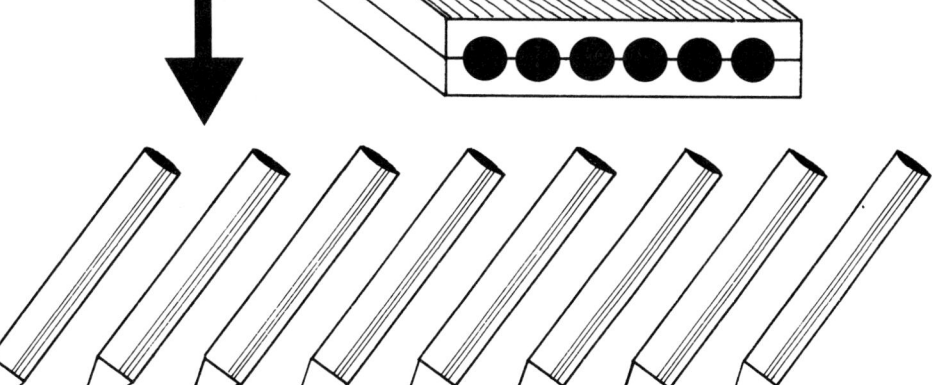

The pencils are cut, sharpened and painted and put into boxes.

Making wool clothes in Scotland

1 Shearing

Sheep have their coats cut once a year. This is called shearing.

2 Baling

The fleeces are packed into bundles or bales and taken to a wool factory.

4 Carding

The clean wool is untangled by a machine called a carder.

3 Scouring

The wool is cleaned to make it pure.

5 Spinning

The wool is then wound into large balls.

6 Knitting

Knitting and weaving are done using huge machines.

Making iron and steel in Wales

Inputs

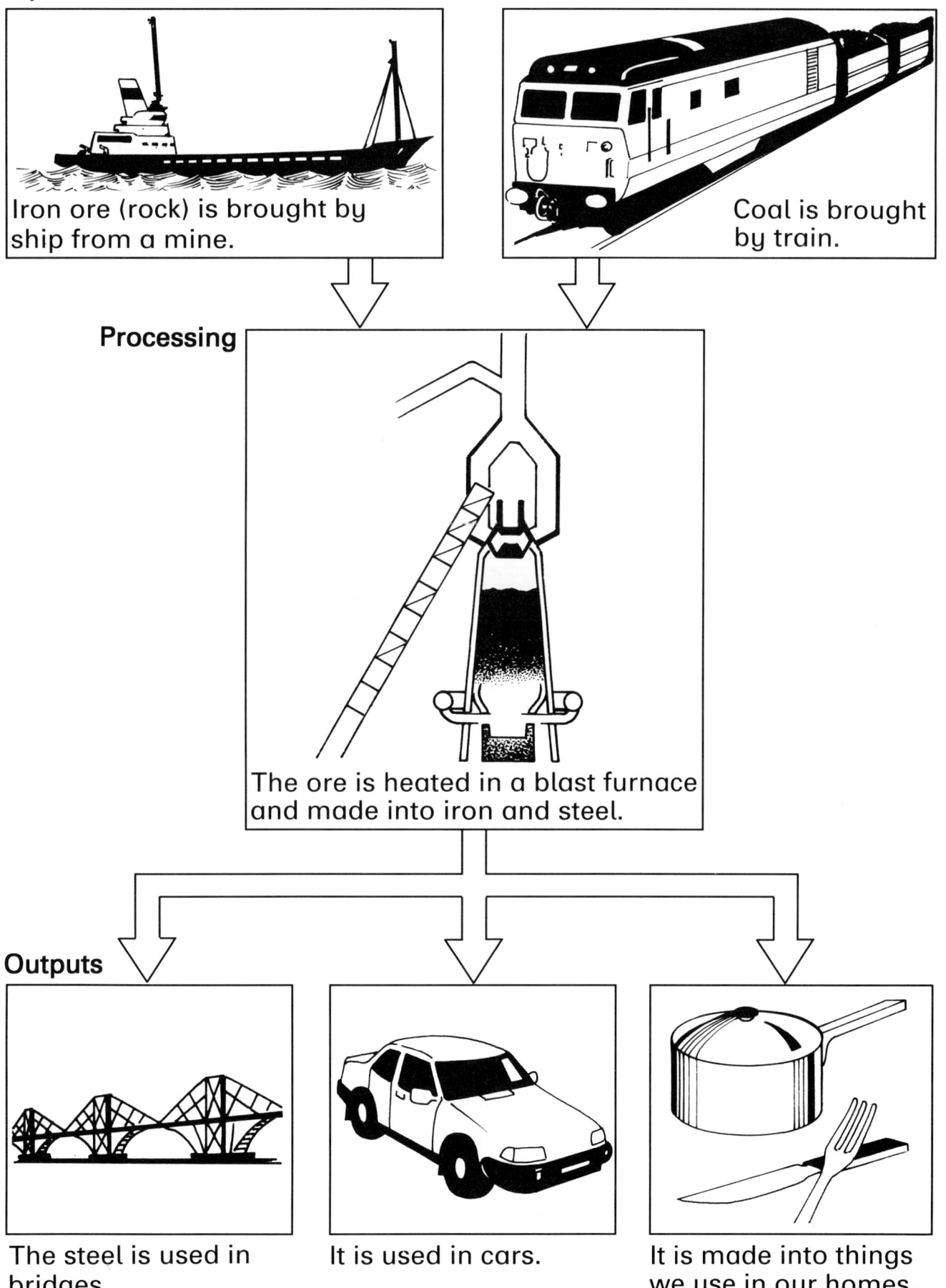

Iron ore (rock) is brought by ship from a mine.

Coal is brought by train.

Processing

The ore is heated in a blast furnace and made into iron and steel.

Outputs

The steel is used in bridges.

It is used in cars.

It is made into things we use in our homes.

Making electricity

Generating electricity

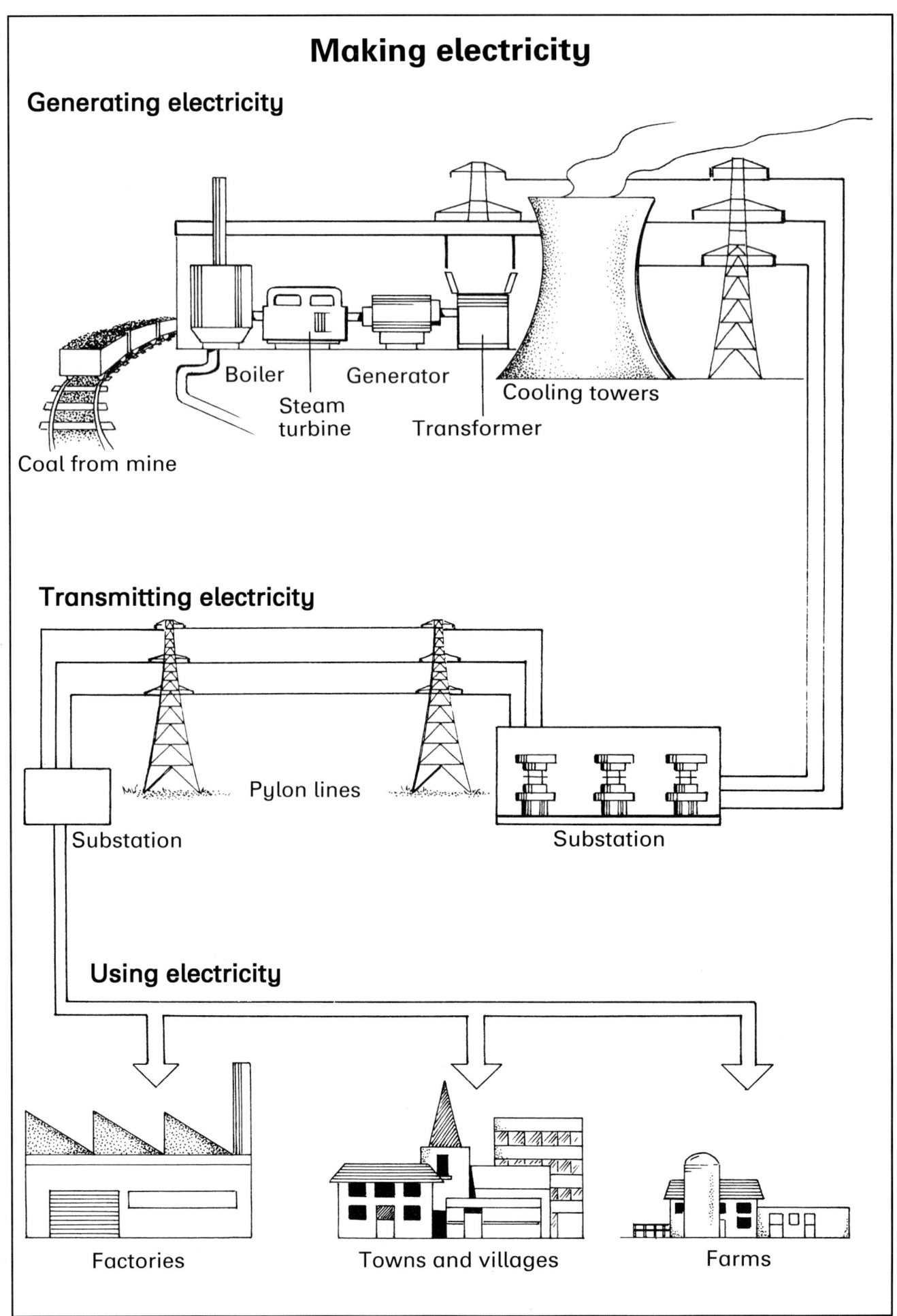

Boiler

Steam
turbine

Generator

Transformer

Cooling towers

Coal from mine

Transmitting electricity

Pylon lines

Substation

Substation

Using electricity

Factories

Towns and villages

Farms

Using oil

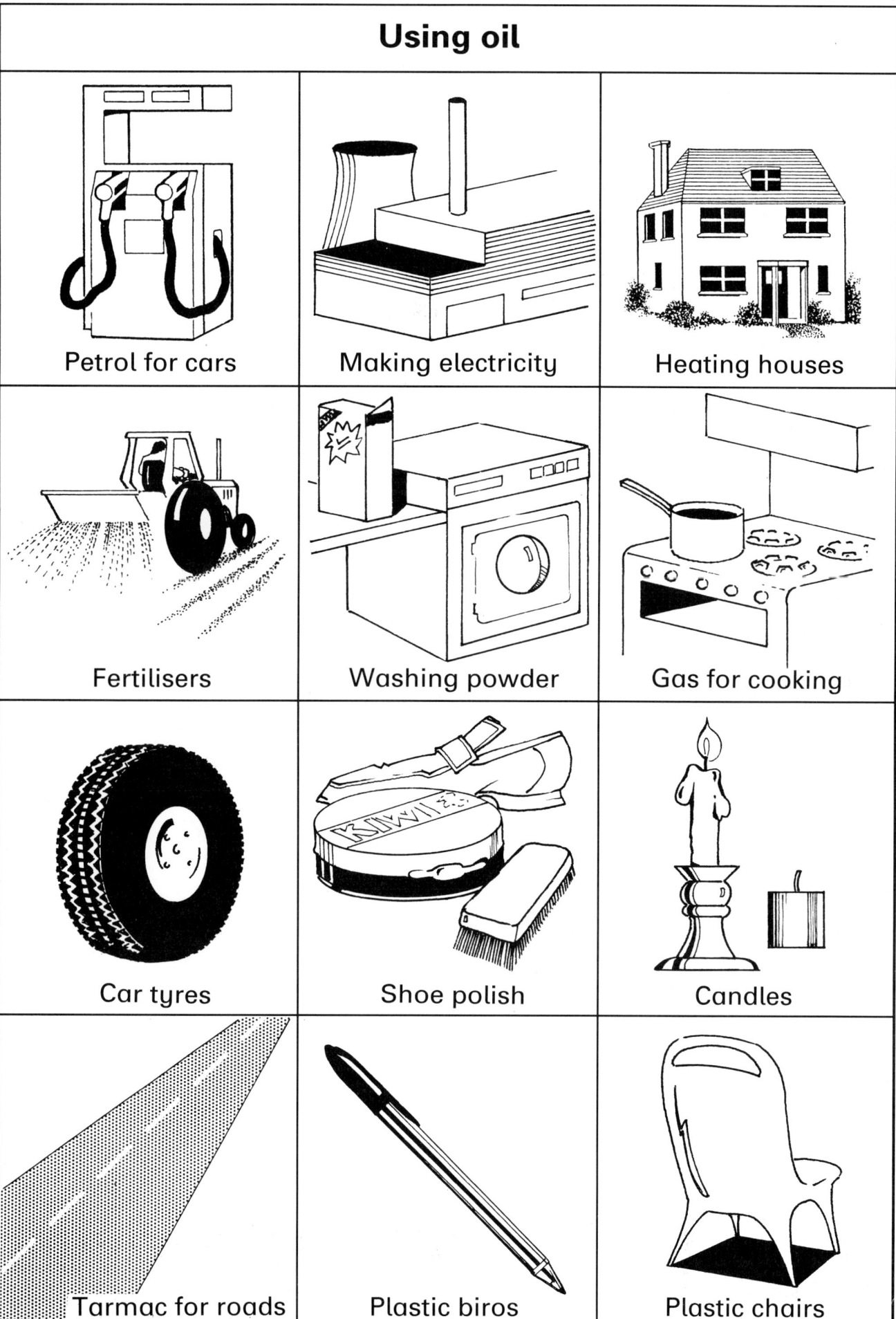

Petrol for cars	Making electricity	Heating houses
Fertilisers	Washing powder	Gas for cooking
Car tyres	Shoe polish	Candles
Tarmac for roads	Plastic biros	Plastic chairs

Oak tree

Grey squirrel	Ladybird	Wolf spider	Ghost moth	Long-eared owl
Great tit	Centipede	Beetle	Leopard moth	Ant

Threatened creatures

North America

Buffalo

Europe

Swallowtail butterfly

Asia

Giant panda

Asia

Snow leopard

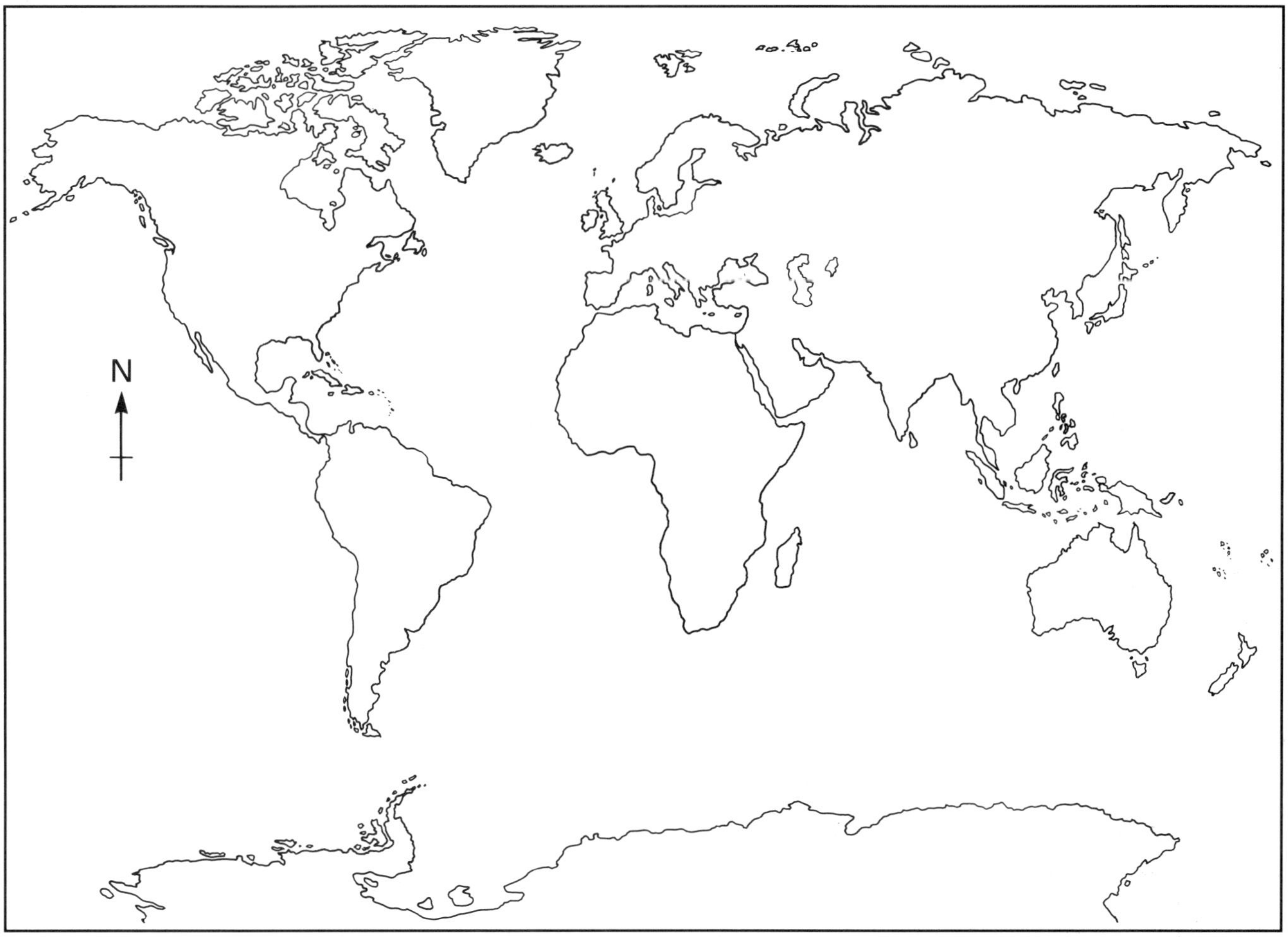

N

South America

Alligator

Africa

Rhinoceros

Antarctica

Whale

Australasia

Parrot

Copymaster 81

Threatened landscapes

Floods	Spreading deserts

Trees cut down in the mountains and taken to factories.

Trees cut down for firewood.

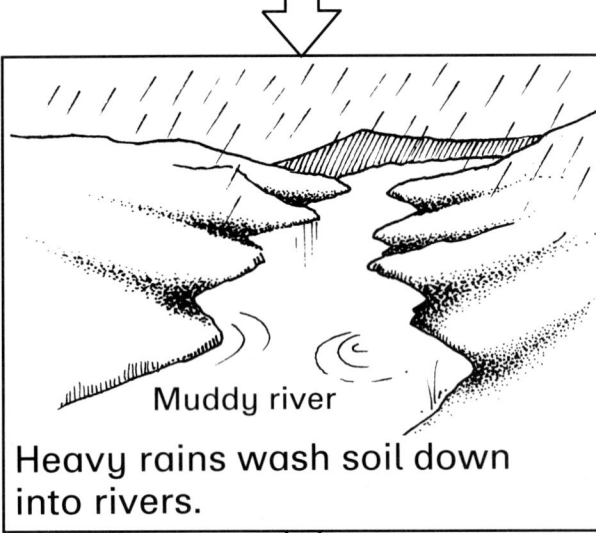

Heavy rains wash soil down into rivers.

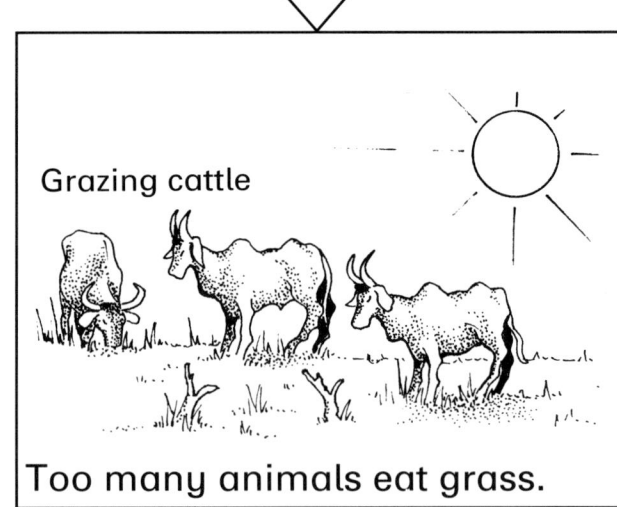

Too many animals eat grass.

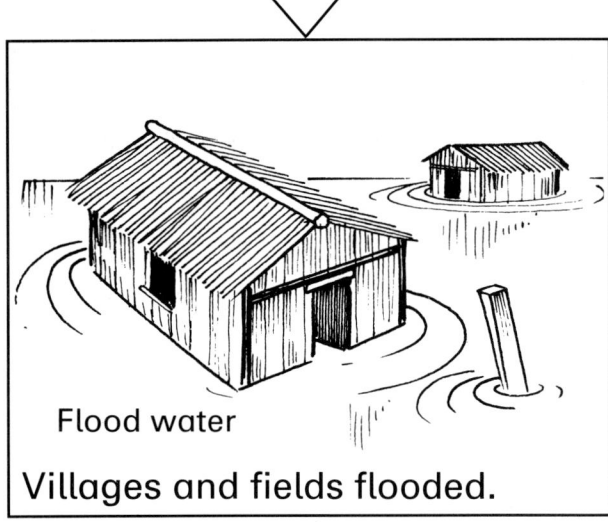

Villages and fields flooded.

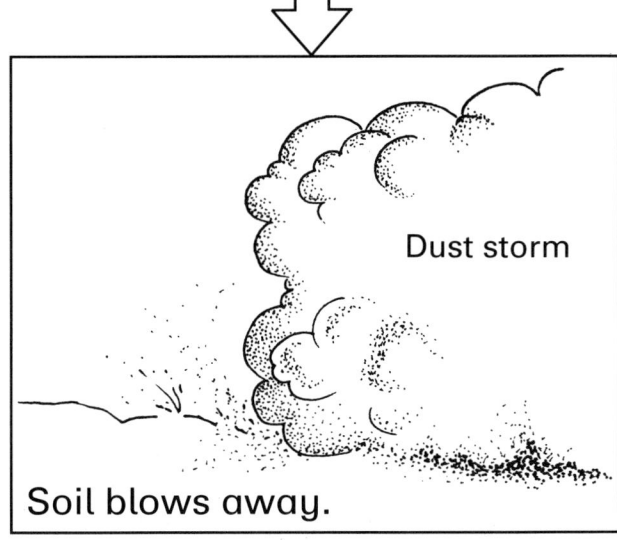

Soil blows away.

Place where this is happening: Bangladesh

Place where this is happening: Kenya

Copymaster 82

Pollution problems

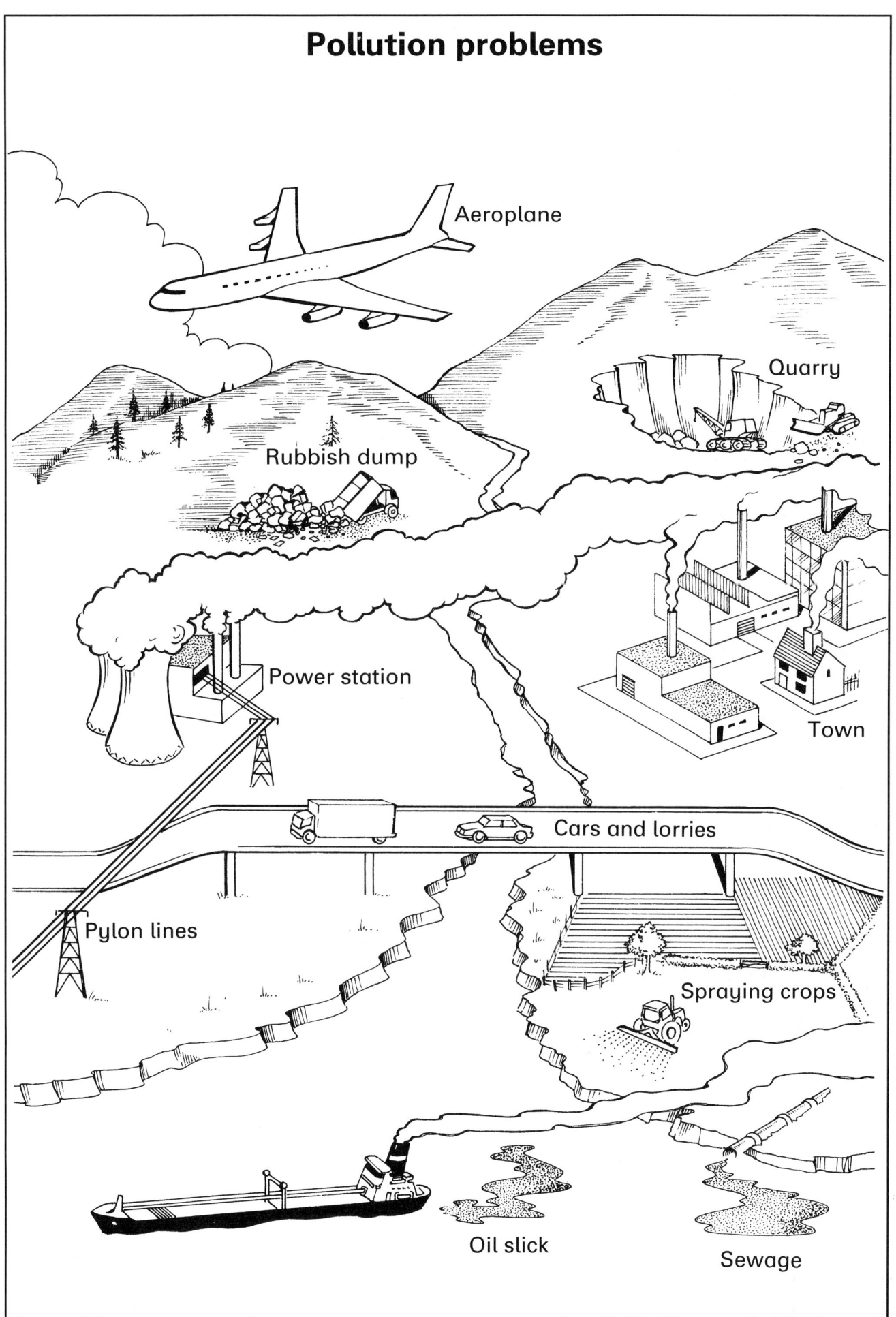

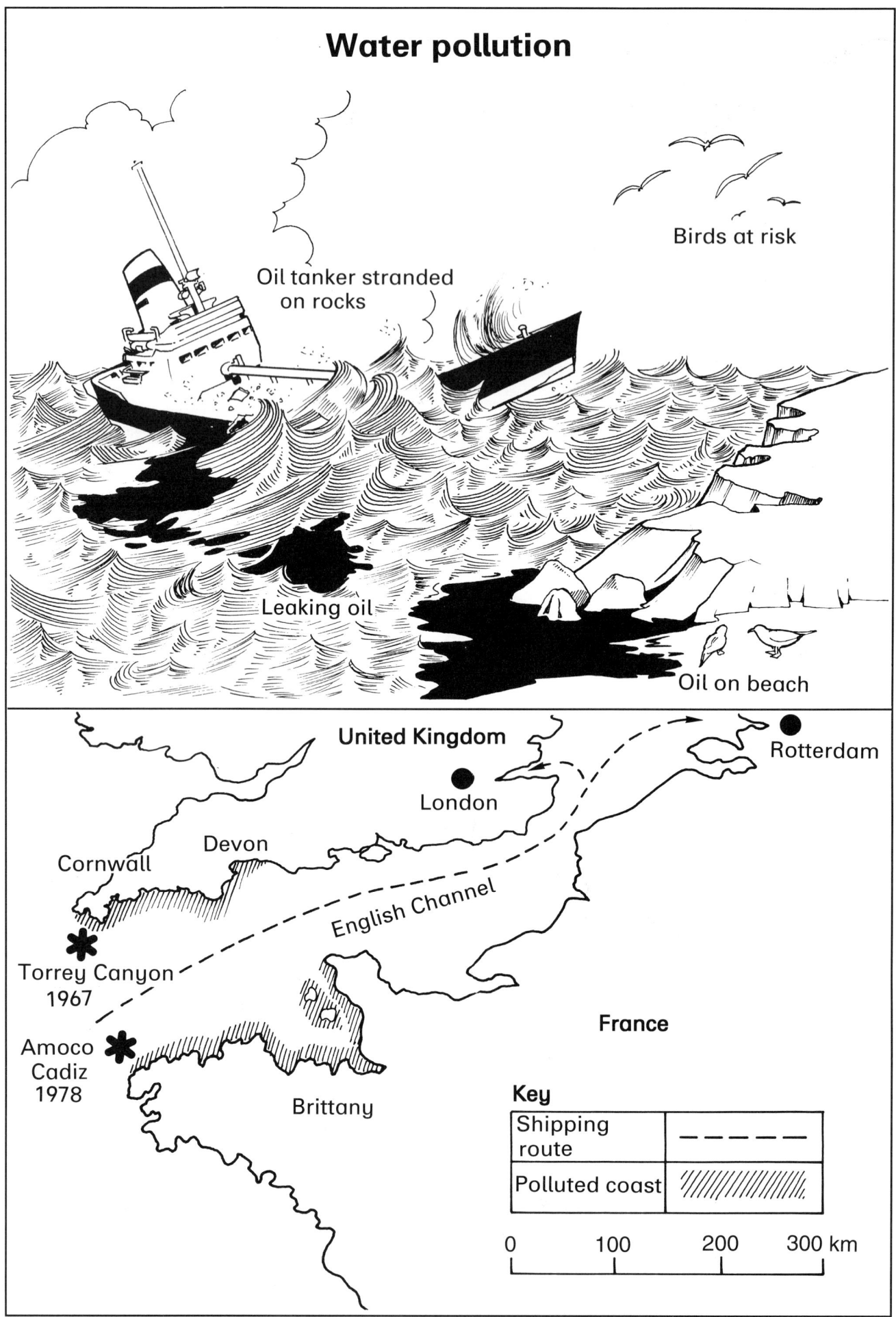

Water pollution

Air pollution

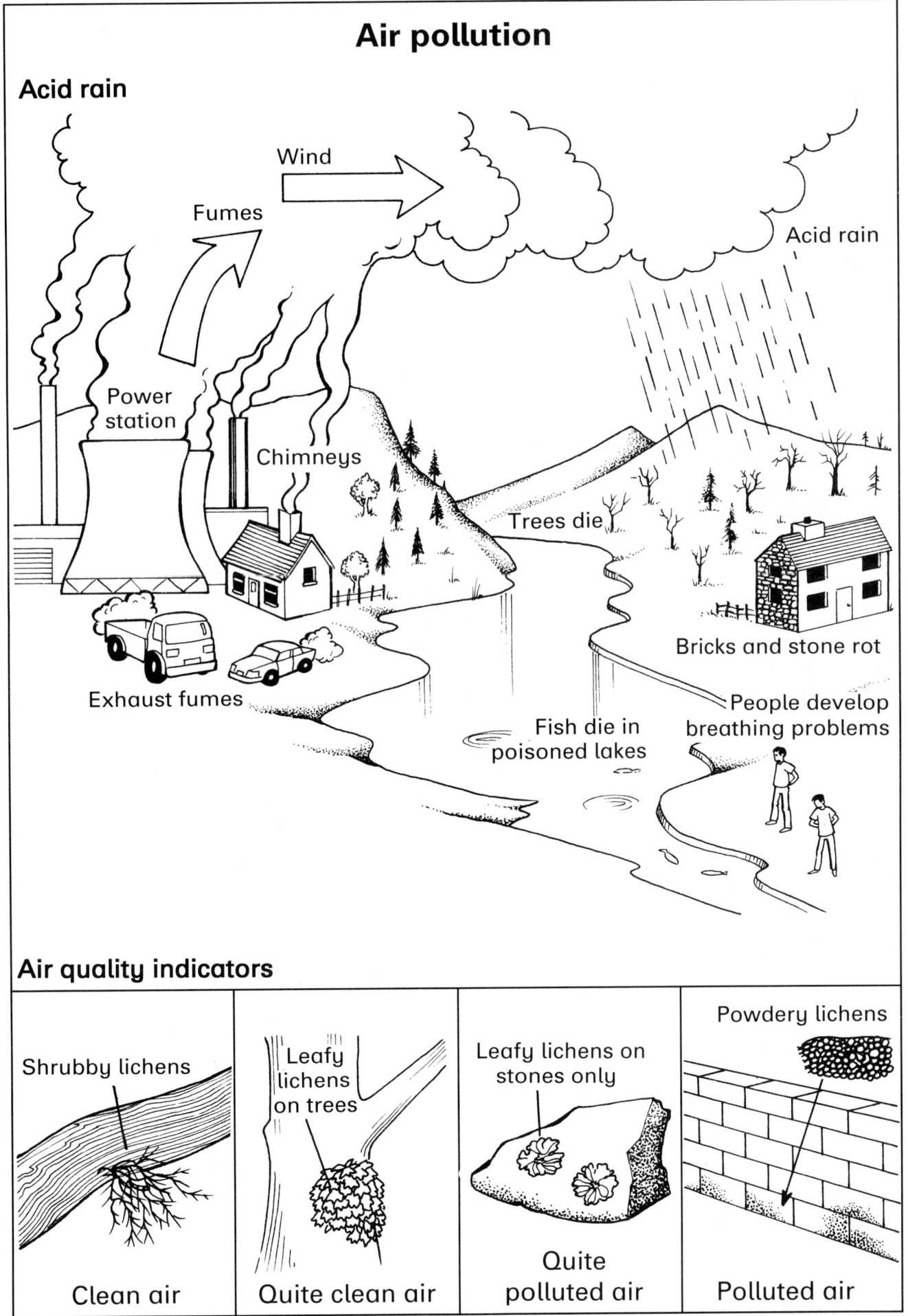

Acid rain

Wind

Fumes

Acid rain

Power station

Chimneys

Trees die

Exhaust fumes

Bricks and stone rot

Fish die in poisoned lakes

People develop breathing problems

Air quality indicators

Shrubby lichens

Leafy lichens on trees

Leafy lichens on stones only

Powdery lichens

Clean air

Quite clean air

Quite polluted air

Polluted air

Copymaster 85

Global warming

What is global warming?

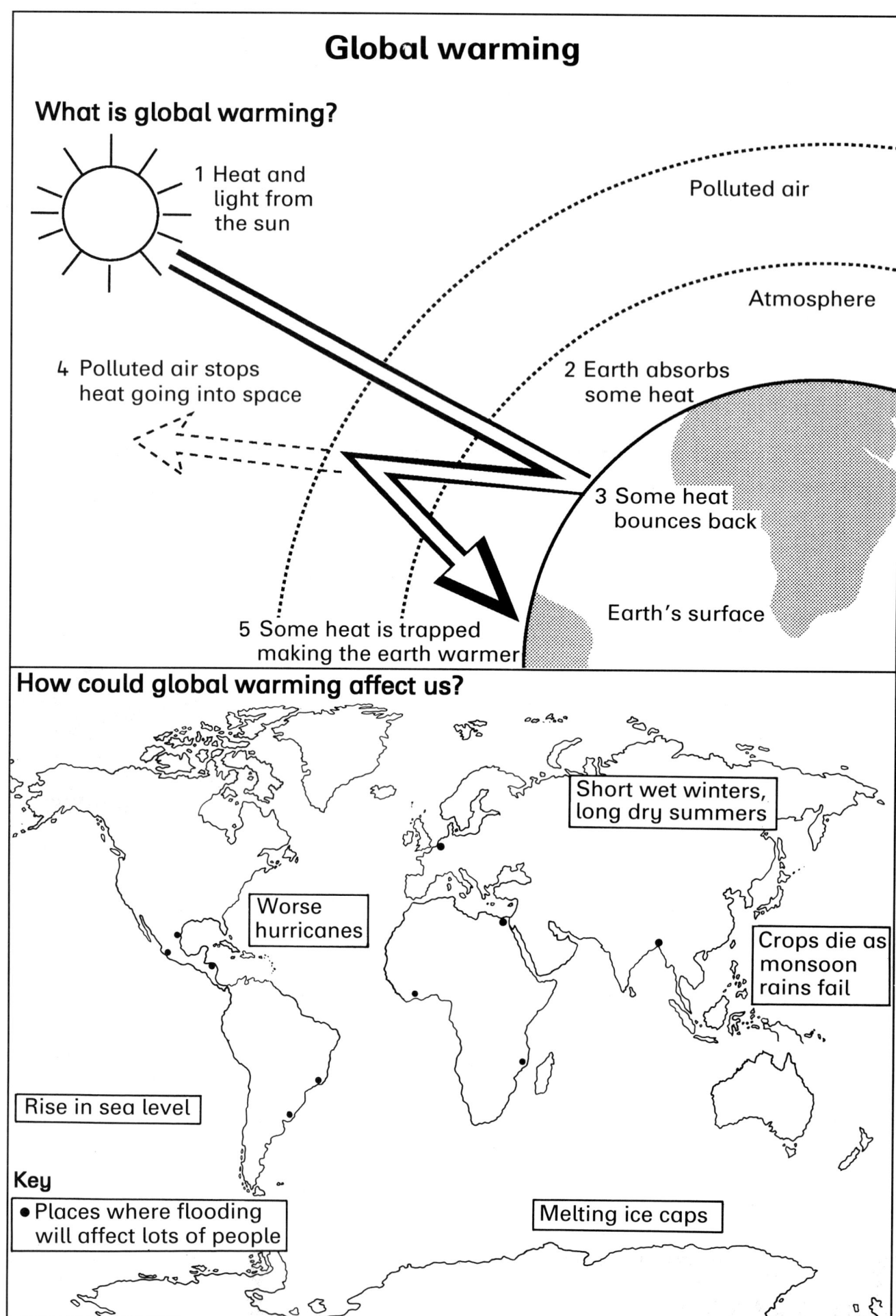

1 Heat and light from the sun

Polluted air

Atmosphere

4 Polluted air stops heat going into space

2 Earth absorbs some heat

3 Some heat bounces back

Earth's surface

5 Some heat is trapped making the earth warmer

How could global warming affect us?

Short wet winters, long dry summers

Worse hurricanes

Crops die as monsoon rains fail

Rise in sea level

Key
● Places where flooding will affect lots of people

Melting ice caps

Improving the school environment

Set up flower tubs

Put up bird boxes

Make a pond

Plant trees

New seats

Set up school garden

Build a statue

Paint a mural

New play equipment

Recycling

Paper

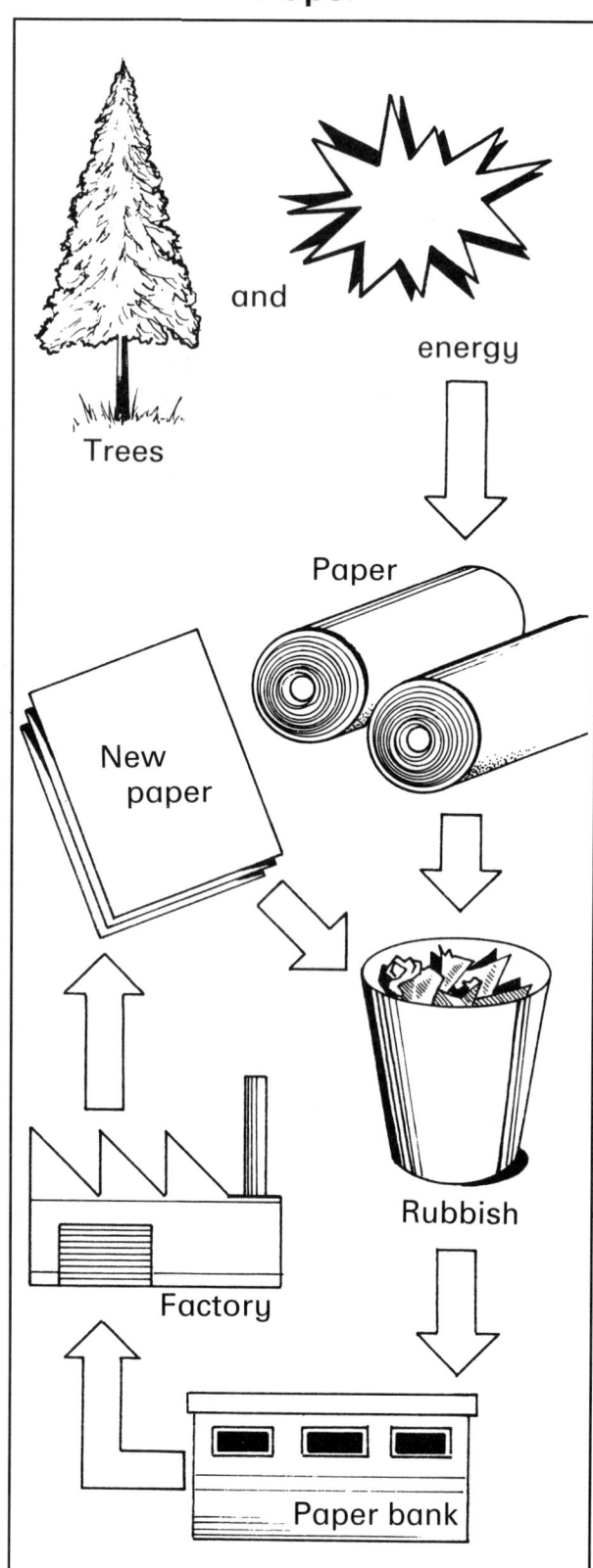

We each use two trees worth of paper a year.

Glass

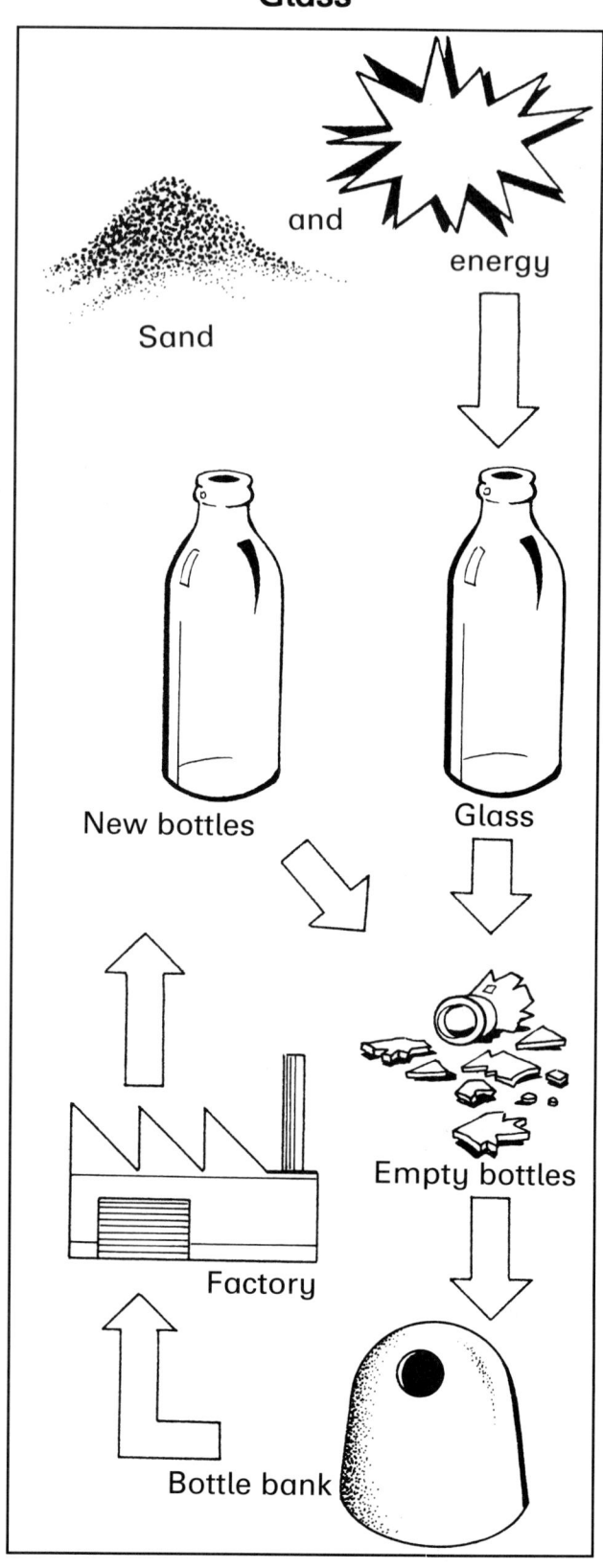

Each household uses a bottle or jar every day.

National parks

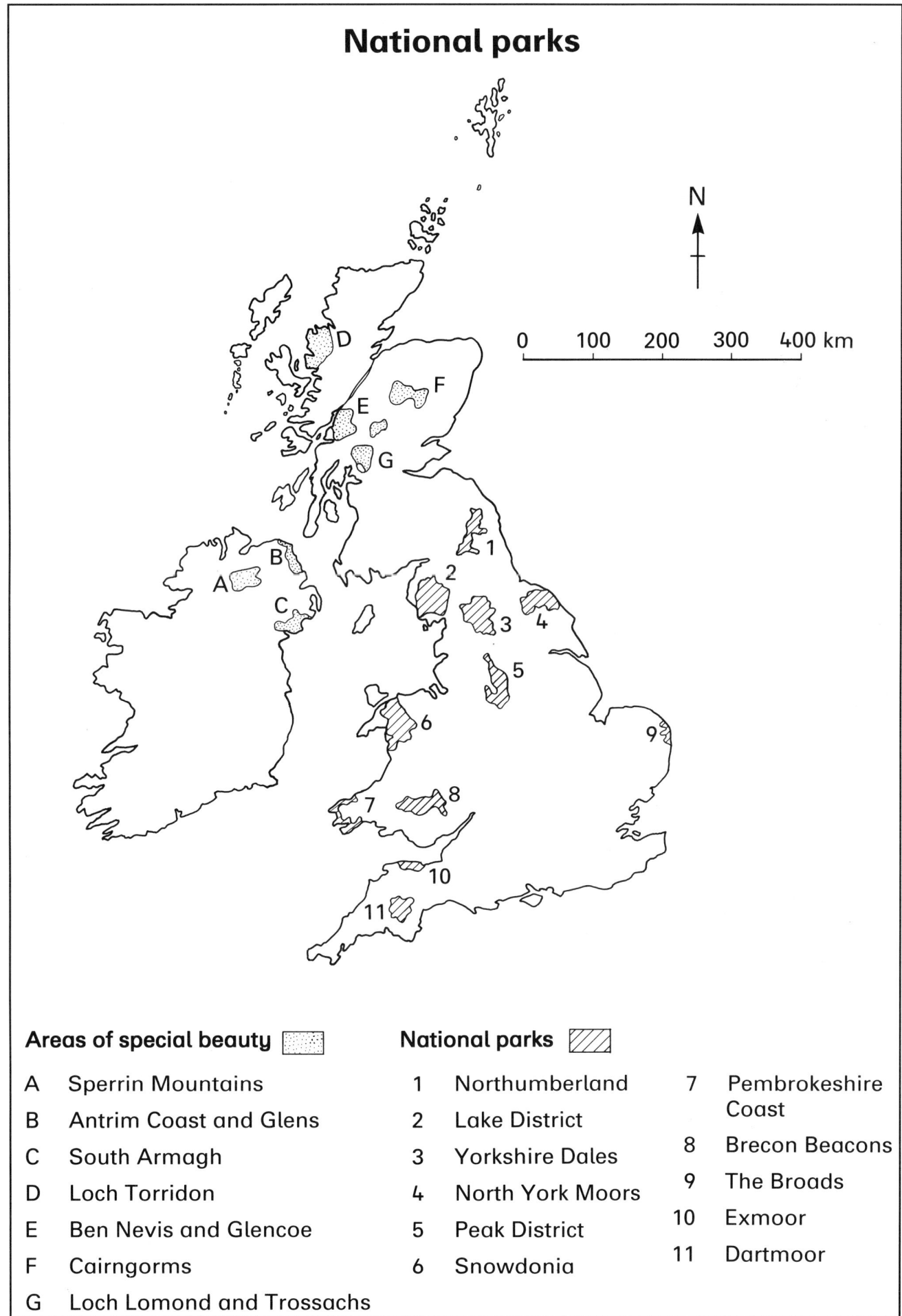

0   100   200   300   400 km

Areas of special beauty   **National parks**

A   Sperrin Mountains

B   Antrim Coast and Glens

C   South Armagh

D   Loch Torridon

E   Ben Nevis and Glencoe

F   Cairngorms

G   Loch Lomond and Trossachs

1   Northumberland

2   Lake District

3   Yorkshire Dales

4   North York Moors

5   Peak District

6   Snowdonia

7   Pembrokeshire Coast

8   Brecon Beacons

9   The Broads

10   Exmoor

11   Dartmoor

Keswick

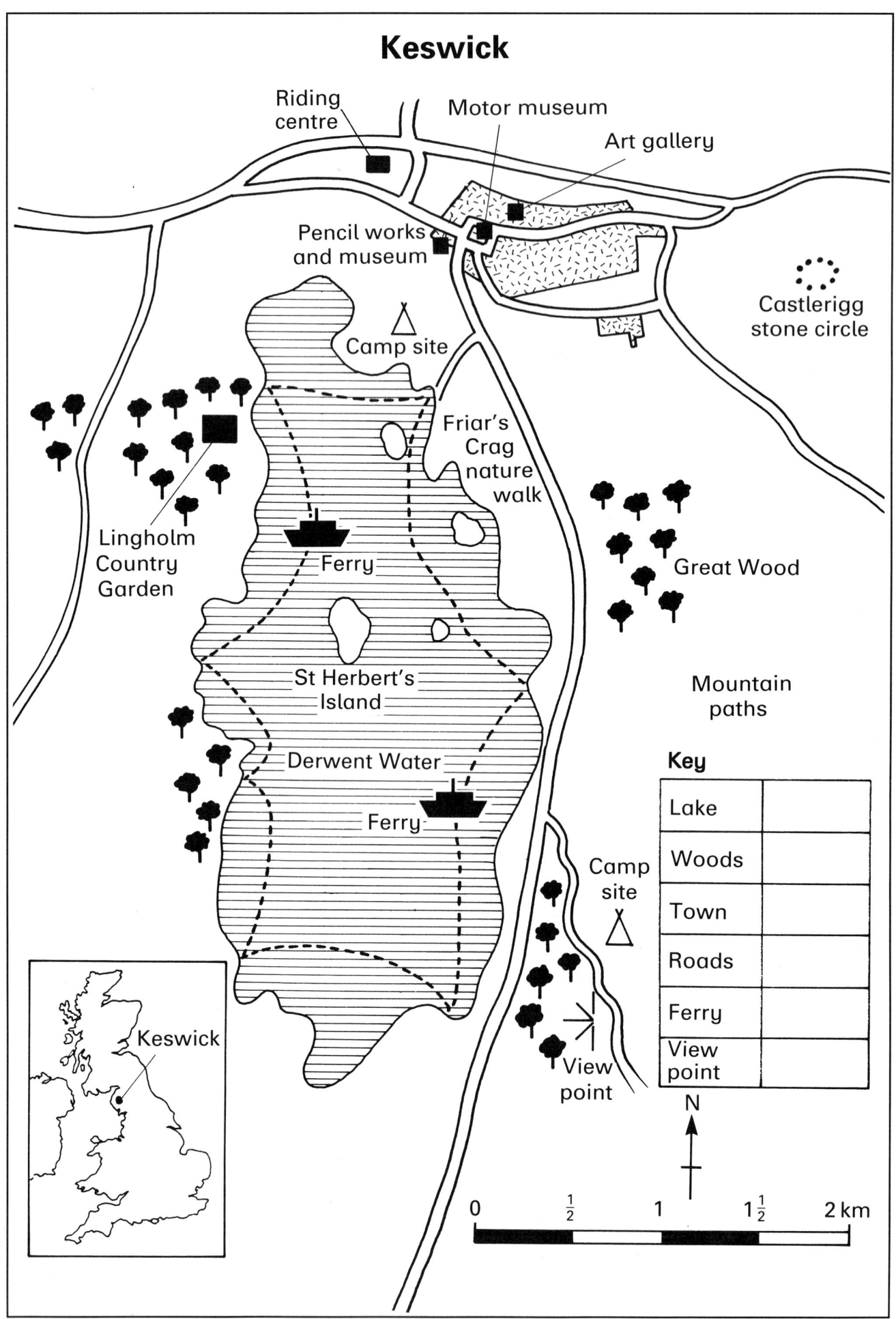

Riding centre

Motor museum

Art gallery

Pencil works and museum

Castlerigg stone circle

Camp site

Friar's Crag nature walk

Lingholm Country Garden

Ferry

Great Wood

Mountain paths

St Herbert's Island

Derwent Water

Ferry

Camp site

Key

Lake	
Woods	
Town	
Roads	
Ferry	
View point	

N

View point

Keswick

0   ½   1   1½   2 km

Copymaster 90

Derwent Water

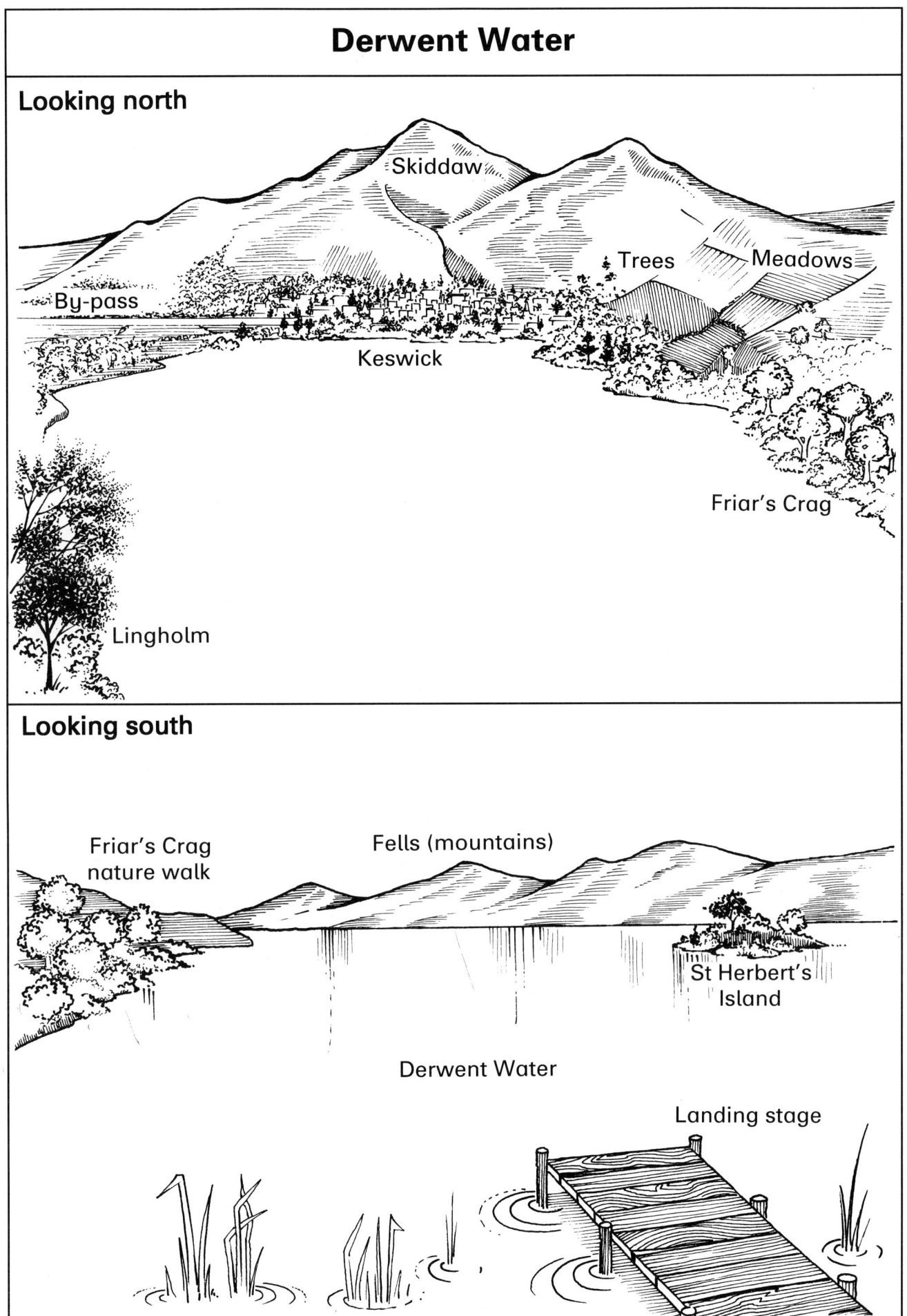

Looking north

Skiddaw

Trees

Meadows

By-pass

Keswick

Friar's Crag

Lingholm

Looking south

Friar's Crag
nature walk

Fells (mountains)

St Herbert's
Island

Derwent Water

Landing stage

Classroom plan

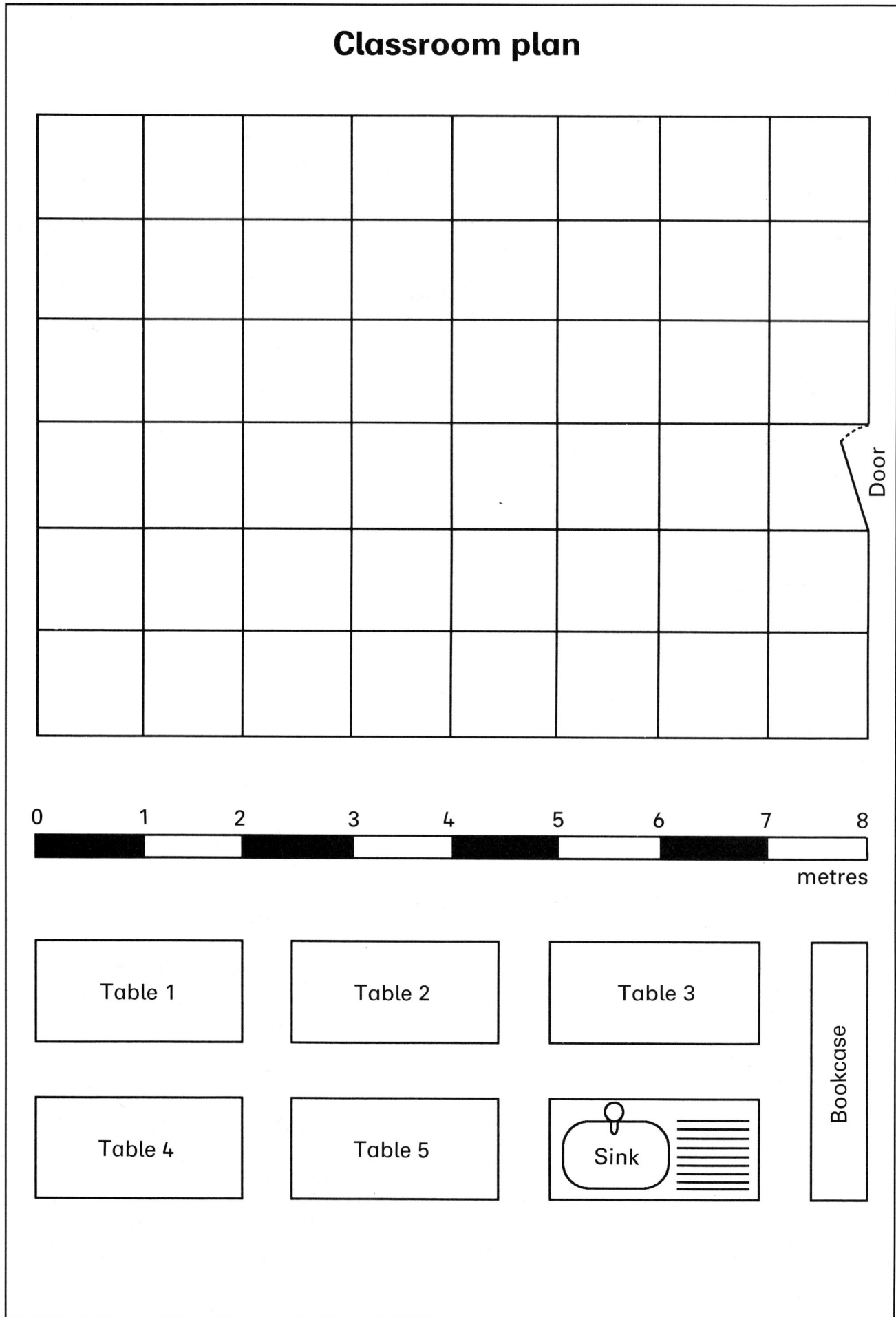

0   1   2   3   4   5   6   7   8

metres

Table 1

Table 2

Table 3

Table 4

Table 5

Sink

Bookcase

Door

Copymaster 92

Canterbury street plan

1 Westgate

2 Old Weavers' Houses

3 Cathedral

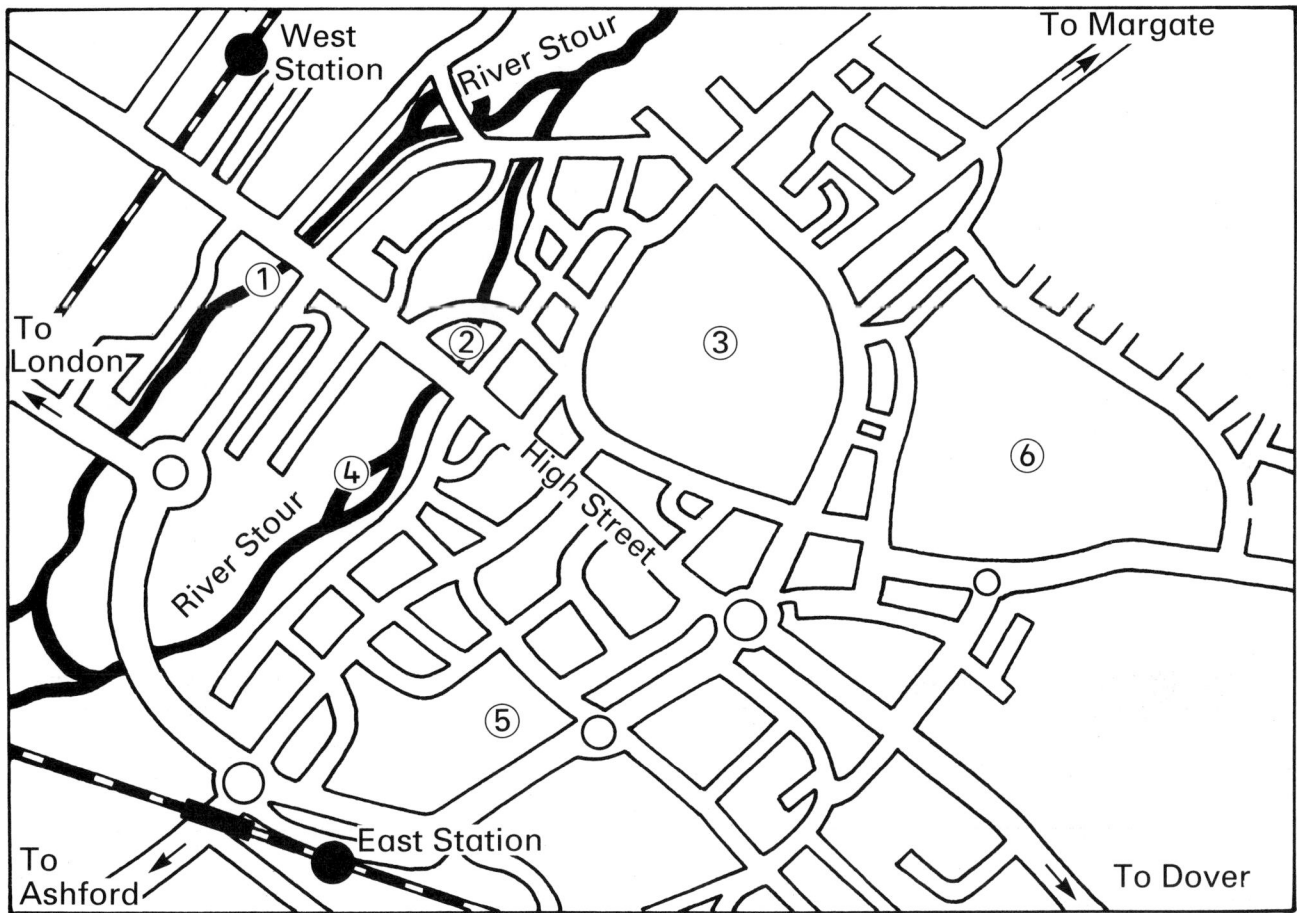

4 Grey Friars

5 Dane John Gardens

6 St Augustine's Abbey

Copymaster 93

Picture map

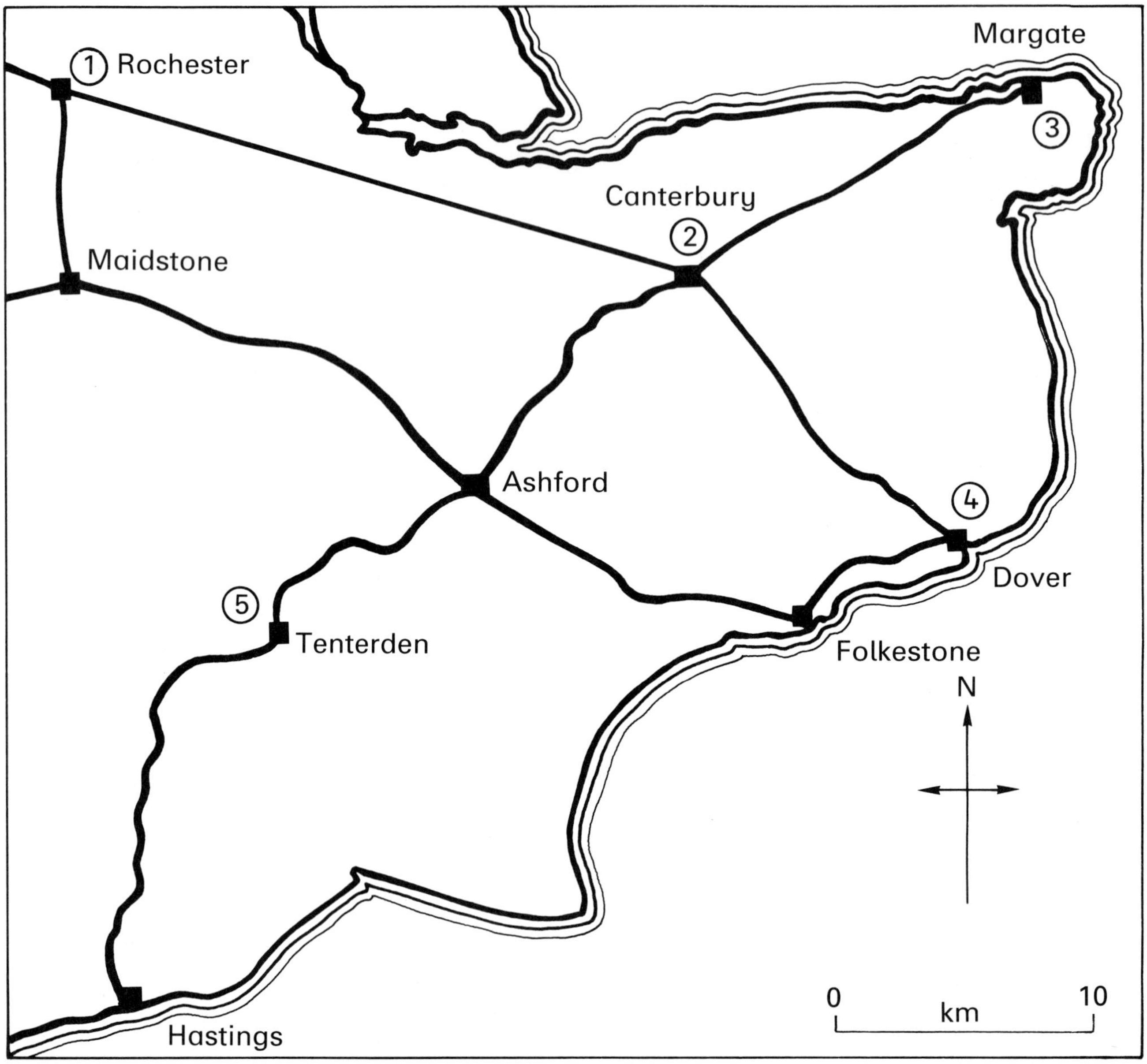

Rochester ①

Margate

Maidstone

Canterbury ②

③

Ashford

④

Dover

⑤

Tenterden

Folkestone

N

Hastings

0   km   10

| 1 Rochester Castle | 2 Canterbury Cathedral | 3 Margate Pier | 4 Dover cliffs | 5 Tenterden Railway |

Copymaster 94

Map symbols

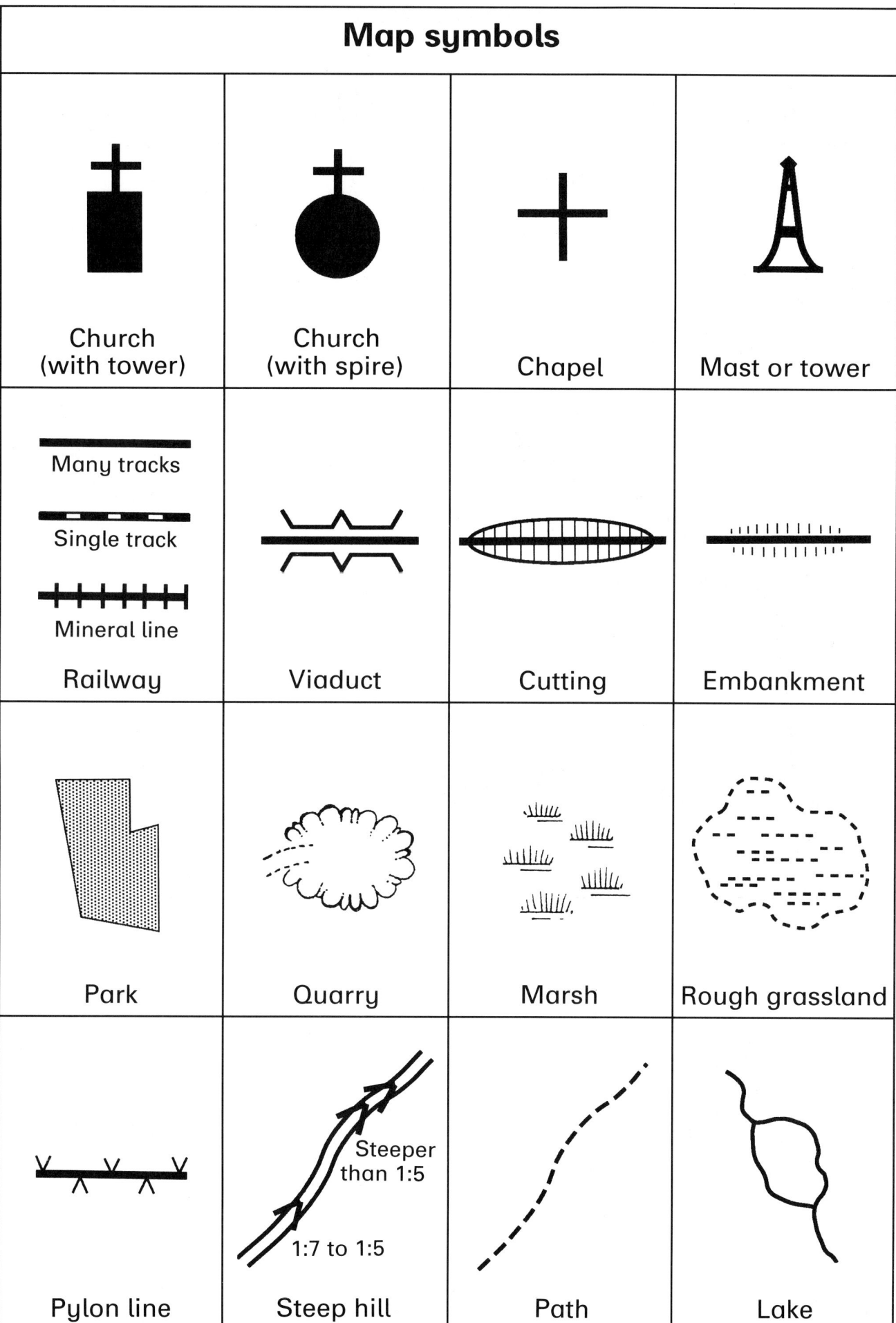

Church (with tower)	Church (with spire)	Chapel	Mast or tower
Many tracks / Single track / Mineral line — Railway	Viaduct	Cutting	Embankment
Park	Quarry	Marsh	Rough grassland
Pylon line	Steep hill — Steeper than 1:5 / 1:7 to 1:5	Path	Lake

British Isles

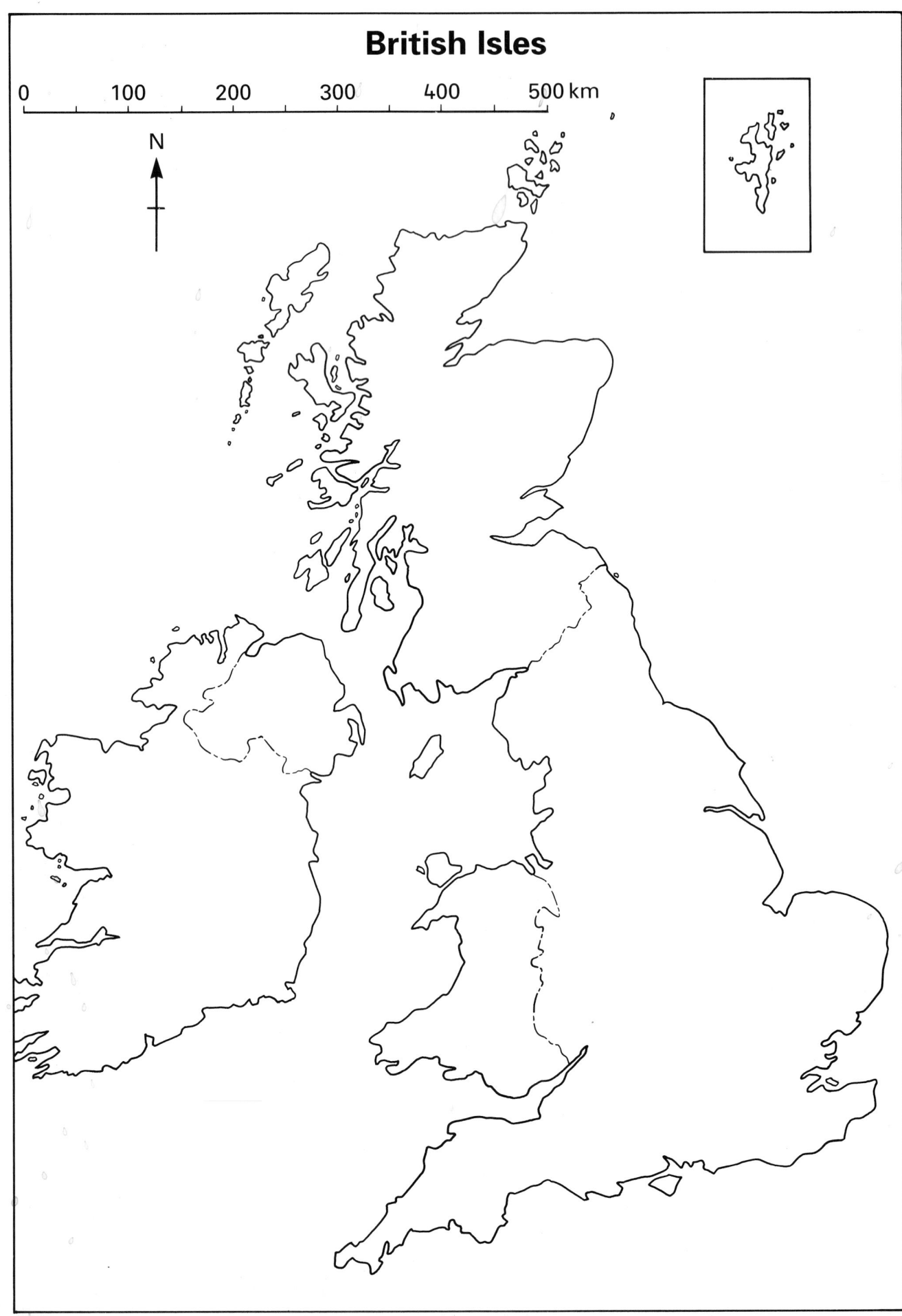

0   100   200   300   400   500 km

N

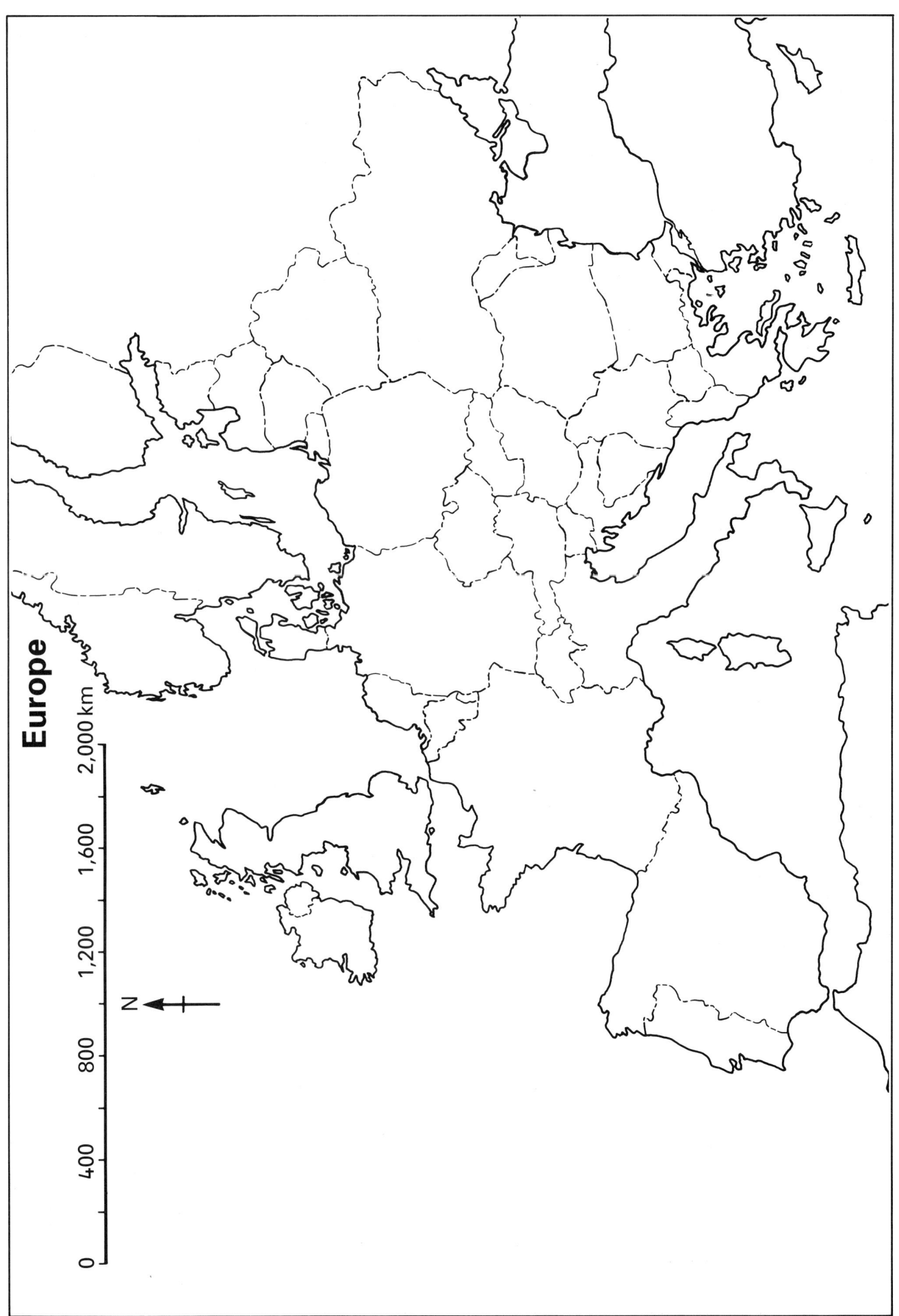

Europe

2,000 km

1,600

1,200

N

800

400

0

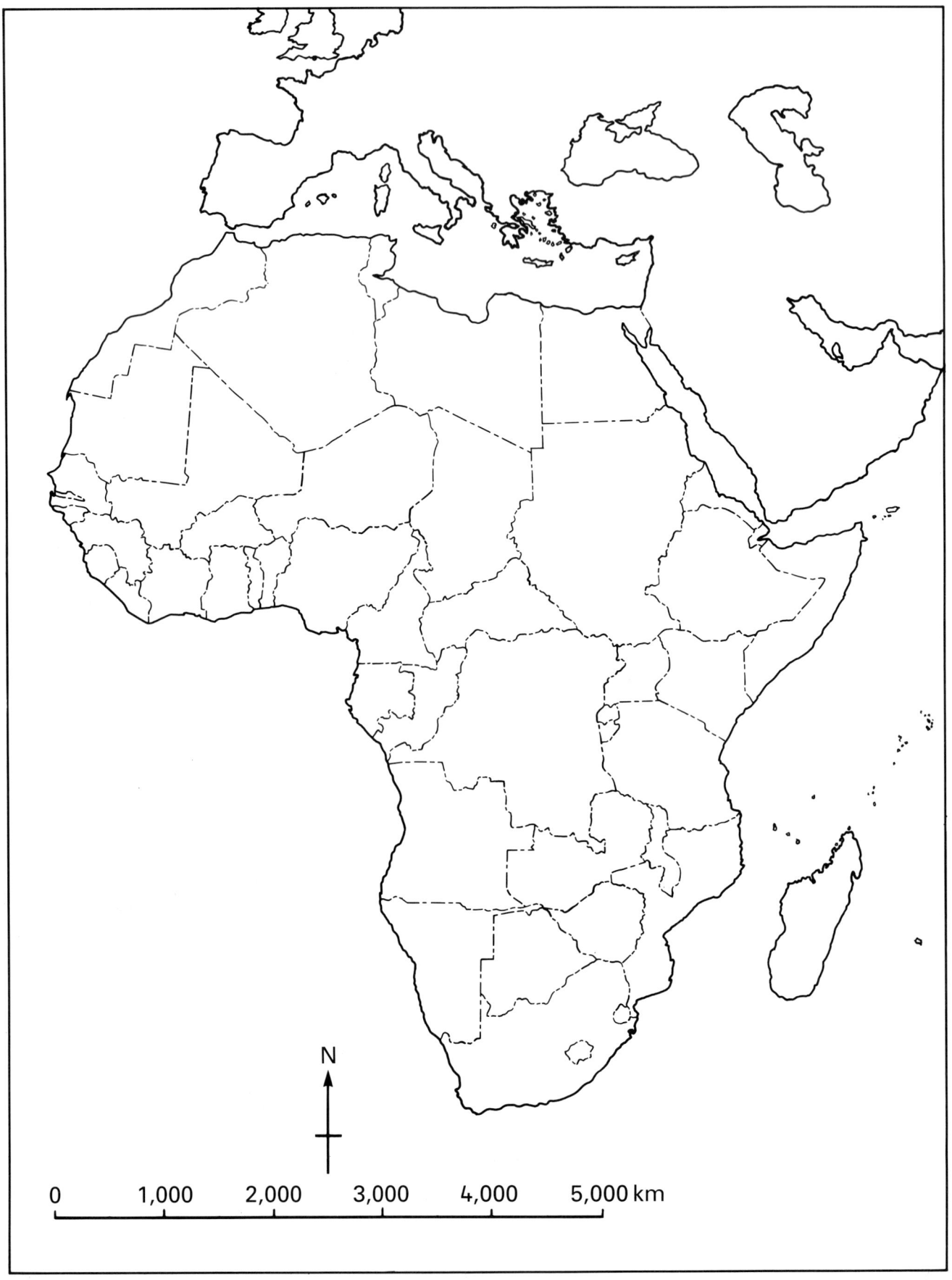

Africa

N

| 0 | 1,000 | 2,000 | 3,000 | 4,000 | 5,000 km |

North America

N

| 0 | 1,000 | 2,000 | 3,000 | 4,000 km |

South America

N

0   1,000   2,000   3,000   4,000 km

West Indies

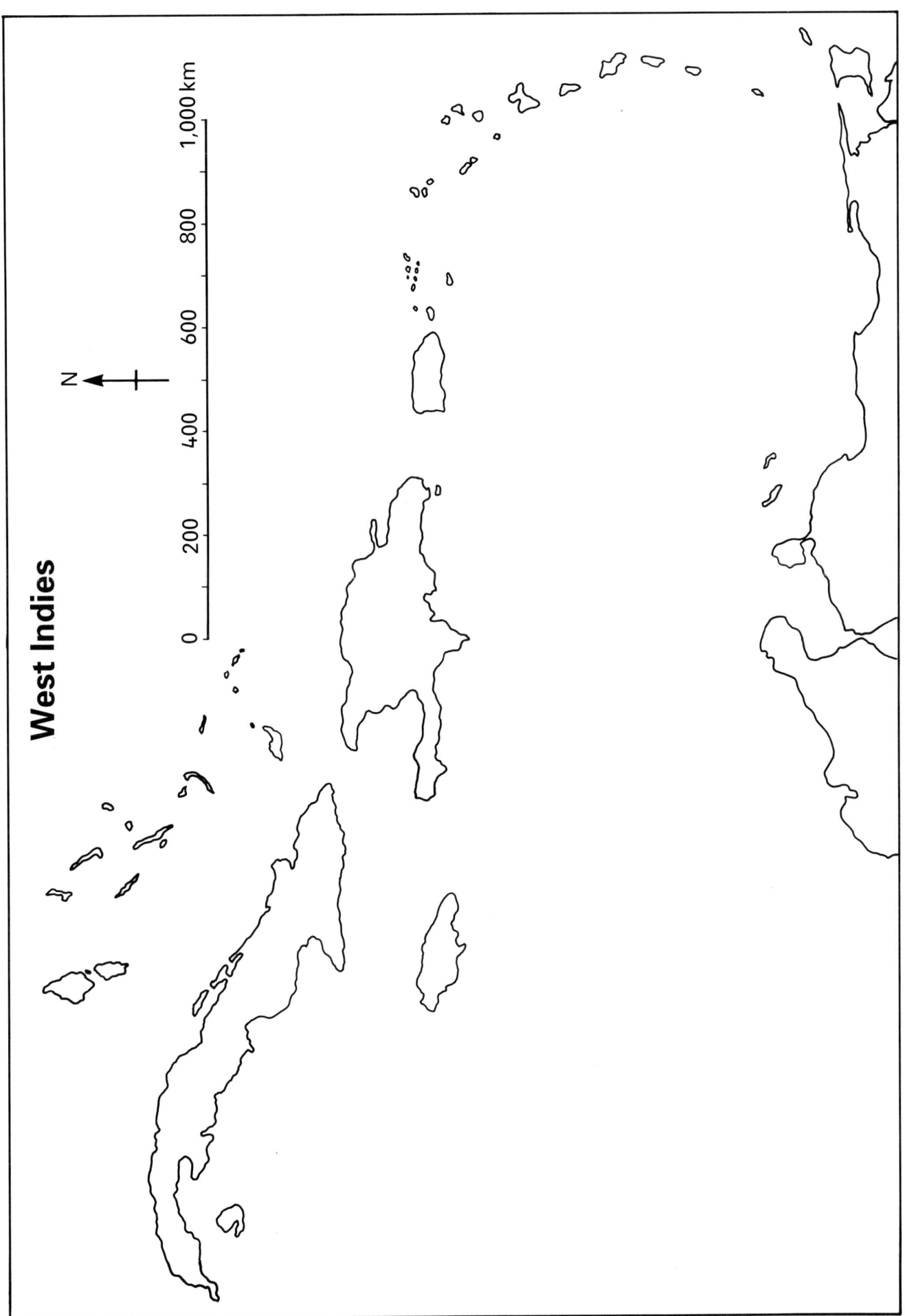

1,000 km

800

600

400

200

0

N

Middle East

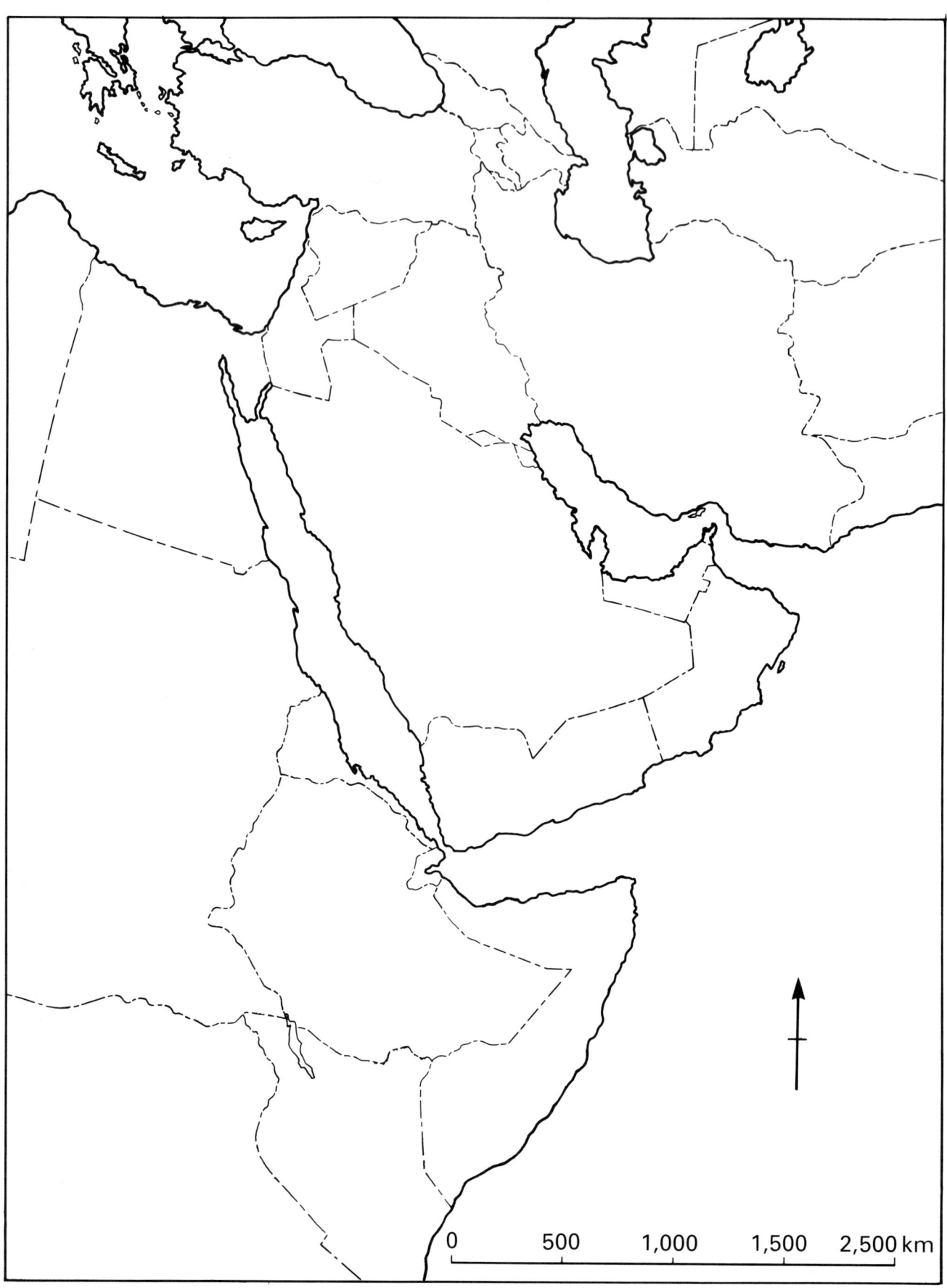

0   500   1,000   1,500   2,500 km

India

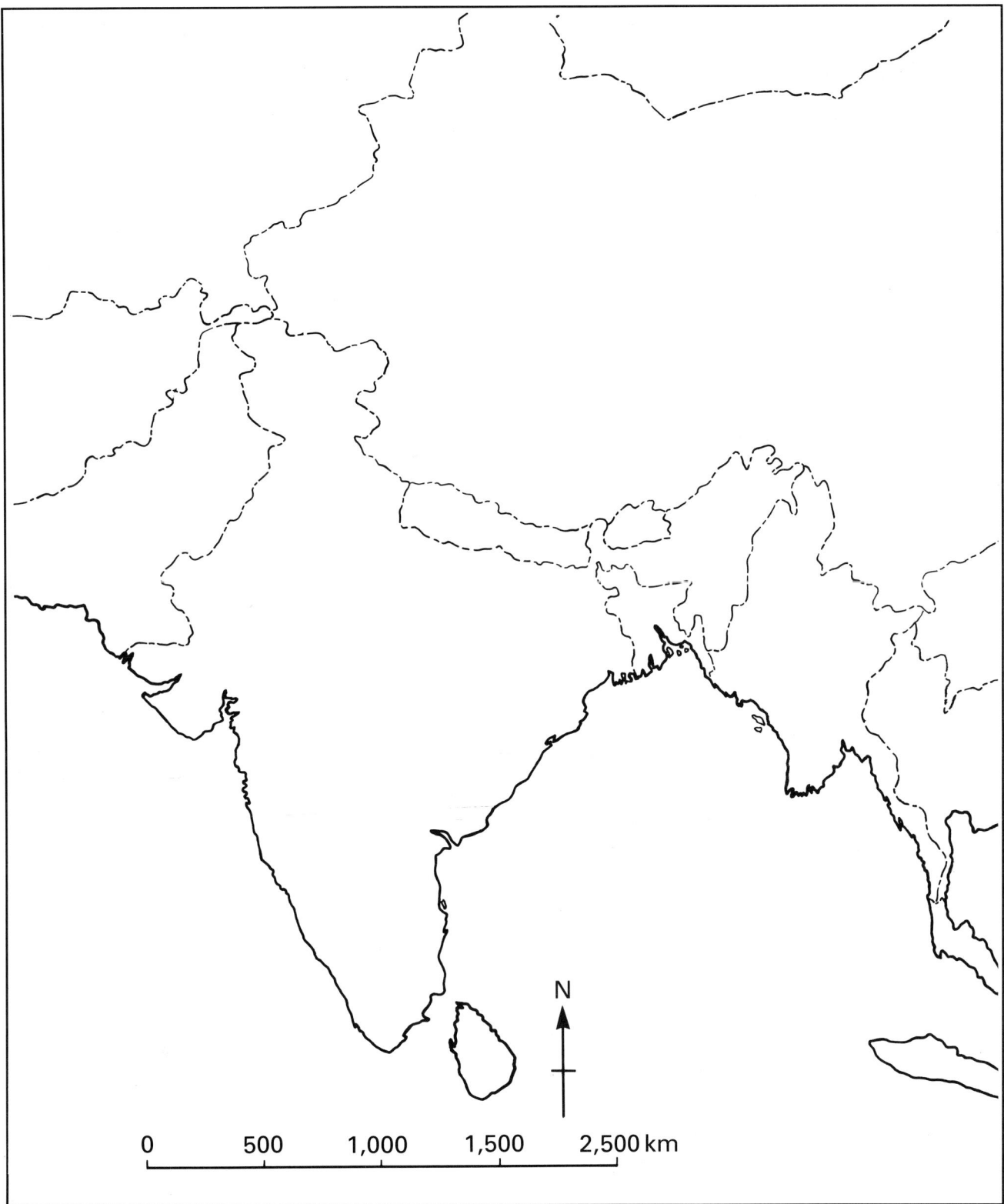

0   500   1,000   1,500   2,500 km

N

Asia

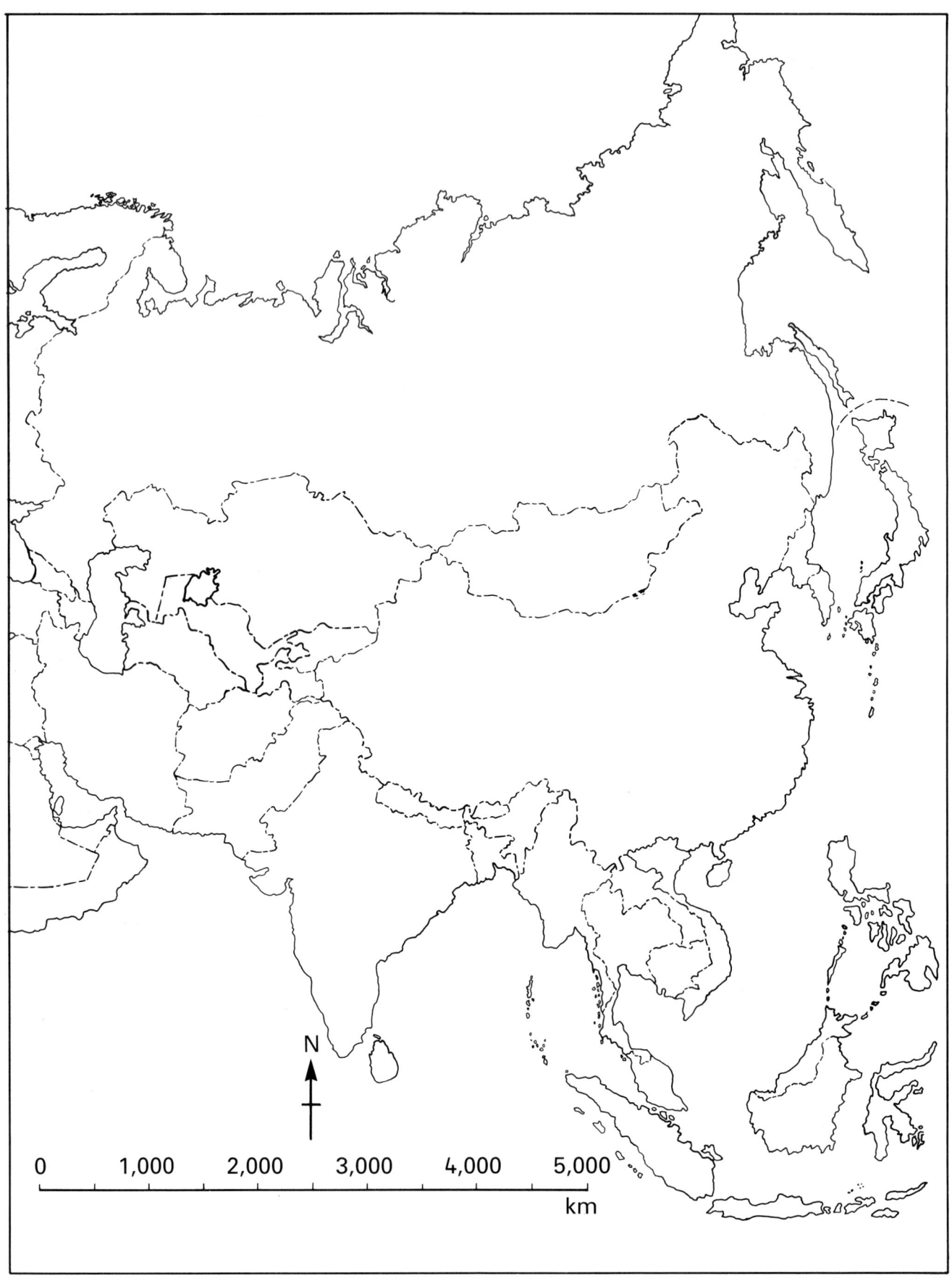

0   1,000   2,000   3,000   4,000   5,000

km

N

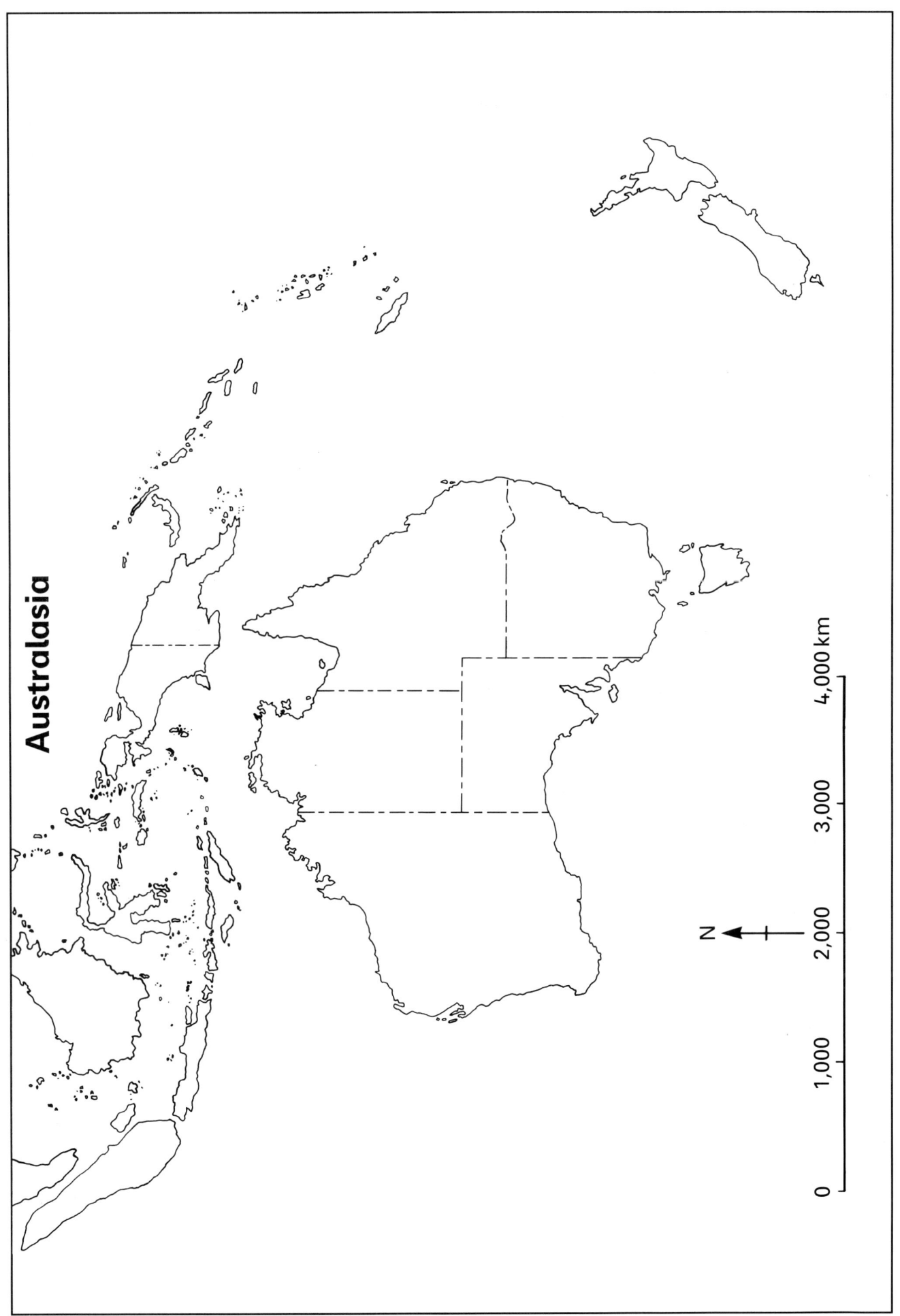

Australasia

N

0   1,000   2,000   3,000   4,000 km

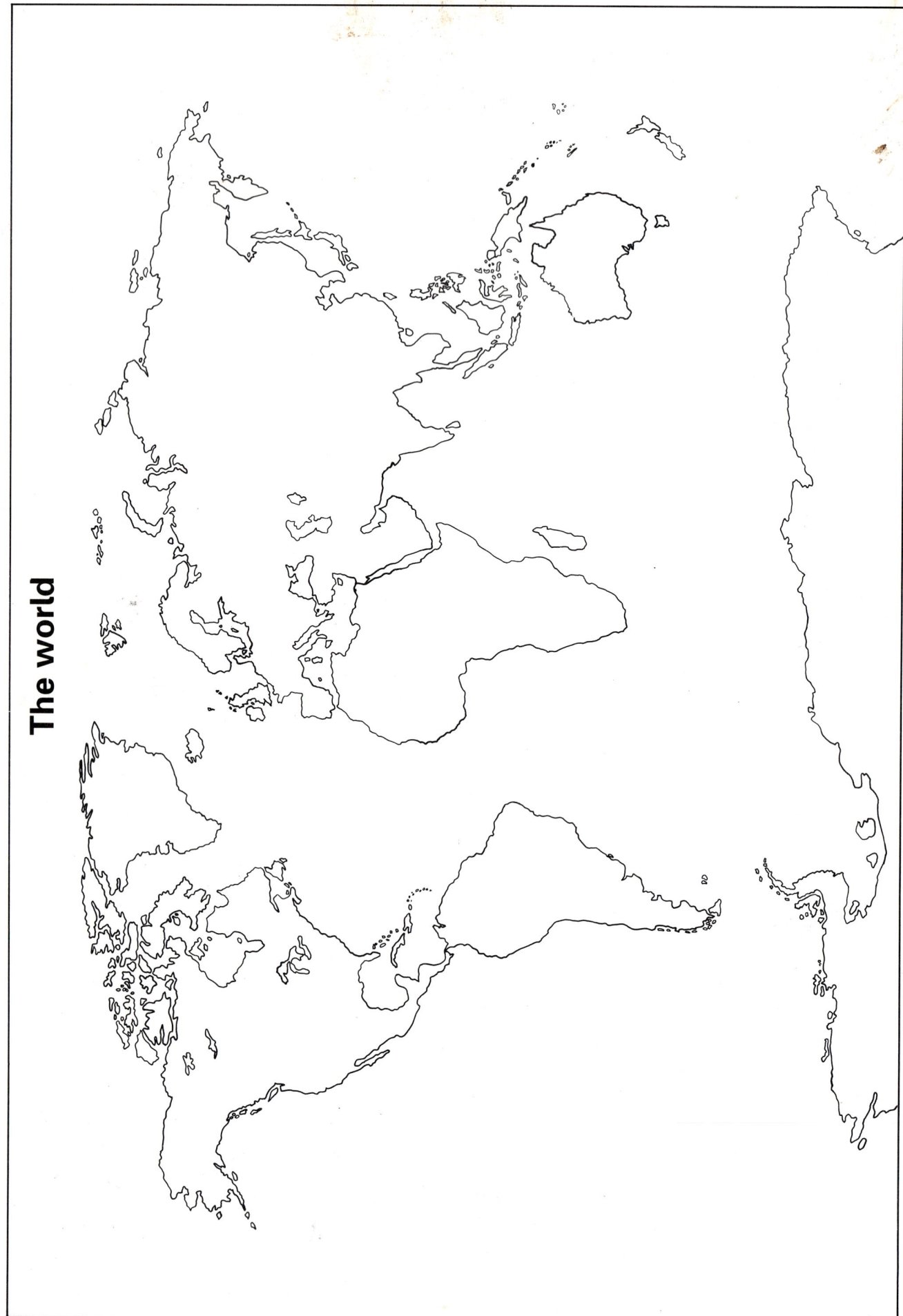

The world